The Institutionalization of Social Welfare

Routledge Advances in Sociology

The Institutionalization of Social Welfare

A Study of Medicalizing Management

Mikael Holmqvist

Routledge
Taylor & Francis Group
New York   London

Routledge
Taylor & Francis Group
270 Madison Avenue
New York, NY 10016

Routledge
Taylor & Francis Group
2 Park Square
Milton Park, Abingdon
Oxon OX14 4RN

© 2008 by Taylor & Francis Group, LLC
Routledge is an imprint of Taylor & Francis Group, an Informa business

Printed in the United States of America on acid-free paper
10 9 8 7 6 5 4 3 2 1

International Standard Book Number-13: 978-0-415-95802-8 (Hardcover)

Library of Congress Cataloging-in-Publication Data

Holmqvist, Mikael, 1970-
    The institutionalization of social welfare : a study of medicalizing management / Mikael Holmqvist.
        p. cm. -- (Routledge advances in sociology ; 30)
    Includes bibliographical references and index.
    ISBN 978-0-415-95802-8 (hardback : alk. paper)
    1. Public welfare administration. 2. Organizational behavior. 3. Institutions (Philosophy) I. Title.

HV40.H636 2007
361.0068--dc22   2007001213

Visit the Taylor & Francis Web site at
http://www.taylorandfrancis.com

and the Routledge Web site at
http://www.routledge.com

For My Son Gabriel Mikaelsson Lind

No one is socially poor until he has been assisted. And this has a general validity: sociologically speaking, poverty does not come first and then assistance ... A person is called poor who received assistance or should receive it given his sociological situation, although perchance he may not receive it ... The poor, as a sociological category, are not those who suffer specific deficiencies and deprivations, but those who receive assistance or should receive it according to social norms. Consequently, in this sense, poverty cannot be defined in itself as a quantitative state, but only in terms of the social reaction resulting from a specific situation.

Georg Simmel, The Poor (1908)
Reprinted in Simmel, G. (1971)

Contents

Figures

Preface

Today most developed countries rely on formally organized welfare programs—in some cases to the extent that they are labeled welfare states. These programs, which have been constructed over the last several decades, make up a larger national and international system of good intentions. Whether or not welfare programs take the shape of financial support, work, housing, health services, or other means of assistance, they are dedicated to helping individuals to live a normal life, adapted to their individual requirements. In many countries there is a more or less formalized expectation in regard to helping the impaired, the sick, the elderly, and other needy persons to participate more fully in the economic, social, and cultural life of society. Overall, it appears inconceivable to imagine civilized society without a comprehensive organizational system of social welfare. When social welfare programs are challenged, the general reaction is therefore often one of resistance and defense of the present order. Social welfare has become a holy cow in many societies; an institutionalized aspect of modern life. For many people—the public at large, academic specialists, journalists, politicians—no alternative to the present road of formally organized social welfare paved with good intentions, seems possible. Since it exists in most countries and makes up a significant part of contemporary social and economic life, it is commonly taken as *prima facie* evidence of its necessity.

In 2005 I published a report in Sweden on a state-owned Swedish welfare organization called Samhall, renowned since the early 1980s for its comprehensive program of vocational rehabilitation of so-called 'occupationally disabled persons' (Holmqvist, 2005). Internationally, Sweden is often considered a model welfare state that has been the subject of intense, worldwide interest; Samhall can be seen as the crown jewel of that system. Among Swedes, its existence is largely taken for granted. One could even say that Samhall is more uncontested than the institution of the Royal Swedish Court that despite its overwhelming popularity nevertheless is subject to some public questioning.

In my own independent study of Samhall I observed that Samhall is more responsive to the needs of its own activities, through which its services are offered, than to the unique needs of its clients. I stated that Samhall appears to influence its clients to learn the role of 'occupationally disabled', thus educating them to eventually start demanding the particular welfare services that the organization is competent to provide. Drawing on C. Wright Mills's thesis of 'the sociological imagination', I argued that Samhall illustrated how a modern welfare state essentially 'solves' social issues of, for instance unemployment, poverty, and criminality, by viewing and treating them as personal troubles in terms of individual disabilities:

> *Troubles* occur within the character of the individual and within the range of his immediate relations with others; they have to do with his self and with those limited areas of social life of which he is directly and personally aware. Accordingly, the statement and the resolution of troubles properly lie within the individual as a biographical entity and within the scope of his immediate milieu—the social setting that is directly open to his personal experience and to some extent his willful activity. A trouble is a private matter: values cherished by an individual are felt by him to be threatened. *Issues* have to do with matters that transcend these local environments of the individual and the range of his inner life. They have to do with the organization of many such milieus into the institutions of an historical society as a whole, with the ways in which various milieux overlap and interpenetrate to form the larger structure of social and historical life. An issue is a public matter: some value cherished by publics is felt to be threatened. (Mills, 2000: 8)

Specifically, the transformation of social issues into personal troubles at Samhall is done by classifying and treating unemployed people as 'medically problematic' through a number of management activities. As a result, clients are eventually considered to suffer from various medical disorders that require a certain kind of help that the Swedish welfare state is competent to provide. Essentially this transformation illustrates how a needy individual is made responsible for his or her social predicament by looking upon it as a consequence of his or her disability. Hence, the target for society's intervention becomes individuals' personal troubles in the form of mental or physiological disorders rather than any social issues. The overwhelming focus of Samhall's vocational rehabilitation is on individual problems. As sociologist Peter Conrad (1987; 2007) has suggested, this unit of intervention risk, however, muddles the reality of social behavior. Clearly, the individual is not solely responsible for the development of, for example, unemployment, yet this becomes the unintentional effect of such a welfare program. The social reality, including class, education, gender, race, and global factors such as competition and technological change, all known to affect unemployment—is collapsed into handy individual disorders that can be remedied by the rehabilitation offered by Samhall.

The ideology of welfare programs for the disabled in Sweden suggests that people are responsible for their problems and that they ought to be able to do something about it. This ideology based on good intentions does not include improvements of other factors that potentially can strengthen needy people's ability to find solutions for their troubles, such as improving the business environment, financial support for education, and so on. Instead, it may help people adapt to unsatisfactory social situations by promoting a view of them as disabled. Not only does this absolve society from pressing social issues, it creates a moral dilemma for the individual. With the existence of social welfare programs for the disabled such as Samhall, disadvantaged persons may be blamed both for their condition as disadvantaged and for not doing something about it. Thus, these programs may unwittingly contribute to creating increased personal dependency and need among already disadvantaged individuals.

Despite the familiarity of this conclusion, it came as no surprise to me that my report became the subject of debate in Sweden. Nevertheless I was surprised by the intensity of the reactions: Obviously my report had challenged some taken for granted ideas of social welfare as they are currently being practiced in Sweden and doubtless in many other countries as well, given the common activity of labeling and classifying disadvantaged people as 'disabled' in order to distribute welfare in the most rational way possible. In trying to make sense of the reactions following upon the publication of my report I began to explore the idea that Samhall illustrates some of the institutionalization of social welfare that can be experienced on a global basis; the result of it prompted me to write this book. How can we explain the fact that social welfare is the continuous subject of an extraordinarily successful institutionalization in contemporary society? What is the key explanatory mechanism for better understanding this common phenomenon?

In completing this project I have been very lucky to rely on the wise judgment and sharp-sighted critiques of a number of friends and colleagues in Sweden and the United States. I am particularly grateful to Konstantin Lampou, Richard Swedberg, Johan Hansson and Per Skålén. I also owe much gratitude to Alexander Styhre, Peter Korp, Christian Maravelias, James G. March, Mikael Holmgren, Torkild Thanem, Bino Catasús, Peter Dobers, W. Richard Scott, Hans Rämö, Roland Almqvist, Hervé Corvellec, Torkel Strömsten, Dick Forslund, Lars Strannegård, Nina Granqvist, Hans Hasselbladh, and Fredrik Sjögren. Likewise, I have benefited by the review process as organized by Routledge's Research Editor Benjamin Holtzman; I am thankful for the helpful remarks raised by the three anonymous reviewers. Thanks are also due to the School of Industrial and Labor Relations of Cornell University for generously accommodating me during the completion of this project. I particularly appreciate the support by Susanne Bruyère and Michael Lounsbury. Funding for this project has been provided by the Jan Wallander and Tom Hedelius Research Foundation for Social Sciences in Sweden.

Finally, I am indebted to my amazing wife Maria Lind—my most important interlocutor.

Mikael Holmqvist

1 Problems of Institutionalization

This is an organizational study of the institutionalization of social welfare. In this book I explore how a social welfare organization becomes an institution. I am analyzing this formal organization as something that takes on a life of its own, and that primarily seems to be concerned with maintaining itself as a result of continuously adapting to its experiences of the demands and requirements of prospective and current clients. There is, of course, a large literature on organizational institutionalization, some of which has analyzed the substantive area of social welfare. This literature raises significant questions and reveals central insights. Nevertheless, my study suggests some important revisions of the general understanding of organized institutionalization and of the institutionalization of social welfare in particular. This revision is based on the observation that essentially social welfare organizations do not adapt to any objective needs in their environments; rather they enact them through 'medicalizing management' that becomes the foremost means by which they become institutions.

Before discussing the theoretical and substantive research problems pertinent to my study of the institutionalization of social welfare, I wish to outline some initial definitions regarding the concepts of 'individual,' 'organization,' and 'environment' that are crucial to the ensuing analysis.

My interest in organization is limited to the extent that it is a 'formal organization.' A formal organization consists of formal plans, routines, rules, instructions, and programs for generating, interpreting, and governing behavior that are jointly managed by two or more individuals. By 'behavior' I mean changes of a human being's position or attitudes that can be described as movements or actions in relation to a particular environment; hence it is a relational phenomenon. To produce coordinated human action, there must be some form of coupling between humans. Hence, an appropriate definition of formal organization is the following:

> [A formal organization] refers to the formal ways in which human con-
> duct becomes socially organized, that is, to the observed regularities in
> the behavior of people that are due to the formal conditions in which
> they find themselves rather than to their physiological or psychological
> characteristics as individuals. (Blau and Scott, 1967: 77)

By 'organization' I do not mean something in nature that must correspond to it, something that is able to enter subject–predicate relations
with things. What is meant is instead interlocked human behaviors; that
is, human behaviors that are 'eventful, process-like, and that possess some
kind of distinctive quality that make it reasonable to call them organizational' (Weick, 1979a: 34). According to this view of organizations, the
following specification is of critical importance:

> There is no such thing as a collective personality which 'acts.' When
> reference is made in a sociological context to a state, a nation, a corpo-
> ration, a family, or an army corps, or to similar collectivities, what is
> meant is, on the contrary, only a certain kind of development of actual
> or possible social actions of individual persons. (Weber, 1978: 14)

An organization is a complex of social interactions of individual human
beings, and it consists 'in the fact that the action of various individuals is
oriented to the belief that it exists or should exist' (Ibid.). There is only
human behavior; if one looks for an organization one will only find it by
observing human behavior grounded in individual experience. When referring to an 'organization that acts,' I refer to interlocked human behaviors
based on shared human experience; that is, individual behaviors that are
oriented to the experience of others' behavior, and that are of a repetitive
and eventful character (March and Simon, 1993: 104ff; Pfeffer and Salancik, 2003: 31; Weick, 1969: 46). The behavior of an organization does
not depend on individual characteristics and personal conditions *per se*,
but on individual experiential behavior that is initiated, dominated, and
controlled in a particular way. From a conceptual point of view, it is not
people of flesh and blood that constitute organizations, it is human experiential behavior. Degree of interaction (i.e., degree of behavioral coupling),
determines the limit of organization, and what should instead be referred
to as the 'environment' (Simon, 1996; Stinchcombe, 1968). Whether or
not an actor is part of a specific organization or of its environment is not
a matter of kind but of degree: 'To the extent that two systems [organiza-
tion and environment] either have few variables in common or share weak
variables, they are independent of each other' (Weick, 1976: 3). According
to this familiar view, an organization is only interlocked human behaviors;
to this extent 'the environment' of an organization is always made up of
loosely coupled human behaviors.

THE THEORETICAL RESEARCH PROBLEM

The idea that once an organization has been established, it tends to perpetuate or transform beyond the original purpose was originally conceptualized by Weber (1978: 69–71) and has been central to the analysis of organized institutionalization ever since. The expansionist tendency is a hallmark of all organizations. Beginning as a tool to accomplish certain ideas, goals, and aims, eventually the organization becomes valued for itself. This phenomenon of institutionalization is legendary, and has been the central concern in much important theorizing by students of organizations (e.g., Clark, 1956; Scott, 1969; Selznick, 1949). The following two definitions of institutionalization are relevant:

> [Institutionalization] involves the taking on of values, ways of acting and believing that are deemed important for their own sake. From then on self-maintenance becomes more than bare organizational survival; it becomes a struggle to preserve the uniqueness of the group in the face of new problems and altered circumstances. (Selznick, 1984: 21)

> Institutionalization involves the processes by which social processes, obligations, or actualities come to take on a rulelike status in social thought and action. (Meyer and Rowan, 1991: 42)

There exist a large number of informative studies on organizations' goal displacement, subversion of core ideas, and deviation from initial ambitions as illustrations of institutionalization (for an overview, see Perrow, 1979: 177ff). The major message in this literature 'is that the organization has sold out its goals in order to survive and grow' (Ibid: 182). Indeed, organizational self-maintenance and expansion are the primary consequences of institutionalization.

Organizational change of a radical and explorative character becomes all the more unlikely when institutionalizing. Institutionalization is characterized by formalization, routinization, refinement, and habituation, making the organization more and more enduring and taken for granted. In his ideas on bureaucracy and the process of 'bureaucratization,' Weber argued:

> Once fully established, bureaucracy is among those social structures which are hardest to destroy...where administration has been completely bureaucratized, the resulting system of domination is practically indestructible. (Weber, 1978: 987)

According to Weber, the member of a true bureaucracy 'is chained to his activity in his entire economic and ideological existence' (Ibid: 988). Hence, even bureaucracy, the most rational *organon*, becomes an institution; that is, the most enduring feature of social life by humans reproducing specific behavior in an interlocked way through shared experience.

The process of infusing organizations with value beyond the technical requirements at hand (Selznick, 1984: 151–152) makes commitment and loyalty among organizational members central to the process of institutionalization. It is not surprising that the concepts of the 'total institution' (Goffman, 1961) or 'totalitarianism' (Arendt, 1968) are often used to describe this phenomenon. Perrow (1979: 186) argued that in institutionalized organizations 'people build their lives around them, identify with them, become dependent upon them'; thus concurrently contributing to their further institutionalization by reproducing dominant rules and routines (Giddens, 1984: 16–34). Institutionalization can be described as a process of inducing individuals to give their full commitment to an organization—thus at the same time making them the subject of comprehensive organizational control. An institutionalized organization is *per se* something that becomes hard to question; it becomes valued for its own sake and its disappearance would be unthinkable to most of its members as a result of their personal identification with the organization's core values and ideas.

There is sometimes a distinction in the literature between 'the new institutionalism' and the 'old institutionalism' in organizational analysis, implying that the differences between them are considerable (e.g., DiMaggio and Powell, 1991a: 11–15). Others argue instead that the ideas in the new institutionalism 'do not represent a sharp break with the past, although there are new emphases and insights' (Scott, 1995: 24). The main difference between 'old' and 'new' approaches to the organizational analysis of institutionalization does not seem to lie in the conceptualization of institutionalization, but instead in the level of analysis: what in the organization is being institutionalized (DiMaggio and Powell, 1991a: 13f; Nee, 2005: 64; Scott, 1995: 55f). To the 'old' institutionalists, the focus is primarily on the institutionalization of formal organizations (corporations, schools, universities, etc.); to the 'new' institutionalists, the focus is primarily on organizations in terms of fields, networks, and societies; that is, more general sociological entities undergoing institutionalization. According to my earlier definition of organization as interlocked human behaviors there are, however, basically no conceptual differences between these two approaches; both concern the institutionalization of human activity.

A common and powerful idea in both the 'old' and 'new' organizational analysis of institutionalization is that environments shape and condition organizations. Organizations are seen as being 'embedded in larger systems of relations' that they inexorably are affected by (Scott and Meyer, 1991: 137). There are hardly any substantial conceptual differences between the two 'schools' of institutionalism regarding the core conceptualization of the process of institutionalization—it is largely seen as being driven by organizations adapting to their external environments that are held to be objective and real. This idea is crucial both to 'neo-institutionalism' (e.g., Powell and DiMaggio 1991; Scott, 1995) and to 'old institutionalism' (e.g., Clark, 1956; Selznick, 1949). As Perrow (1979: 194) argued in his review of the latter literature: 'Parts of the "environment" are seen as affecting organizations, but the organization is not seen as defining, creating, and shaping its environment.'

A key problem in much theorizing on organizations' institutionalization is then how organizations incorporate environmental demands and requirements in order to prosper and survive. A standard idea is that a 'successful organization' is an organization that is largely structured by phenomena in its environment, thus demonstrating that it is adapting to some institutionalized features in the surroundings. The fact that much of these organizational adaptations are largely ceremonial (Meyer and Rowan, 1991), does not mean that they are inconsequential for organizations' concrete operations through humans' behavior. It is commonly argued that organizations' behavior tends to become all the more similar when confronted with the same environmental demands (DiMaggio and Powell, 1991b). Most hospitals, for instance, are said to share the same basic internal features by adapting to the same laws, regulations, and general trends in society (Flood and Scott, 1987).

Of course, institutional theory maintains that 'organizations, and the individuals who populate them, are suspended in a web of values, norms, rules, beliefs, and taken-for-granted assumptions that are at least *partially of their own making*' (Barley and Tolbert, 1997: 93, emphasis added; see also Meyer and Rowan, 1991: 48). There is a well-established idea among students of institutions that actors contribute to create the institutions to which they subsequently respond. As Scott (1987: 496) argued, institutionalization is a 'social process by which individuals come to accept a shared definition of social reality.' However, more often than not, 'institutionalists have concentrated on an institution's capacity to constrain' (Barley and Tolbert, 1997: 95), thus *de facto* resulting in an analysis that largely ignores organizations' ability to construct their environments. In their model of institutional change, Greenwood et al. (2002: 59–61) suggested that '[i]nstitutional theory neither denies nor is inconsistent with change. On the contrary, many institutional accounts are about isomorphic convergence'; that is, change conceptualized as adaptation to objective and external requirements.

Indeed, this standard analysis has much conceptual validity and has been the subject of considerable empirical research. Increasingly, however, students of institutionalization are focusing their attention on how organizations exercise agency through recording, registering, neglecting, translating, and interpreting their environments when adapting to them (e.g., Blackler and Regan, 2006; Brunsson and Olsen, 1997; Phillips et al., 2004; Sahlin-Andersson, 1996; Sévon, 1996; Zilber, 2002). Greenwood and Hinings (1996: 1032) stressed that 'this line of thought leads to the conclusion that the role of intraorganizational dynamics in accepting or rejecting institutionalized practices is critical,' thus analyzing institutionalization as a process of organizations actively managing their environments when adapting to them (cf. DiMaggio and Powell, 1991b: 63; Meyer and Rowan, 1991: 54). This perspective aims to give the issue of institutionalization full attention. Phillips et al. (2004: 635) have noted: 'institutional research has tended to focus on the effects rather than the process of institutionalization, which largely remains a "black box".' Hasselbladh and Kallinikos (2000) criticized institutional theory for its tendency to treat the process of institutionalization in terms of adaptation alone: 'organizations, organizational action and structure have been seen as responses to various objective conditions surrounding organizations' (697) and institutional theory 'bypasses the central issue of the social construction of rationalization, which it treats in terms of structural isomorphism' (700).

Certainly, by emphasizing organizations' interpretation, sense-making, and selective attention when adapting to external pressures and demands, a perspective that focuses the activities of the organization has become all the more accepted in organizational analyses of institutionalization. Environmental models are not likely to be internalized whole cloth by organizations being passive in relation to their environments. Czarniawska and Joerges argued that organizations react to their environments by 'translating' external demands to make them fit organizational (i.e., local) norms and needs:

> The perceived attributes of an idea, the perceived characteristics of a problem and the match between them are all created, negotiated or imposed during the collective translation process. All three are the results, not the antecedents of this process. (Czarniawska and Joerges, 1996: 25)

Thus, adaptation to an environment involves to some extent organizational agency; there is no one-sided determinism in this approach.

This important development of institutional theory can be further extended through the concept of 'enactment' as offered by organization theory (e.g., Smircich and Stubbart, 1985; Starbuck, 1976; Weick, 1979a). Enactment means basically that an organization does not *react* to an environment (whether completely or partially); it *enacts* it (Weick, 1969: 64); hence in an enacted world, there are as many environments as there are enactors (Pfeffer and Salancik, 2003: 73). The reason why many organizations behave similarly is not that they are subject to the same external pressures of conformity, but rather that they enact their environments similarly (Starbuck, 1976: 1069). The enactment concept stresses the need to understand how organizations fully produce the world that they experience through their own dynamics.

Students of organizations have indicated the relevance of the enactment concept for institutional analysis (Jennings and Greenwood, 2003:
203–205; March and Olsen, 1989: 46–47; Weick et al., 2005: 417). This is
promising since an 'enacted environment model' (Smircich and Stubbart,
1985) has the potential to further develop a much needed 'agency perspective' in institutional theory, not least by bringing down the often highly
abstract macro-analyses of institutional change to the micro-level (Blackler
and Regan, 2006; Barley and Tolbert, 1997). Potentially, the concept of
enactment embodies a strong recognition of how agency and concrete, constructive, cognitive processes are critical elements in institutionalization.

The assumption that organizations *react* (certainly, in a selective way)
to their objective environments, is still a prominent one in most organizational analyses of institutionalization. But this view does not sufficiently
take into account how organizations act upon their own experience of
'external phenomena' (Oliver, 1991; Tolbert and Zucker, 1996). Despite
the recent emphasis among students of institutionalization on organizations' interpretation of their environments, the idea of the environment
as an independent and external entity to which organizations react is still
dominating. It is generally believed that the 'objective environment' may be
accurately or inaccurately perceived, but in either case organizations must
strive to maintain congruence between objective environmental constraints
and organizational needs.

According to an 'enactment view on institutionalization,' institutionalized environments to which organizations adapt would be the more or less
perfect product of the organizations themselves, not the other way around.
Students of organizations that have drawn on the enactment concept when
analyzing organizations assume that separate objective environments simply do not exist. Organizations do not adapt to any 'external' phenomena, but to their own experience; thus blurring the traditional distinction
between the 'organization' and the 'environment.' As Starbuck argued:

> Organizations' environments are largely invented by organizations
> themselves. Organizations select their environments from ranges of
> alternatives, then they subjectively perceive the environments they
> inhabit. (Starbuck, 1976: 1069)

Following this line of thought, enactment 'is the feedstock for institutionalization' (Weick, 1995: 36) by organizations managing what environments to adapt to based on their own experience. A central idea is that
an organization can only make sense of its environment by observing
and relating to its own experience. The 'external environment' is a void;
there is only an 'inner world' of experience. Enactment is, of course, not
understood here as an organization alone creating the environment it then
interprets to understand;[1] but it is seen as the result of bargaining between

the organization and the environment. It is assumed that the behavioral changes that result from the interaction between an organization and its environment may be *triggered* by the environment, but they are always *determined* by the organization based on its experiences.

The idea that organizations enact their environments on experiential grounds can be associated with the 'Carnegie School' of organization theory that emphasizes how organizations continuously try to *manage* their environments rather than passively respond to them (e.g., March and Simon, 1993; Pfeffer and Salancik, 2003; Starbuck, 1976; Weick, 1979a). Cyert and March (1992: 168) stressed: 'Rather than treat the environment as exogenous and to be predicted, [organizations] seek ways to make it controllable.' The environment is not something that can simply be observed, classified, and interpreted as such; instead it is created by experiential management procedures of classification, naming, tabulating, and description (March and Olsen, 1979). Largely, it is the result of organizational power and authority that generate certain experiences. Certainly, the Carnegie School's emphasis on organizations' influencing, manipulating, and negotiating their environments has repeatedly been acknowledged as a critical source of inspiration by students of institutionalization (e.g., Czarniawska and Sévon, 1996: 5; DiMaggio and Powell, 1991a: 18f; Selznick, 1984: x), but its core ideas regarding the potential of organizations to experientially shape and create the environments to which they subsequently adapt has remained obscure as a framework for systematic analysis of institutionalization.

In this regard, analytic guidance and inspiration can be found in March and Olsen's conceptualization of institutionalization as a process of organizations *creating* their environments:

> Institutions create their environments in part, and the resulting complications are significant.... When environments are created, the actions taken in adapting to an environment are partly responses to previous actions by the same actor, reflected through the environment. (March and Olsen, 1989: 46)

Refining this theory of institutionalization, the authors concluded the following:

> Institutions create their environments by the way they interpret and act in a confusing world. It is not simply that the world is incompletely or inaccurately perceived, but also that actions taken as a result of beliefs about an environment can, in fact, construct the environment. (Ibid: 47)

According to March and Olsen, retrieved experiences in the form of organizational routines and rules for managing human behaviors stand at the center of attention, making certain activities possible based on experiential learning that contributes to enacting a certain environment.

The relevance of an analysis of institutionalization that emphasizes organizations' management of their environments through the concept of enactment seems obvious, since it reverses the causes of organizational institutionalization from primarily being found in the organization's external environment, to the active management by the organization of its experiences of the environment. Organizations do not adapt to their 'objective' environments, but to their experience of their environments. The enactment concept does not negate loose coupling between the organization and its environment, thus avoiding an unproductive tautology where organizations can only adapt to their environments if the environments are adapted to the organizations, and vice versa (cf. March and Olsen, 1979: 56–59; Weick, 1976). Instead, the enactment concept stresses that organizations typically strive towards 'closing' any behavioral differences between the organization and the environment on experiential grounds.

By organizations enacting their environments they are in the business of institutionalizing themselves as a result of their experienced activities that are not necessarily a response to any *a priori* 'external' pressure to conform: 'Managers and other organization members create not only their organization, but also their environment' (Smircich and Stubbart, 1985: 727). Certainly, 'the core institutionalist contribution is to see environments and organizational settings as highly interpenetrated' (Jepperson and Meyer, 1991: 205); to the extent that institutionalized organizations are isomorphic with their environments, this is not the result of organizations adapting to external forces, but the result of them effectively managing their experiences of their environments. This is the reason why Weber (1978: 973) stressed that institutionalization thrives on a technically rational management whose 'precision, speed, unambiguity, knowledge of the files, continuity, discretion, unity, strict subordination, reduction of friction and of material and personal costs' can accomplish a fundamental requirement in the process of institutionalization; namely, shaping the environment in a way that the organization is created for.

THE SUBSTANTIVE RESEARCH PROBLEM

One of the potentially most relevant areas for analyzing organized institutionalization according to the theoretical framework that was discussed above is *social welfare organizations*. The phenomenon of social welfare organizations in contemporary society reflects the fact that the distribution of much social welfare is a formally organized affair. Some of the welfare is disseminated by ordinary organizations such as companies, schools, churches, government agencies, military organizations, to mention a few. Other welfare services are offered by organizations that are exclusively dedicated to providing welfare, such as blindness agencies, sheltered work organizations, rehabilitation clinics, and similar organizations. According to one popular definition, social welfare organizations 'operate primarily to further the common good and general welfare of the people of the community (such as by bringing about civic betterment and social improvements).'[2]

How does the institutionalization of social welfare in modern society come about through the organized programs and activities of social welfare organizations? What are its implications and consequences? What will a close and critical study of the institutionalization of social welfare tell us about these problems? These questions are important since the distribution of welfare is so contingent upon formal organization and management in modern society. It is especially important to examine the institutionalization of social welfare organizations because these organizations are proposed as contributions to the technique of 'normal life.' Paraphrasing Philip Selznick's (1949) classic study of institutionalization, *TVA and the Grass Roots: A Study of Politics and Organization*: a social welfare organization is obviously many things, but most important for this study's purposes is its status as a social instrument. It is this role as instrument with which this study is concerned; in other words it is the organization to which my attention is directed. Hence it is the nature of the welfare organization as an organized group of working individuals, as a living organization, which is under scrutiny.

A key problem for any social welfare organization is its ability to help and assist disadvantaged people. This requires an ability on the part of the organization to understand and adapt to disadvantaged people's individual requirements and demands:

> The purpose of social welfare is to promote the social betterment of a class or group of people who are defined as disadvantaged, handicapped, or deprived. A set of common problems is attributed to such persons based upon the nature of the trait or quality which sets them apart from the rest of society. Programs of social welfare are then planned to meet the needs which arise out of these problems. It is believed that the form and content of such programs should be determined by the needs of the client. As his needs change, the programs themselves must change; conversely, the welfare of the client should be the primary factor to consider in making any policy decisions about change in such programs. (Scott, 1980: 97)

Any social welfare organization can be assumed to face an immense complexity in their environments as a result of clients' varying and changing personal needs, requirements, and demands. On the one hand, adapting to all clients' needs is the ultimate indicator of a social welfare organization's effectiveness, without which it soon will lose its legitimacy. A blindness agency that doesn't respond to the concerns and demands of sight-impaired people is bound to perish. Eventually it will not be regarded as a credible and legitimate actor in providing social welfare. On the other hand, responding to all individual requirements and needs among its clients seems impossible if any concern about the overall organizational performance is to be secured. If a blindness agency would attempt to adapt completely to every client's needs, it would soon be swamped by too conflicting and incommensurable demands. This well-known dilemma in analyses of organizations' adaptation to their environments (e.g., Cyert and March, 1992; Meyer and Rowan, 1991; Pfeffer and Salancik, 2003) seems to be particularly acute with social welfare organizations, given their primary task to address people's individual needs and concerns in an organizationally rational way.

Despite the common idea in the literature on organized social welfare—that 'successful' social welfare organizations should be efficient in managing their adaptation to the requirements as experienced by their clients (e.g., Hasenfeld, 2000; Schmid, 2000; Slavin, 1985)—a number of empirical studies of organized social welfare have suggested that in their efforts to adapt to the needs of their clients, they have instead increasingly become more concerned with their own needs. For instance Scott (1980: 97) argued that clients' requests and the kinds of available welfare services often run in two separate orbits. He claimed that the services which are offered to needy persons do not necessarily apply to all of them, nor can it be assumed that they are necessarily benefited by them. According to Scott, the preservation of the organization itself is a vital factor when analyzing the behavior of organized social welfare. Similarly, Stone (1985: 183) claimed that the 'paradox' of social welfare organizations is that they on the one hand seek to reduce the number of problem cases who need their services, but on the other hand demonstrate that problem cases abound. 'A rehabilitation agency, for example, needs clients in order to survive and grow.' Lane (1997: 155) stated in his study of social welfare services for deaf children that 'organizations espousing each construction of deafness compete to "own" the children and define their needs. Their very economic survival depends on their success in that competition.'

Fundamentally, how can we understand how a social welfare organization adapts to its most important environment; that is, its prospective and existing clients? Potentially, this issue can be approached by analyzing how clients are enacted as 'disabled' by social welfare organizations. In the standard literature on welfare programs and the welfare state it is emphasized that *medical classification of disability* has become one of the major paths to aid and assistance in most countries today (e.g., Butcher, 2002; Considine, 2001; Drake, 1999; Lane, 1997; Lindert, 2004). As Stone argued in her book *The Disabled State*:

The very notion of disability is fundamental to the architecture of the welfare state; it is something like a keystone that allows the other supporting structures of the welfare system and, in some sense, the economy at large to remain in place. (Stone, 1985: 12)

Potentially medical concepts and ideas pertinent to disability, such as clinical testing, diagnosing, and rehabilitation of individuals, are particularly efficient management practices that act to institutionalize social welfare in society. Increasingly, modern social welfare organization has joined hands with medical practice in order to rationally carry out its main objective, which is to administer and manage social welfare (Abberley, 2002; Albrecht, 2002; Thomas, 2002). In his study *The Medicalization of Welfare,* Schram (2000) analyzed how welfare organizations devoted to reducing poverty are ever more drawing on medical ideas (e.g., clinical procedures in diagnosing illnesses) in order to organize their clients as legal and administratively legitimate recipients of aid. He noted how these organizations evaluate their clients' ability to get a job on medical, rather than professional grounds: 'Health and mental health screening become critical features of welfare administration' (87). Schram concluded that 'the medicalization of welfare is part of the rise of a larger therapeutic culture' (83) and that 'welfare dependency is itself increasingly being redefined from an economic problem to a medicalized one' (81).

By managing social welfare through medical concepts and ideas social welfare organizations have an interesting potential to enact their environments and hence to effectively institutionalize themselves. This potential can be explored through the concept of 'medicalization' (e.g., Conrad, 2007; Lupton, 1997; Pitts, 1968). Medicalization is commonly regarded as a process by which all the more human behaviors become defined and treated as medical problems and issues; thus becoming the subject of a medical organization's experience. Medicalization thrives on discipline and control, making people's learning of the 'sick role,' for instance, a rational and effective enterprise (Loe, 2004; Parsons, 1951; Schram, 2000). But medicalization is not only an effect of formal organization and management, it is also a function of management by providing a clinical template for authority and control. In this way medicalization is a potentially important mechanism of organizations' enactment as the effective management of organizations' experience of their environments.

As will be explored in this study, medicalization constituted through such standard management practices as examinations, diagnoses, training, and testing, is a crucial mechanism for managing organizations' environments in terms of their experience of human behaviors. As such it does not only compose an important management mechanism in its traditional 'technical' sense of controlling and influencing human behavior to carry out various activities in a rule-bounded way; it also constitutes a mechanism of institutionalization by which people's fundamental identity become transformed in a way the organization is created for.

There is a need for analyzing both how social welfare management medicalizes, and how social welfare management is being medicalized—both the management of medicalization and the medicalization of management. On the one hand, medicalization has the potential to facilitate the management and administration of social welfare organizations by relying on a medical model's aura of impartiality and exactness both in order to effectively address the classic problem of the 'distributive dilemma' in social welfare (e.g., Gummer, 1990; Patti, 2000; Slavin, 1985); that is, who are the needy that should enjoy help and assistance; and by addressing the process of rehabilitation and restoration of selected clients to a 'normal life' (e.g., Abberley, 2002; Albrecht, 1992). By enacting clients as disabled (i.e., medically problematic), individuals can be managed as 'productive' actors that can contribute to the organization's effective accomplishment of its purpose; namely to provide social welfare in an ongoing and repetitive manner to the benefit of disabled individuals.

On the other hand, the medicalization of social welfare may contribute to generating the legendary pathological effects of institutionalization in terms of organizational pressure to expand the definition of who are the disabled. By all the more human behaviors becoming identified and treated as medically problematic by an expanding social welfare system, all the more people are likely to be asking for welfare support that they experience themselves as being in need of given their disabilities. The result may, in the end, be a self-fulfilling prophecy: Based on experience, the institutionalization of social welfare organization generates the problems among people to which social welfare organizations have the 'only' and 'obvious' solutions. What may happen is that social welfare organizations eventually start shaping the environment by becoming increasingly responsive to their experiences of prospective and existing clients, and all the more unresponsive to the experiences as held by clients themselves. By managing through medicalizing, management itself may become all the more medicalized by social welfare organizations increasingly adapting to people's disabilities that are the result of their own enactment; by managing social welfare by medicalizing welfare clients' behavior, social welfare may become all the more medicalized (see Schram, 2000); by managing citizens of a society as medical cases, society may eventually become medicalized (see Conrad, 2007). As Schumpeter (1955: 25) laconically said: 'Created by the wars that required it, the machine now created the wars it required.'

2 Medicalizing Management
A Framework of Analysis

In the present study, the significance of the concept of medicalization for organizational analysis is examined as the intersection of two sets of conceptions of institutionalization: those associated with management and those associated with medicine. In defining this framework of institutionalization there is, first, a need to discuss the critical relationship between medicine and management. What does a 'medical perspective' on management imply; and what does a 'management perspective' on medicine imply? What are we seeing with the linking of medicine and organization? What are we ignoring? Such evaluation requires reflection on the ways that medical ideas inform us about management; but also about the ways management informs us about medicine.

Modern medicine rests on two fundamental ideas: That it builds on methods that are elaborated within the natural sciences, and that it is effective. In this regard medicine comes close to a common quest of management as illustrated by, for instance, Weber's (1978) ideas on rational-legal domination and authority, Taylor's (1998) principles of 'scientific management,' and Simon's (1997) theories of decision making. Weber stressed the following:

> Bureaucracy develops the more perfectly, the more it is 'dehumanized,' the more completely it succeeds in eliminating from official business love, hatred, and all purely personal, irrational, and emotional elements which escape calculation. (Weber, 1978: 975)

Regarded as a form of legal domination that rests on a belief in the legality of enacted rules, medicine necessarily becomes a formally administrated, bureaucratized enterprise. The ethos of bureaucracy seems to fit modern medicine's tendency toward imperialism particularly well (see, e.g., Conrad, 2007; Illich, 1975). To the extent that medicine is successful in expanding its domain, it is due to its claims for scientific, rational, and legal legitimacy. To a large extent the history of medicine is the history of formal organization, where a trained expert displaces old trial procedures which are bound to tradition or irrational presuppositions (Foucault, 1989: 45;

Weber, 1978: 975). The result is a technical superiority of medical organizations that have training and experience, and the likelihood that they will continue acting medically because of this superiority. Instead of entrusting medical practice to the mercy of mountebanks and gossips, it has become a formally managed affair.

According to *The Concise Oxford Dictionary* (1999: 864), the word 'management' denotes at least three things:

(a) 'The process of managing,' i.e., the control, regulation, supervision, hence organization of certain activities;
(b) 'The people managing an organization,' such as executives, managers, and other formally appointed leaders; and
(c) 'The treatment or control of diseases or disorders, or the care of patients who suffer from them.'

It is no coincidence that management is a key concept in both medical and organizational discourse: both deal with regulating and addressing potential or existing threats to the effective operation of human or social organisms, irrespective of whether these practices are labeled 'human resource management' as in the typical management discourse, or 'clinical management' as is typical in medical discourse. Some well-known clinical management activities are diagnosis, classification, documentation, examination, rehabilitation, treatment, and therapy; some standard human resource management practices are recruitment and selection, performance appraisal, training and development, testing, and exiting.

The relation between management and medicine can be explored by extending Weber's (1949) famous typology of 'economic institutions' and their relation to 'non-economic' phenomena. On the one hand, there exist events or institutions that were deliberately created for medical ends, such as hospitals or rehabilitation clinics. There are other non-medical institutions, for instance the political system, that insofar as they influence medicine have consequences which are of interest from a medical point of view; for example, through the regulation of medical practice and research. These can be called 'medically relevant' phenomena. Then there are institutions which are not medical but that still are influenced by medical factors; for instance, the area of legislation; in contemporary society, many areas of social life are legally prohibited by referring to medical science. These can be called 'medically conditioned' phenomena.

On the other hand, there exist institutions that were deliberately created for the purpose of management, such as administrative entities in corporations. There are other institutions of a non-managerial character that insofar as they influence management have consequences which are of interest from a management point of view; for example, management research. These can be called 'management relevant' phenomena. Finally, there are institutions which are not management in a traditional sense, but that still are influenced by standard managerial factors; for instance, religious organizations concerned with assisting people in crises. These can be called 'management conditioned' phenomena.

Of course, the boundary between 'medical' and 'non-medical' institutions is vague; the 'medical' aspect of a particular phenomenon is never only 'medically conditioned' nor only 'medically relevant.' Likewise, the boundary between 'management' and 'non-management' institutions is vague; the 'managerial' aspect of a particular phenomenon is never only 'management conditioned' nor is it only 'management relevant.'

In relation to medical institutions, management may be a relevant phenomenon, or a conditioned phenomenon. In relation to management institutions, medicine may be a relevant phenomenon, or a conditioned phenomenon. To be more specific, the following areas of analysis of the relationship between medicine and management is possible: (1) the ways in which management is a 'medically relevant' phenomenon (i.e., how management practices and activities in society may affect medicine and medical institutions); (2) the ways in which management is a 'medically conditioned' phenomenon (i.e., how management is influenced by medicine); (3) how medicine is a 'management relevant' phenomenon (i.e., how medical practices and activities in society may affect management and management institutions); and (4) how medicine is a 'management conditioned' phenomenon (i.e., how medicine is influenced by management). A 'relevant phenomenon' *influences* something; a 'conditioned phenomenon' is *being influenced* by something. The difference between something that is 'relevant' to something, and something that is 'conditioned' by something was not explained by Weber; however, he argued that both deal with 'influencing.' Swedberg (2005: 75) explained Weber's theory on economic institutions in the following way: *Economically conditioned phenomena* are 'non-economic phenomena...which are influenced to an important extent by economic phenomena.' *Economically relevant phenomena* are 'non-economic phenomena...which influence economic phenomena.' When management influences medicine, this can be called *managementization*. When medicine influences management, this can be referred to as *medicalization*. The interplay between medicine and management can thus be divided into two processes: 'managementization' and 'medicalization' (see Figure 2.1).

The relation between managementization and medicalization can be specified in the following way. When medical concepts and ideas, such as clinical testing of illnesses, are applied to medical events or in medical institutions, 'regular' medical activity prevails. Likewise, when management concepts and ideas, such as recruitment and training, are applied to management events or in management institutions, 'regular' management activity prevails. When medical concepts and ideas are applied to management events or in management institutions—in the present study social welfare organizations—a process of medicalization is at hand (i.e., 'medical

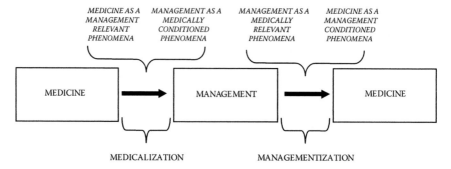

Figure 2.1 A typology of medicine and management.

imperialism'). When management concepts and ideas are applied to medical events or in medical institutions—for example, hospitals—a process of managementization is at hand (i.e., 'management imperialism') (see Figure 2.2).

Students of organizations have already paid a great deal of systematic attention to how management concepts and ideas may influence medical institutions. The 'managementization of medical activity' is a thoroughly researched area where much attention has been paid to the 'effective,' 'intelligent,' and 'rational' management of hospitals, clinics, and other welfare institutions (e.g., Christensen and Laegrid, 2001; Clark and Newman, 1997; McLaughlin et al., 2002). Few, if any studies have, however, devoted attention to how medical ideas and concepts affect the general theory and practice of management; for instance the administration and organization of social welfare (cf. Schram, 2000); and thus how medicalizing manage-

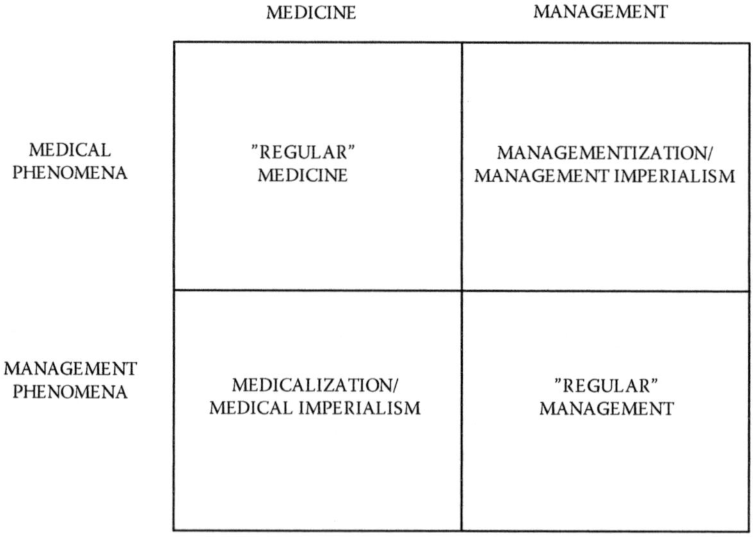

	MEDICINE	MANAGEMENT
MEDICAL PHENOMENA	"REGULAR" MEDICINE	MANAGEMENTIZATION/ MANAGEMENT IMPERIALISM
MANAGEMENT PHENOMENA	MEDICALIZATION/ MEDICAL IMPERIALISM	"REGULAR" MANAGEMENT

Figure 2.2 A typology of medicalization and managementization.

ment practices may contribute to the medicalization of particular organizations or fields of organizations (e.g., social welfare organizations), and the overall medicalization of society (Conrad, 2007; Illich, 1975).

I wish to examine medicine as a management practice concerned with enacting human behaviors. This stresses the need to analyze medicine as a managerial activity by focusing attention on its concrete practices of diagnosing, treating, and organizing humans as medical cases. Hence, the focus is on the 'managerialism' of medicine; that is, the ways medicine can be understood as 'management' in order to produce and reproduce organizations. Implicit in this approach is the idea that when I say that there is a medicalization of management through the dispersion of medical activity to management institutions and the development of a medical rationality in managerial discourse and practice, I also say that there is a widespread managementization of society. As with all organizing through standard operating procedures of sense-making, attention, translation, and interpretation of human behaviors (e.g., March and Olsen, 1979; Weick, 1979), medicine contributes to produce the environment that actors experience. In this sense it is performative. The object of its activities is the human being; hence it aims to enact a certain kind of individual activity. Medicine is not only about understanding and theorizing human behavior, it is also about generating, producing, and creating human beings without which certain organized activity cannot be accomplished. It is assumed that medicine has strongly formative elements in that it sets out to create human behaviors in certain ways; hence it is a potentially important management practice that may enact the kind of environment to which an organization subsequently adapts. The medicalization of an organization's environment may eventually generate the medicalization of the organization that becomes central to its institutionalization.

My attention is focused on medicalization pertinent to the analysis of social welfare organizations—how medical ideas of disability influence social welfare management. 'Medicalizing management' stresses: (1) the *management of medicalization* (i.e., medicine as a management relevant phenomenon); and (2) the *medicalization of management* (i.e., management as a medically conditioned phenomenon). Both can be understood as experiential learning processes that enact medical experiences from which both the individual and the organization adapts; both interact in the institutionalization of organizational behavior regarded as the continuous enactment of interlocked human behaviors. Hence, it is based on the idea that organizations and environments interact; they are always in a state of coupling, acting as mutual sources of perturbation.

In all, in this study I aim to examine how a social welfare organization manages by medicalizing through its formal practices, ceremonies, and procedures, and what the consequences of these activities are on individual and organizational behavior. Hence in this study I am concerned with the problem of 'medicalizing management' in explaining the institutionalization of social welfare; that is, both the management of medicalization and the medicalization of management. This framework addresses the theoretical and substantive research problems regarding how social welfare manages by medicalizing and how social welfare management is being medicalized; that is, how social welfare clients' individual behavior is managed through medicalization concurrently with the medicalization of social welfare.

In the following two chapters I extend the introductory analysis of chapters 1 and 2. In chapter 3, a theory of management is proposed based on an analysis of how experiences are enacted through experiential learning. It is argued that formal organizations manage humans' experience both by providing the content of social identities and roles and by providing cues for evoking them. They define appropriate behavioral rules to attach to appropriate identities and structure the occasions for experientially learning one identity or role over another. This management becomes the basic mechanism of organizations enacting their environments as part of a larger enterprise of institutionalization. In chapter 4, attention is given to theories of medicalization. The ways in which individuals enact themselves as disabled, sick, impaired, or in other ways medically problematic is proposed, based on their individual experiential learning. This learning is organizationally managed as part of formal organizations' enactment of their experience. According to this analysis, medicalization is managed learning derived from individual 'medical experience,' resulting in organizational enactment of human behavior.

3 Management

By what mechanisms can we understand how organizations adapt to their enacted environments? In their seminal analysis Cyert and March (1992: 118) proposed that 'an organization is an adaptive institution. In short, the firm learns from its experience.' Ideally the experiential learning by an organization of an environment's total demands requires that the organization can experience the environment perfectly and objectively, (i.e., understand its full variety and complexity). But, since the complexity of the environment is always immensely greater than the computational powers of an organization (Simon, 1996), no organization can experience and thus learn from all potentially relevant experiences of its environment. Instead, organizations largely create the environmental experiences from which they subsequently learn. This is accomplished through a process of organization–environment interaction, where the organization typically influences its environment to generate 'organizationally relevant' experiences that can form the basis of its learning. Hence, organizations 'negotiate their environments' (Cyert and March, 1992) and 'manipulate' them (Hedberg et al., 1976) by managing the process of organization–environment experiencing in order to generate particular experiences that can form the basis of its learning. Why? In order to preserve itself, adding to 'self-maintenance' (Selznick, 1984: 21), organizations experientially 'buffer' themselves from external contingencies (Thompson, 2003: 20–24). By learning organizationally relevant behaviors based on experience, the environment ceases to be a fully 'external' source of uncertainty. In this way organizations' environments are largely the product of organization influence: 'Organizations' environments are not given realities; they are created' (Pfeffer and Salancik, 2003: 13).

Retrieved experiences from earlier organizational learning in the form of standard operating procedures, rules, and routines generate experiences of the environment to which the organization is already more or less accustomed, thus focusing its attention on 'relevant' experiences (March and Olsen, 1979). Learning from the experience of certain environmental demands derives from this; requirements that can be associated to existing organizational experiences in the organizational memory (Walsh and

Ungson, 1991). Existing experience limits the process of learning from new experience, thus enabling the organization to learn 'organizationally appropriate' experience (Weick, 1979b: 42). Without this ability to ignore and select, the organization would merely experience experiential chaos, becoming swamped by incommensurable demands from its environment. Lacking an ability to *manage* relevant experiences through discriminative attention, no lessons from its construction of the environment will be experienced. Organizations operate in a stream of ongoing environmental experience; experiences are made discrete through a process of interpretation and attention that forms the basis for certain experiential learning.

> It is in this sense that members of organizations actually create the environment to which they then adapt. It is actors and actors alone who separate out for closer attention portions of an ongoing flow of experience. It is their making of experience into discrete experiences that produces the raw material for organizing. (Weick, 1969: 91)

This management activity can be called 'enactment,' i.e., 'processes through which learners create their environments' (Hedberg, 1981: 5). Enactment is the conscious coordination of learning from experience of the environment that the organization can understand and act on. Based on learned rules and routines, the organization actively manipulates the environment and then it reacts based on the same rules and routines (March and Olsen, 1979: 13f). There is no experience of any kind of the environment until the organization *does* something with it and then *suffers* its consequences. As already said, the process is one of organization–environment interaction creating certain experiences, where the organization influences the environment to learn from its experiences in an 'organizationally relevant' way. Organizations that learn 'effectively' become well-adapted to their environments, even as their environments become well-adapted to them. The enactment of experience is a reciprocal act between the organization and environment, both of which make demands on each other; but it is always the organization that *determines* what aspects of its experience to attend to as *triggered* by the environment.

This process needs management if it is to create certain organizationally relevant experiences. The environment must be influenced to experience things that are relevant to the organization in order to change its behavior (i.e., learning) in an organizationally attractive way. Management plays a key role in enacting appropriate environmental experiences through dominating experiential learning: 'One function of management...is to guide and control this process of manipulating the environment' (Pfeffer and Salancik, 2003: 18). Organizations' environments are subject to various forms of organizational influence in order for them to generate organizationally appropriate experiences of their own behavior so that they can learn to act as 'instruments' of the organization (Cyert and March, 1992;

Simon, 1997). Managers, acting 'as writers of scripts and providers of cues and prompts' (March, 1994: 72) organize the bargaining-learning that occurs by enacting certain aspects of experience. Hence 'managers construct, rearrange, single out, and demolish many "objective" features of their surroundings' (Weick, 1979a: 164).

The extent to which an organization learns from its experience of its environment is a function of its authority in organization–environment bargaining. Authority, that is, 'the power to make decisions which guide the actions of another' (Simon, 1997: 179), is given by the subordinate actor; he or she 'permits his [or her] behavior to be guided by the decision of a superior' (Ibid: 10). Authority is based on a belief that the superior possesses or has access to some resources that the subordinate needs. This is also to say that power in social bargaining resides in the other party's dependence on specific resources (Emerson, 1962; Pfeffer and Salancik, 2003: 44–52; Stinchcombe, 1968: 162; Weber, 1946: 81–82), thus making the other actor's implicit or explicit claims for obedience appear legitimate (Weber, 1978: 212–215; also 63f). An organization is dependent on its environment in proportion to the organization's need for resources that the environment can provide and in inverse proportion to the ability of other environments to provide the same resource. Such resources are 'behavioral commitments' (Cyert and March, 1992); that is, factors that enable a certain mode of action and essentially constitute rules, routines, and other forms of encoded experience. Hence, the conclusion by Weber (1978) that the bureaucracy, which he regarded as 'the most rational known means of exercising authority over human beings' (223), 'means fundamentally domination through knowledge' (225). The more power an actor has, the more likely it is that the organization has access to the resource that the subordinate needs based on its experiences. The power of organizations in the bargaining process therefore becomes crucial to the outcome of learning regarded as a mechanism for enacting its environment. Being powerful means successfully managing experiential variety in the organization–environment interaction, thus making certain learning possible. Consequently, 'power is a property of the social relation; it is not an attribute of the actor' (Emerson, 1962: 32); it is inherent in the bargaining–learning process. Weber (1978: 36–37) stressed that enactment (i.e., the ability to impose an order as legal), is the most important basis for actors to ascribe legitimacy. Hence, an organization's 'enacted order may be established in one of two ways: by voluntary agreement, or by being imposed and acquiesced in' (Weber, 1978: 50).

'Successfully' managing the (enacted) environment, the organization may eventually generate a behaviorally closed system. As Weick (1979a: 239) argued: 'Organizations can and do act like closed systems.... Organizational attentiveness to one's own past experience can continue unpunished for surprisingly long periods of time.' Eventually the learning of experience from the environment becomes a self-fulfilling prophecy (Watzlawick et al., 1974). As a result of its dominance of the learning from enacted experiences, the environment becomes part of the organization. A distinction between the organization and its environment becomes hopelessly obscured. The organization learns to adapt to its enacted experiences that form the basis of its behavior, and not to any 'objective' experiences as posed by an 'external' environment. Environments come to act 'organizationally' based on organizationally formed experiences. The end result is the generation of positive feedback between experience and competence, potentially creating self-destructive 'competency traps' (Levitt and March, 1988) and excessive exploitation of existing experiences (Holmqvist, 2004). This legendary effect of learning through enacting environmental experiences generates a closed connection between organizational actions and environmental actions (Hedberg, 1981; March and Olsen, 1979). Put differently, the organization has successfully come to manage a source of external uncertainty by fully transforming the environment into a part of the organization on experiential grounds.

MANAGING INDIVIDUAL EXPERIENCING

When referring to 'organizational enactment' it is essentially individuals' managed learning from experience that is at the center of attention. Although individuals are born with certain innately organized patterns of behavior that predispose them towards the world in a certain fashion, most social scientists would agree that behavior is learnt from experience. As Bandura (1986: 20) argued:

> Humans come with few inborn patterns. This remarkable plasticity places high demand on learning.... It is difficult to imagine a social transmission system in which the language, life style, and institutional practices of the culture are taught to each new member just by selective reinforcement and fortuitous behaviors, without the benefit of models to exemplify these cultural patterns.

According to Bandura, 'most patterns of human behavior are organized by individual experience and retained in neural codes, rather than being provided ready-made by inborn programming' (Ibid: 22). But what is experience? Dewey argued that experience includes *what* people do, as well as *how* people act and are acted upon (i.e., processes of experiencing). When *experiencing*, individuals act upon experience and do something with it and then they suffer the consequences of their experience. In this sense, experience has both an active and a passive element; actors do something to it, and experience does something to them:

The nature of experience can be understood only by noting that it includes an active and passive element peculiarly combined. On the active hand, experience is trying—a meaning which is made explicit in the connected term experiment. On the passive, it is undergoing.... The connection of these two phases of experience measures the fruitfulness or value of the experience. Mere activity does not constitute experience. It is dispersive, centrifugal, dissipating. Experience as trying involves change, but change is meaningless transition unless it is consciously connected with the return of wave of consequences which flow from it. When an activity is continued into the undergoing of consequences, when the change made by action is reflected back into a change made in us, the mere flux is loaded with significance. (Dewey, 1916: 139)

To learn from experience is to make a backward and forward connection between what people do to things and what they enjoy or suffer from things as a consequence. 'Meaningful experience,' such as 'medical experience' and more specifically 'sickness,' 'blindness,' or 'deafness,' is the experience that is actively sorted out from an ongoing stream of individual experiencing. On the one hand then, there is experience that is chaotic, fragmentary, and ambiguous. On the other hand there is experience that is refined and distinct. *An* experience gains a unity as a result of certain activity: 'The fact that I become aware of the meaning of an experience presupposes that I notice it and "select it out" from all my other experiences' (Schutz, 1967: 41). Hence, 'contact with experience presupposes an organizing or structuring activity' (Piaget, 1952: 369). Without conscious attention, there can be no experience of any kind. 'No experience having a meaning is possible without some element of thought' (Dewey, 1916: 145). In that regard *'my experience is what I agree to attend to.* Only those items which I *notice* shape my mind—without selective interest, experience is utter chaos (James, 1981: 381). People are 'agents of experiences rather than simply undergoers of experiences' (Bandura, 2001: 4). Once an experience has been caught in the 'cone of light' as Schutz (1967) put it, the experience is 'lifted out' from the ongoing stream of lived experience, and becomes discrete. It is at this moment that the experience acquires meaning. Through activity, individuals 'freeze' some experience that they subsequently reflect upon. As a result of such acts, there are meaning-endowed experience, and meaningless experience underlying any individual's behavioral repertoire.

As already implied, experiencing requires management in the form of reflective attention; it is not experience by only passively living in experience: 'If I call one of these experiences meaningful it is only because, in taking heed of it, I have "selected it out" of and distinguished it from the abundance of experience coexisting with it, preceding it, and following it'

(Schutz, 1967: 41). Consequently, 'consciousness is at all times primarily a *selecting agency*' (James, 1981: 142). An individual 'responds to the pattern of stimuli to which [she] is exposed,' resulting from his or her '*organization* of sensory experience' (Köhler, 1970: 120). By *actively* managing their attention to their living experience, people are no longer only passively living within a flow of real and imagined experience; but the experience is understood, apprehended, and distinguished:

> Meaning does not lie in the experience. Rather, those experiences are meaningful which are grasped reflectively. The meaning is the way in which the Ego regards its experience. The meaning lies in the attitude of the Ego toward that part of its stream of consciousness which has already flowed by.... Ego looks at its experience and thereby renders it meaningful. (Schutz, 1967: 69f)

By managing their individual experiencing, people do not react to experiences; they *enact* them. Obviously this idea, as said above, presupposes that any meaningful experience of an individual is *lived*; it is not living or to be lived. 'Stated bluntly, we can know what we've done only after we've done it. Only by doing is it possible for us to discover what we have done' (Weick, 1969: 64). The only way to lend experiences discreteness, separateness, and distinctiveness (i.e., meaning) is by stepping outside the stream of continuous experience and directing attention to it:

> When, by my act of reflection, I turn my attention to my living experience, I am no longer taking up my position within the stream of pure duration, I am no longer simply living within that flow. The experiences are apprehended, distinguished, brought into relief, marked out from one another; the experiences which were constituted as phases within the flow of duration now become object of attention as constituted experiences. What had first been constituted as a phase now stands out as a full-blown experience, no matter whether the Act of attention is one of reflection or of reproduction (in simple apprehension). For the Act of attention—and this is of major importance for the study of meaning—presupposes an elapsed, passed-away experience—in short, one that is already in the past. (Schutz, 1967: 51)

An experience, for instance 'disability,' always refers to a prior experience that acts as cognitive typification. Without ability to recognize, people will not experience. This is not a passive affair. Prior experience directs (but does not determine) people's attention to situations in a selective manner and thus allows them to experience certain things. Experiencing is backward looking: 'A painter must continuously undergo the effect of his every brush stroke or he will not be aware of what he is doing and where his work is going' (Dewey, 1934: 45). Individuals have the ability to apply a range of schematic rules to manipulate and negotiate experiences. Any situation is 'pre-managed' through existing experiences—people may gain new experiences to the extent that they combine their existing experiences in a novel way. Hence, it is not the case that people encounter new situations which are then interpreted. People enact situations from existing experiences.

MANAGING SOCIAL EXPERIENCING

'Experience does not go on simply inside a person. It goes on there, for it influences the formation of attitudes of desire and purpose. But this is not the whole of the story.... There are sources outside an individual which give rise to experience' (Dewey, 1938: 39). These external sources are real in the sense that they have 'a being independent of our own volition (we cannot "wish them away")'; they are not the products of our enacted experience (Berger and Luckmann, 1966: 13). Creating meaningful experiences that can be learned from is in this way a social rather than an individual process. Things interacting in certain ways *are* experience—the environment is 'whatever conditions interact with personal needs, desires, purposes and capacities to *create* the experience which is *had*'(Dewey, 1938: 43). Learning is socially situated; every experiential learning is the result of interaction between a person and the world in which he or she lives. According to this view, there is no 'one-sided determinism' as in either extreme behaviorism (e.g., Skinner, 1953) or in extreme cognitivism (e.g., Freud, 2001); but rather a 'reciprocal determinism' in managing learning (Bandura, 1986). Experiential learning can be conceptualized as a process of social bargaining where actors make sense of their experiences by reducing the possible meanings of experience. Both inner and external factors determine the ensuing behavior:

> The individual is contained in sociation and, at the same time, finds himself confronted by it. He is both a link in the organism of sociation and an autonomous organic whole; he exists both for society and for himself.... The 'within' and the 'without' between individual and society are not two unrelated definitions but define together the fully homogenous position of man as a social animal.' (Simmel, 1971: 17)

Experience is not an objective entity that exists independently of human consciousness, but neither is an individual's experience a fully private affair. Experience is instead what is known similarly by others. In that regard any meaningful experience is necessarily 'intersubjective' (Schutz and Luckmann, 1973). The socially situated character of experiential learning implies that people take heed of the social context in which they find themselves, by collectively enacting certain social rules that they judge appropriate and legitimate. This socially rule-bound dimension is indispensable to the ability to attend to one's private experience and link it to the 'external world.' Social rules are encoded experience that is crucial to people's collective sense-making of their individual experience.

When individuals learn from experience, they do not follow logic of consequences by evaluating all possible experiences. Instead they act in socially appropriate ways, 'fulfilling identities or roles by recognizing situations and following rules that match behavior to the situations they encounter' (March, 1994: viii). Without this ability of sociality, an individual's learning would be tremendously burdensome; she would remain immature, helpless, without language, beliefs, ideas, or standards. It is by participating in specific social activities—essentially by learning social roles—that one can acquire specific and socially relevant experiences. 'Not only is social life identical with communication, but all communication (and hence all genuine social life) is educative. To be a recipient of a communication is to have an enlarged and changed experience' (Dewey, 1916: 5). An individual can acquire meaningful experience 'only by taking the attitudes of other individuals toward himself within a social environment or context of experience and behavior in which both he and they are involved' (Mead, 1967: 138). Learning invites the individual into certain social patterns; he or she must, to some extent, adapt to already established behavioral norms, which are, in a sense, both controlling and enabling. As Berger and Luckmann (1966: 53) said:

> I cannot use the rules of German syntax when I speak English; I cannot use words invented by my three-year-old son if I want to communicate outside my family; I must take into account prevailing standards of proper speech for various occasions, even it I would prefer my private 'improper' ones. Language provides me with a ready-made possibility for the ongoing objectification of my unfolding experience. Put differently, language is pliantly expansive so as to allow me to objectify a great variety of experiences coming my way in the course of my life.

As a result, 'one has to be a member of a community to be a self' (Mead, 1967: 162). Without behaving socially (i.e., following rules and acting as a member of something social), those experiences relevant to learning within a particular society cannot be enacted; they will remain ambiguous, equivocal, and obscure. In orienting one's own behavior towards that of others, it gains meaning.

The core mechanism of learning, selective attention to experience, is a social process where humans bargain with others in order to enact socially valid experiences (i.e., experiences that are socially meaningful). 'The individual in his isolation is nothing; only in and through absorption of the aims and meaning of organized institutions does he attain true personality' (Dewey, 1916: 94). Hence, 'the self has a character which is different from that of the physiological organism proper. The self is something which has a development; it is not initially there, at birth, but arises in the process of social experience and activity' (Mead, 1967:135). All learning stems from one's own enacted experience; but learning requires social interaction to make an individual aware of experience that otherwise would only have been 'lived through.' Potentially, a person knows herself better than anyone else. Her history of past experiences, most of which remain undisclosed, are part of her unique memory, 'stock of experience' that is basically only accessible to her. But this 'better knowledge' of herself requires attention and reflection. It is not immediately presented to any person. To make it available requires that the person stop, arrest the continuous spontaneity of her experience, and deliberately turn her attention back upon herself. 'What is more, such reflection about myself is typically occasioned by the attitude towards me that *the other* exhibits. It is typically a "mirror" response to attitudes of the other' (Berger and Luckmann, 1966: 44). Socially managed experience is necessary to form any individual experience; the attitude and behaviors of others are crucial to an individual's understanding of herself. In social processes, an individual learns to attend to her private experiences in a sensible and meaningful way.

ORGANIZED EXPERIENCING

As already indicated, the idea of social experiencing is basically not an idea of mutual adjustment but of social dominance, authority, and influence. Formal organization is contained in the very practices of interacting by people enacting social rules and routines (i.e., encoded experience). The necessary 'sorting out' of currently lived-through experience in learning processes is in essence an organizational affair, aimed at *certain* behavioral changes by the human actor. The importance of understanding experiential learning not only as a social, but also as a formally managed organizational process cannot be underestimated; it is only by formally organizing individuals' stream of experience, by consciously controlling and directing it, that experiences can be effectively enacted by associating them to earlier experiences. Unfocused, everyday, haphazard social interaction is not helpful in enacting specific experiences.

If, for instance, an individual is to become a patient at a hospital, he or she must learn 'relevant' experiences that are compatible with dominant social norms. Moreover, this learning must be efficient and rational, thus not being left to individual trial-and-error or random social interpretation. Socially valid experiences can only be enacted under specialized conditions, such as are found in highly organized settings in which people are members either by choice (e.g., corporations and other work organizations), by force (e.g., prisons and some hospitals), or by birth (e.g., families and some churches). 'The high specificity of structure and coordination within organizations—as contrasted with the diffuse and variable relations *among* organizations and among unorganized individuals—marks off the individual organization as a sociological unit' (March and Simon, 1993: 4).

'Organization' is *educative*, that is, influential and authoritative, in the sense that it acts as attention-cues to experience. First of all, organization provides people with rules of how to act and behave that affects what experiences they generate. Secondly, it has the potential to limit the stream of ongoing experience through social isolation. Thirdly, it can simplify attention to experience by organizing people's activities according to an idea of 'each individual having her own place.' Fourth and most importantly, it directs attention according to a system of hierarchy, making sequential attention to experience possible. Organization not only aims at reducing complexity in experience; it also aims at wedding out what is undesirable, which is a key requirement in any experiential learning:

> Organizations shape individual action both by providing the content of identities and rules and by providing appropriate cues for evoking them. They not only define appropriate behavioral rules to attach to appropriate identities...but also structure the occasions for evoking one identity or rules or another. (March, 1994: 71)

In essence, management constitutes the primary mechanism in individual experiential learning by constituting routines, procedures, conventions, strategies, codes, and other encoded experience around which any meaningful human behavior is constructed. This activity is crucial to any organized enactment. By directing attention, it provides a system of discipline, reducing any inefficiency in social phenomena. This discipline is absolutely necessary to learning by guiding people's efforts to draw lessons 'from relevant experience.' Indeed, organization (i.e., dominance), is indispensable in people's learning to overcome their own limitations in understanding their private experience. When learning meaningful experiences in contemporary formally organized society, people are basically learning organizational roles. At the same time they become selves, by rendering their experiences socially meaningful. In this regard experiential learning derives neither from the experience of the isolated individual actor, nor from the existence of any form of social totality; but from formally organized management practices, ceremonies, and procedures (Lave and Wenger, 1991; Tsoukas, 1996).

Organizations can be defined as collective behavioral plans, recipes, rules, instructions, and programs of argumentation, interpretation, naming, and sense-making of experience, as 'consensually validated grammar for reducing equivocality by means of sensible interlocked behaviors'

(Weick, 1979a: 3). Through their members' activities, organizations operate on experience that is ambiguous, uncertain, and equivocal; in formal
organizations individuals spend much time negotiating among themselves
an acceptable version of what is happening in various organization–environment situations. This process of striving for behavioral consensus is
also a process striving for reducing equivocality in direct experience, thus
enacting it as meaningful. Organization increases people's ability to learn
by minimizing experiential ambiguity, thus providing informative guidance
in their learning. They 'provide the general stimuli and attention-directors
that channelize behaviors of the members of the group' (Simon, 1997: 110).
By people acting according to organizational rules, their individual experience is organized into manageable proportions, hence making a relatively
swift and effective learning possible.

The central notion of 'bounded rationality' (e.g., March and Simon,
1993; Thompson, 2003) assumes that it is impossible for the single, isolated
individual to reach any high degree of intelligence. In living in an ongoing
stream of experience, the number of alternatives to explore is too great,
the information she must evaluate too vast. Therefore individual learning
takes place in an environment of 'givens,' premises that are seen as legitimate by the subject as bases for her attention to experience; and behavior
is adaptive within limits set by the 'givens.' Not only is this organized management of individual experiencing fundamental to human learning and
change; it is also fundamental to the reproduction of sociality, and hence
of organization:

> It is the social process in group life that creates and upholds the rules,
> not the rules that create and uphold group life.... A network or an insti-
> tution does not function automatically because of some inner dynamics
> or system requirements; it functions because people at different points
> do something, and what they do is a result of how they define the situ-
> ation in which they are called to act. (Blumer, 1969: 19)

Organization places humans in a psychological environment that will
adapt their individual experiencing to organization objectives; that is, to
organizationally enacted experience. By acquiring these, the individual
learns how to make sense of her individual ongoing stream of experience,
thus adding to the reproduction of certain organizational experiences. In
a sense then, by learning organizationally, an individual acts as an instrument to an organization, and in a way, meaningful behavior is never individual, it is always organizational. Individual skills, the behavioral result
of learning, '[are] the analogue of organizational routines' (Nelson and
Winter, 1982: 73). Hence, 'the organization member acquires knowledge,
skill, and identifications or loyalties that enable him to make decisions, by
himself, as the organization would like him to decide' (Simon, 1997: 112).

By organizations generating positive feedback between experience and competence, the individual becomes specialized in carrying out certain behaviors. Not only does organization simplify humans' experiential learning and make it manageable, they specialize it as well:

> When the stimuli is of a kind that has been experienced repeatedly in the past, the response will ordinarily be highly routinized.... The stimulus will evoke, with a minimum of problem-solving or other computational activity, a well-structured definition of the situation that will include a repertory of response programs, and programs for selecting an appropriate specific response from the repertory. (March and Simon, 1993: 140)

In the individual there is reinforcement through selective perception of experience and rationalization, so that eventually the individual will learn to experience situations organizationally, not personally. By having internalized organizational rules, routines, codes, and programs, people's behavior will act to generate organizationally appropriate experiences in a repetitive and taken-for-granted way. 'Having become true believers of a specific schema, group members direct their attention toward an environment and sample it in such a way that the true belief becomes self-validating and the group becomes even more fervent in its attachment to the schema' (Weick, 1979a: 156). The propensity of organization members to see those things that are consistent with their previous experience is a well-known observation among psychologists (e.g., Janis and Mann, 1977; Kahneman et al., 1982). Experiences that are discordant with the dominant frame of reference are filtered out before they reach consciousness, or are reinterpreted or 'rationalized' so as to remove the discrepancy. The organizationally molded individual frame of reference serves just as much to validate individual experience as the experience does to validate the frame of reference.

This legendary activity of organizational enactment is not accomplished by individual people, but by collective experiences that generate interlocked behaviors. The learning of a specific role, such as 'disabled,' is an organized activity taking place in particular organizational practices. It is only by acting organizationally that specific experience can be enacted, which is the reason why, for example, Scott (1969) concluded that it is primarily in blindness agencies people become blind or why Goffman (1961) argued that mental hospitals cannot fail to produce mental patients. Experiential learning stems from the specific practice at hand and in relation to the structuring resources of local conditions. Learning is not instruction or teaching, but the process of enacting self in a particular organization. Hence, what is learned is profoundly connected to the organized conditions under which it is learned:

The central issue in learning is becoming a practitioner, not learning about practice. This approach draws attention away from abstract knowledge and cranial processes and situates it in the practices and communities in which knowledge takes on significance. (Brown and Duguid, 1991: 48)

As already stressed, to learn from experience is to participate in particular activities, which are made possible through people's interlocked behaviors (i.e., organization). To *have* a medical experience, such as illness that can form the basis for learning of 'the sick role' in an organized system (Parsons, 1951) requires that this experience is sorted out from the constant flow of individual experience, which is accomplished organizationally rather than through tedious individual effort.

4 Medicalization

It is a standard observation that medicine has become all the more influential and powerful in society. Medical research, practice, and industry constantly elaborate new diagnoses, techniques, and treatments of human problems and disorders. Medicine deals increasingly with behaviors that are said to be physiologically or psychologically pathological, abnormal, or deviant. The popular notion of 'rehabilitation,' restoration to health and normal functioning, signifies some of this enterprise. Likewise, medicine increasingly deals with controlling the conditions that allegedly produce various behavioral disorders through 'preventive medicine,' 'health promotion,' and related activities of 'healthism.' Indeed, for a long time there has been a steady increase in the supply of medical services in coping with potential or existing disturbances to the health, well-being, and 'normal' functioning of individuals. People are examined by the medical profession at every stage in life; medical criteria often define what is acceptable in town planning, office structures, automobile design, food retailing, and many other areas. A medical interpretation of smoking defines the use of public space; medical examinations determine who is able to enter certain employments, benefit from welfare, take out insurance, and enjoy full civil rights.

Progressively medicine's expansion has become the focus of attention for sociological analyses. These enquiries examine the transformation of all the more human expressions, attitudes, and behaviors into medical issues and problems, and investigate its implications for individual and social life. The phenomenon under scrutiny is popularly called 'medicalization.' Literally, medicalization means 'to make medical.' According to *The Concise Oxford Dictionary* (1999: 885), to medicalize is to 'treat as a medical problem, especially without justification.' A standard definition of medicalization in sociological analyses is the process by which human behaviors become defined and treated as medical problems and issues (e.g., Ballard and Elston, 2005; Bull, 1990; Conrad, 2005; Schram, 2000). Zola (1972: 487) explained it as follows: 'Making medicine and the labels "healthy" and "ill" *relevant* to an ever increasing part of human existence.' Medicalization can be illustrated by the phenomenon of transforming such behaviors as menopause, eating disorder, suicide, infertility, melancholia, pedophilia, child abuse, impotence, criminality, hyperactivity, dying, and childbirth into medical cases, thus turning them into legitimate issues for medical intervention and control. Although some behaviors seem more completely medicalized than others a number of studies have stressed a considerable variety of human behavior that is increasingly being treated and organized as medical issues.

Some examples of classic studies of medicalization are Ervin Goffman's *Asylums* (1961), Michel Foucault's *The Birth of the Clinic* (1989/1963), Eliot Freidson's *Professions of Medicine* (1970), Robert A. Scott's *The Making of Blind Men* (1969), Ivan Illich's *Medical Nemesis* (1975), and Thomas S. Szasz's *The Myth of Mental Illness* (2003/1974). During the last several years the number of analyses of medicalization has surged. Andrew J. Polsky's *The Rise of the Therapeutic State* (1991), Richard Wertz and Dorothy Wertz's *Lying In:A History of Childbirth* (1989), Mieka Loe's *The Rise of Viagra* (2004), James Le Fanu's *The Rise and Fall of Modern Medicine* (2000), Gary Albrecht's *The Disability Business* (1992), Jan Branson and Don Miller's *Damned for Their Difference. The Cultural Construction of Deaf People as Disabled* (2002), Deborah Lupton's *The Imperative of Health* (1995), Peter Conrad's *The Medicalizaiton of Society* (2007), and Michael Fitzpatrick's *The Tyranny of Health* (2001), are but a few examples of recent studies dealing with medicalization.

The fact that medical sociology is one of contemporary sociology's most vibrant domains is but one of several testimonies to the importance of medicine as a field of inquiry for social scientists. Even though the majority of studies of medicalization so far have been grounded in a sociological frame of reference, and even though most studies of medicalization have so far been undertaken by sociologists, medicalization is today an issue for most social scientists. Increasingly, students of medicalization come from various fields such as psychology, criminology, history, ethnography, and anthropology. Even in medicine, increasing attention is being paid to medicalization. The special issue of the *British Medical Journal* (2002), 'Too Much Medicine,' is but one witness to this. Indeed, several important analyses of medicalization have been proposed by physicians (e.g., Le Fanu, 2000; Szasz, 2003).

MECHANISMS OF MEDICALIZATION

More specifically, what is medicalization? By what mechanisms does it take place and unfold? In his study of blindness agencies, Scott gave some answers:

> Many of the attitudes, behavior patterns, and qualities of character that have long been assumed to be given to blind people by their con-

dition are, in fact, the result of ordinary processes of socialization.... Organized intervention programs for the blind play a major role in determining the nature of this socialization. Blindness then is a social role that people who have serious difficulty seeing or who cannot see at all must learn how to play. (Scott, 1969:3)

Scott concluded that one of the most important, but least recognized, functions performed by organizations of the blindness system is to teach people who have difficulty seeing how to behave like blind people, thus embracing a view of themselves as 'medical cases' that need rehabilitation. According to Scott's analysis, blindness is not a 'bio-medical' condition; it is a learned social role that has been enacted in a formal and systematic way by sight-impaired people as a result of their participation in certain activities tied to specific social environments, in this case blindness agencies. In his study of the medicalization of mental illness, Szasz made the following point:

We think and speak of diseases as having 'causes,' 'treatments,' and 'cures.' However, if a person speaks a language other than our own, we do not look for the 'cause' of his peculiar linguistic behavior.... To understand such behavior, we must think in terms of learning and meaning. Accordingly, we might conclude that speaking French is the result of living among people who speak French. It follows, then, that if hysteria is an idiom rather than an illness, it is senseless to inquire its 'causes.' As with languages, we shall be able to ask only how hysteria was learned and what it means. (Szasz, 2003: 146)

As a result, Szasz concluded, mental illness is not something a person *has*, but is something he *does* or *is*. According to Szasz, being mentally ill is a particular behavior, linked to certain social rules that are enacted in activity. To understand mental illness, it is not sufficient to analyze who people are, but what they do; *how* they experientially learn social roles in a particular culturally and socially bounded way.

These studies are both representative of many classic and recent studies of medicalization. They shift away from the study of illness or health as a bio-medical attribute of people (a standard idea in medicine), to how medical conditions are enacted by people as a result of them participating in various social contexts. 'The disabled,' 'the healthy,' 'the sick,' and so on, are, according to this sociological perspective, not natural but social constructions, which result from certain medicalizing activities; a 'medical condition,' demanding medical intervention, is nothing but an effect of medicalization. As Foucault put it in his analysis:

A condition does not consist in a more or less pronounced trait but essentially in a sort of general deficiency of the individual's level of coordination.... This notion of condition offers two big advantages. The first is that it allows any physical element or deviant behavior whatever, however disparate and distant they may be, to be connected with a sort of unified background that accounts for it—a background that differs from the state of health but nevertheless is not an illness. Consequently, this notion of condition has a formidable capacity for integration: It refers to nonhealth, but it can also bring in its field any conduct whatsoever as soon as it is physiologically, psychologically, sociologically, morally, and even legally deviant. The notion's capacity for integration in this pathology, in this medicalization of the abnormal, is clearly marvelous. (Foucault, 2003: 312f)

In his 'sick role theory,' Parsons (1951) suggested that being sick or healthy is not necessarily a bio-medical status: as has already been said, it can also be regarded as a social role learned from experience. According to this perspective, a 'sick' person is not a unique personality; he or she is enacting a role provided by others, much as any other *homo sociologicus* would do. The role is linked to certain collective activities that are being reproduced by people carrying out their roles. A person acting as patient enacts certain organized activities (e.g., medical treatment). In that regard the concept of medicalization is not primarily concerned with the 'objective' state of an organism as a biological system, but with experiential learning of social roles that are grounded in individual experience. By emphasizing the social side of health, illness, and related medical concepts to explain the increase in medical conditions among people in contemporary society, students of medicalization have brought attention to how illness, health, disease, and related 'personal conditions' are in fact created in medically-oriented social practices and are, as a consequence, sociological rather than bio-medical in character (Corker and Shakespeare, 2002; Thomas, 2002). Thus students of medicalization have not been concerned so much with health or non-health *per se* but with the social processes through which certain forms of medical behaviors are enacted in individual experience through learning.

MEDICALIZATION AND ORGANIZATION

Students of medicalization have suggested that medicalization is not only a social affair in general. They have also argued that medicalization is a formally organized venture as a result of medically-oriented activities of such formal organizations as clinics, hospitals, rehabilitation agencies, social welfare organizations, medical professionals, pharmaceutical industries, and other sociologically unique actors. A standard idea is that the more powerful a medical organization in society, the more medicalized human behavior.

There exist a number of studies that illustrate this point that are worth mentioning in some detail. For instance, Loe's (2004) study of the pharmaceutical Viagra is an analysis of the role of organization for medicalizing men's erectile dysfunctions. By inducing men to learn the role of 'impotent,' they become legitimate consumers of Viagra, which is a pharmaceutical manufactured and sold to 'impotent men.' Albrecht (1992) claimed that a commercial industry is behind the expansion of the medical concept of disability in the United States, teaching people how to think and act as disabled in order for them to become 'legitimate consumers' of a rehabilitation industry's services. In his classic study of mental hospitals, Goffman proposed how people became mental patients as a result of certain organizational practices and ceremonies related to mental hospitals:

> In the mental hospital, the setting and the house rules press home to the patient that he is, after all, a mental case who has suffered some kind of social collapse on the outside, having failed in some over-all way, and that here he is of little social weight, being hardly capable of acting like a full-fledged person at all. (Goffman, 1961: 151f)

According to Goffman, a mental patient's 'career' is a learning process where individuals' initial experience of themselves as sane is gradually being re-defined according to a medical norm of mental illness (for another classic example of this, see Rosenhan, 1975). Eventually, the patient must 'insightfully' come to take the hospital's view of himself: 'The patient becomes the kind of object upon which a psychiatric service can be performed. To be made a patient is to be remade into a serviceable object' (Goffman, 1961: 379). Goffman concluded that psychiatric workers are not seen as discovering whether people are sick, but as making them sick. Finally, Bull analyzed the religious organization Seventh-Day Adventism's social control by medicalizing its environment:

> Adventists not only campaigned for the state to regulate the health of the population; they also started their own medically-based schemes for social improvement.... It is clear that Adventism operates as a dynamic and effective instrument for extending and defending the medical regulation of society. (Bull, 1990: 256)

The experiential learning of the social role as, for instance, blind or impotent, is a formally organized affair taking place within formal organizations, such as hospitals, clinics, welfare agencies, churches, and so on. Certainly, some people suffer from certain bio-medical problems, but this cannot alone explain how they become medical cases and how they eventually start experiencing themselves as, for instance, sick or disabled. Single organizations and the organizational networks in which they are members are instead assumed to be the primary agents of their medicalization of self.

By stressing the role of 'organization' in processes of medicalizing people's behavior, students of medicalization have suggested that medicalization is not a haphazard process, but the result of certain intentions and purposes (i.e., management). In his analysis of the history of medicine, Foucault (1989) emphasized that 'medical experience' can only be created in formally integrated contexts, where a 'medical gaze' systematically and deliberately, by acts of classification and diagnosis, brings into focus those experiences in individuals that are necessary for them to experience themselves as 'medical cases.' Hence, before the advent of medicine as an organized and unitary practice offered by clinical organization, 'an indispensable structure was lacking: a structure that might have given unity to a form of experience already defined by individual observation' (Foucault, 1989: 60). To experience oneself as a medical case requires a certain organization. Illness, disease, disability, and related medical experiences are always formed in correlation with a set of formal organizations and institutions of control that operate according to certain experiences.

CONSEQUENCES OF MEDICALIZATION

In his critique of medicine's growing imperialism, Illich (1975) claimed that society is being characterized by a 'medicalization of life.' Illich argued that 'the medical establishment has become a major threat to health' (11), by transforming more people into medical cases, irrespective of their bio-physiological status. As a result, individuals increasingly become the subject of medicine's management, reducing their individual power to manage themselves, Illich argued. In a medicalized society, 'to be healthy becomes an enlightened task. It also turns into an anti-social activity' (168). Regarded as a key mechanism of social control in contemporary society, medicalization is often analyzed in negative terms. In his article on medicalization, Pitts (1968: 391) emphasized: 'Medicalization is one of the most effective means of social control that is destined to become the main mode of *formal* social control.' If more and more 'normal' human behaviors become defined as medical problems, more and more people, it is said, are likely to learn to become medical cases that are systematically controlled, treated, and organized according to a medical model. Hence they will become cases for medical definition and intervention.

All social management requires vocabularies and ways of representing that which is to be governed and controlled. Medicalization can be seen as a mechanism by which certain human expressions, attitudes, and behaviors are enacted through a medical model's programs and techniques. That which is to be controlled, human behaviors, are brought out in relief, are made visible, and are conceptualized; that is, made manageable. 'Sickness,' for instance, is not a pre-given entity, but something being enacted in certain formally managed relations that aim to control people. Through processes of medicalization they become both an object of knowledge and a target of organizational management; they are not something 'discovered' but something enacted. By people learning from experience the role of 'healthy person' or 'sick person,' or any other medical experience in a formally managed way, they become tied to a social experience of health or non-health as conceptualized in certain organizational practices and institutions. As such, medicalization is essentially not repressive or negative; it is productive and positive by enacting certain behaviors that are functional in certain contexts (Lupton, 1997).

In order for an organization to control its environment by medicalizing, individuals' behavior must first become medical issues and problems. They must become known to themselves and to others as sick or healthy. Paraphrasing Simmel's (1971: 175–176) axiom on poverty, no one is socially healthy or non-healthy until he has been organized as such. And this has a general validity: sociologically speaking, health or non-health does not come first and then medical intervention. A person is called healthy or non-healthy who receives assistance or should receive it given her sociological situation, although perchance she may not receive it. The non-healthy person, as a sociological category, is not one who suffers specific deficiencies and deprivations, but one who receives assistance or should receive it according to social norms. In this sense, health or non-health cannot be defined in itself as a quantitative state, but only in terms of the social reaction resulting from a specific situation. Medical norms found and legitimize a certain exercise of management and are always linked to techniques of learning. By medicalizing all the more human behaviors through experiential learning, they become aligned to established medical and social norms of functioning and behaving. On a general level, this control concerns the construction of such social ideas as who is healthy, and thus 'normal'; medical control also concerns the promotion of health and rehabilitation of illness through concrete management activities of division of labor, counseling, examining, and diagnosing.

5   Samhall of Sweden

Based on a study of the Swedish sheltered work organization, Samhall (http://www.samhall.se), it is hoped that a contribution can be made here toward a better theoretical and empirical understanding of the institutionalization of social welfare. This contribution revolves around an analysis of how this particular organization adapts to its most important environment; its prospective and existing clients.

Although this is a study of the institutionalization of a Swedish welfare organization, the primary interest is in theoretical considerations. Therefore, the choice of research site is, perhaps, not as consequential as it might otherwise be. Of course, Samhall is deeply embedded in a unique political, social, and economic context, namely, Swedish welfare (e.g., Bengtsson, 1994; Lewis, 2004; Lindert, 2004). Internationally, Sweden has often been the source of much interest in conversations on the organization and management of social welfare. 'The Swedish Model'—originally designed by Gunnar Myrdal, the author of *An American Dilemma* and a Nobel Laureate in economics and his wife Alva Myrdal, a Nobel Laureate in peace— still remains an enigma in some of the international debate on welfare. It is not my intention to discuss the relative merits of this model as it is currently being exercised through Samhall. Rather, my intention is primarily to use Samhall as a case through which to explore the general theoretical and substantive research issues pertinent to the institutionalization of social welfare.

In the appendix, my study is outlined in detail. In brief, the main study was carried out from 2003 through 2005, with some complementary data gathering during 2006. The core of the data consists of an ethnographic study where I participated in Samhall's activities by working together with its clients for several months doing cleaning, producing food, manufacturing furniture, micro-filming documents, doing archival work, manufacturing closets, and other work, thereby participating in some of the many business activities in which Samhall is involved. The participant observation was complemented with about 100 interviews with managers and clients of Samhall, as well as with 20 interviews with administrative officials at the National Employment Office in Sweden. Both organizations granted me free access to their files, which enabled me to rely also on archival sources. In addition, a number of government reports and documents with reference to Samhall and social welfare policies were used.[1]

Overall, Samhall can be seen as an organization imbued with political goals regarding the distribution of welfare; social goals regarding rehabilitation of 'people with disabilities'; and economic goals pertinent to its business operations. Samhall's official assignment is 'to produce goods and services that are in demand [on the market] in order to provide meaningful and developing employment for persons with disabilities, where there is a need.' Founded in 1980 through a mandate by the Swedish Parliament, Samhall is today one of Scandinavia's leading corporations, selling a range of goods (e.g., medical technology, telecoms, and furniture) and services (e.g., cleaning, property-services, municipality-run home-help services, and staffing with complete teams for private business) in competition with other corporations serving consumers and organizations. It is also Sweden's largest subcontractor, working in close partnership with major international corporations, municipalities, and government agencies. With a presence in most of Sweden's municipalities, it is Sweden's most geographically spread welfare organization. Samhall employs around 22,000 individuals (2006) and has a turnover of approximately $1.1 billion; the organization receives an annual grant from Parliament of around $600,000 to compensate for its employees' alleged needs for a work environment 'specifically adapted to their individual disabilities.' Samhall can be described as an organization clothed with the power of government but possessed of the flexibility and initiative of a business organization.

As an important feature of contemporary Swedish welfare policy, Samhall is an organization that recruits the least attractive people on the job market, the so-called *occupationally disabled* and offers them employment according to the same conditions as in any work organization. In Samhall's documents it is stressed that the majority of the employees have one or several disabilities. The term 'occupationally disabled' ('arbetshandikappad' in the original Swedish)[2] was created in 1975 by the National Employment Office. According to a government ordinance, an occupationally disabled person is regarded as a needy individual due to his or her functional disorders, which impair the person from competing successfully with other people for jobs.

The core ideas of Samhall are 'social inclusion' and 'empowerment' through work. These ideas are not unique to Samhall and Sweden, but are central to many countries as part of their national welfare policies (e.g., Lewis, 2004; Shionoya, 2005). Internationally sponsored programs of inclusion and empowerment by, for instance, the United Nations, the International Labor Organization, and the European Union, aim at 'integrating people in need' in society by offering them work adapted to their unique demands and requirements. Indeed, 'work for the disabled' is commonly emphasized as a human right, stressing 'equal opportunities' for people in society (Albrecht, 2002; Corker and Shakespeare, 2002). Samhall is one of the founding members of Workability International, a global network of social welfare organizations 'dedicated to providing work and employment services to people with a disability' (http://www.workability-international. org). The organization is engaged in various European Union-sponsored programs on rehabilitation and employment, and is an active member of Rehabilitation International (http://www.rehab-international.org).

Samhall's current operational plan (2006) for the next few years 'is based on the following strategic objectives' established by Samhall's Board of Directors:

> Samhall shall be the leading company for long term employment for people with disabilities and a leading player in temporary employment;

> Samhall shall combine a strong individual perspective that focuses on each employee's potentials, with a profitable business structure that offers a variety of duties;

> Employment by Samhall shall generate value through high employment, training, and other development activities;

> The rest of the world shall perceive Samhall as the leading company in Sweden for development through employment for people with disabilities.

Besides offering occupationally disabled persons regular employment according to conditions that apply in any other work organization in Sweden, Samhall's purpose is to provide 'professional and personal rehabilitation, for instance, strengthening of self-confidence, increasing independence and developing valuable competence,' as it is stated in one of Samhall's documents. Thus, Samhall draws on the internationally popular idea of 'vocational rehabilitation.' Rehabilitation aims at 'normalizing'; that is, making people independent from welfare support in the future (e.g., Albrecht, 1992; Considine, 2001; Stone, 1985). The ultimate goal is that the employment at Samhall should end: 'Work within Samhall is organized in such a way that it enables the employee to eventually find employment at another employer.' Thus, a central idea of Samhall as an organization is rehabilitation of that which is problematic. In a government study it was laid down that Samhall has a special role 'in society's rehabilitation activities,' where it was pointed out that 'the rehabilitation undertaking must be regarded as being central to Samhall's activities.' This is said to imply 'helping sick people and people with a functional disorder to obtain the best functional capacity possible and conditions for a normal life...and is aimed at people who for medical, social or other reasons have difficulties in obtaining and retaining a job.'

In order to accomplish its goal of both offering *all* occupationally disabled individuals in society employment with Samhall, and rehabilitating those already employed, work activities in Samhall must be focused on effectively managing the unique needs and requirements of its clients. As maintained in one document, the company has therefore developed a 'quality-assured personnel development process' that describes how Samhall 'should carry out, follow up and improve personnel development in such a way that the requirements of the State are satisfied.' This process should originate from 'a unified personnel development methodology' for the entire organization, which, according to Samhall's personnel manager, requires 'concepts and systematization.' In this connection, it has been essential to formulate a 'theory' for Samhall, 'where the assumptions, values, goals and visions for the development for the work organization are made concrete,' emphasizing that 'conceptual coordination' is implemented within the company. Samhall's CEO formulated this challenge in the following way:

> To successfully tackle our primary assignment, we are heedful of the rehabilitative forces that are in action in the working environment. We attempt to counteract those forces that pull in the wrong direction and strengthen those forces that have a rehabilitative effect. The development of methodology is an ongoing process. It can be said that the development of methodology is our strategic center—our core.

These ideas are in accordance with the concept that Samhall offers, 'Development in daily work,' which is expressed in several Samhall documents, such as 'Rehabilitation through Work' and 'The Healing Force of Work.' In one of them it is established that 'the primary task of Samhall is to develop people' and that 'the specific thing with Samhall is that we are rehabilitated through work.' In another document, the following was pointed out:

> A job at Samhall provides an opportunity for personal and working life development as well as learning. The work itself, participation in production, is the basis for personal development. In addition to the daily work, different support actions and training are offered that have importance both for work at Samhall and for our employees' possibilities in the rest of the labor market. By operating a business enterprise, Samhall creates work that gives employees opportunities to develop their capacity for working based on individual prerequisites.

Overall, Samhall's methodology is based on the concept 'The Individual at the Center.' This is explained in one document: 'With the individual at the center, employment at Samhall should constitute a positive and goal-oriented opportunity for the client. This entails that the prerequisite, expectations, and needs of the individual for developmental and supportive efforts should serve as a guide during each employment situation.' The idea of putting individuals' unique needs and requirements first, and then adapting a welfare system to them, is core to social welfare organizations' operations (e.g., Hasenfeld, 2000; Patti, 2000; Scott, 1980). In order to accomplish this, the organizations are encouraged to systematically learn about their clients' needs and preferences in order to offer them an individually-adapted rehabilitation to a 'normal life' (Abberley, 2002; Davis, 1997). The general emphasis on the 'individual at the center' at Samhall is said to suppress the feeling among the disabled that they 'have little influence over their rehabilitation process,' which a government study pointed out. Learning about the abilities and personal qualities of clients are proverbially about the ability of Samhall to identify the limitations and problems of an individual with the aim of organizing the individual's need for help and assistance, and in so doing offer ' help to help oneself.'

A member of Samhall's corporate management declared: 'We should create a distinctive image of ourselves as a personnel development company, where people are employed after careful mapping.' This idea was explained in a Samhall brochure: 'The work tempo is adapted to the individual's prerequisites. Functional disorders are compensated by specially designed work environments and work adaptation.' The mapping of the individual is instituted before employment has taken place; and is about offering an adapted working environment based on the medical difficulties and problems that every employee of Samhall is presumed to have on the basis of his or her occupational disability. Hence, examination and assessment of the occupationally disabled are recurring activities throughout individuals' careers with Samhall in order to place them in an environment that is adapted to their unique needs, so that the best rehabilitative effect can be attained.

According to the organization, 'Samhall's assignment is based on personal development through employment. Samhall has a continuous personnel development process consisting of three components: recruitment, development, and transition.' **Recruitment** refers to the process through which 'the employment office refers unemployed job seekers with disabilities' to Samhall; **Development** refers to activities in which 'employees play an active role, accepting personal responsibility for their work and their own development'; and **Transition** is the process through which the client leaves the organization; 'the ultimate goal is a job outside of Samhall.' These activities are described in the following three chapters.

Chapter 6 describes how clients are recruited by Samhall based on an idea of 'occupational disability' among prospective welfare recipients. Chapter 7 reports the developmental activities that Samhall manages in rehabilitating its clients from their functional disorders that are assumed to explain their disabilities. A core idea is that clients develop through various work-related activities. Chapter 8 describes the issues involved when Samhall clients are to leave the welfare organization for a job outside Samhall, thus not relying on social welfare any longer.

6   Recruitment

Normally, employment as an occupationally disabled person at Samhall takes place via the auspices of the National Employment Office. All unemployed people in Sweden must register with the National Employment Office as unemployed in order to receive their unemployment compensation. Before discussing the recruitment program at Samhall, it may be relevant to mention something about the persons the National Employment Office judges to be potential candidates for assignment to Samhall. Among other things, this assessment is based on a government ordinance, 'Special Measures for Persons with an Occupational Disability.' In that ordinance it is specified that the target group for sheltered work at Samhall is those whose work capacity is reduced due to medical problems. 'Functional disorders' are problems that have been medically diagnosed by doctors or other medical experts that designate a person as in need of welfare services in relation to the rest of the unemployed population: 'A person is occupationally disabled if a functional disorder impairs or prevents participation in working life,' as it is expressed in a government report.

Staff at the National Employment Office, who are trained to match job applicants with available jobs, base their judgement of potential Samhall clients on the same criteria they use for other job applicants; that is, the applicant's capacity for work. In reaching the conclusion that an applicant is unable to hold down a job in the open labor market for medical reasons and would be best suited to a sheltered job with Samhall, they examine a number of factors about the applicant's conduct, such as repeated, lengthy, but unsuccessful efforts to find work themselves or with the help of National Employment Office staff; problems in holding down a job; deviant behavior during meetings with the National Employment Office; difficulties in reading information from the National Employment Office or in understanding information given verbally; physical abnormalities; problems in completing a written job application or in using computers when searching for job opportunities at the National Employment Office; or difficulties in communicating in Swedish.

According to one administrative official of the National Employment Office, these and other forms of behavior on the part of the job applicant can 'indicate' that a person has or can be expected to have difficulties in finding work in the 'normal' fashion; that he or she needs assistance and help. It can also be assumed that the applicant has or will have difficulties in functioning 'normally' in a typical workplace—that he or she in effect has one or several 'occupational disabilities.' Another administrative official stressed that others among the unemployed probably share many of the problems that certain recruits for Samhall experience, yet the National Employment Office would never consider them as potential Samhall employees. But since the problems of potential Samhall clients are 'demonstrated more intensely' and give 'clearer indications' of occupational disability, such as having been long-term unemployed or long-term sick, the National Employment Office tends, on the basis of its experience, to regard these persons as more legitimate candidates than others for employment with Samhall. To assume that a person *suffers from* a medical disorder, which makes the person handicapped in comparison with others who clearly have not failed to get and keep a job, is not only a reasonable but also a necessary conclusion for the National Employment Office to reach given the organization's focus on providing welfare services to people that are experienced as disabled on medical grounds.

An administrative official of the National Employment Office said to me in one of my interviews that 'when we sit discussing cases [among colleagues], we can say that "this is a typical Samhall case" and then everybody in the group understands. It's a kind of intuition; we've made enough attempts, and it [the person applying for work] makes no demands either, it [sic] is just happy to get a job, and so it [sic] can have this kind of employment.' One of his colleagues was of the opinion that in order to be considered for employment at Samhall, it may 'not only be due to a medical problem, but also be about how persons function socially, personality-wise, that they need much more deliberate and stronger labor management to be able to cope with their work tasks, and then Samhall comes to mind.'

If a person has problems with sight or hearing, if he or she has lost one leg or both, or arms and hands, has hydrocephalus or other physical deviations, or if he or she behaves in a manner that the National Employment Office, based on its routines and rules of 'normal conduct' among job seekers, recognizes as a deficit in motor control and perception (DAMP), attention deficit hyperactivity disorder (ADHD), the person suffers from cerebral palsy, or similar typical medical problems, Samhall staff will assume that the person will have problems obtaining work in the regular labor market. These 'obvious cases' as an administrative official called them, consist of persons who many times can submit written documentation supporting their problems, such as statements from a doctor, statements from special schools, and certificates from counselors, where experts have experienced them as functionally disordered in roughly the same way as the National

Employment Office is now doing. In other cases, it becomes apparent to the National Employment Office that the person has or can be expected to have problems when he or she 'has been referred here from the prison and probation service, the social services or regional social insurance office,' as one administrative official put it, and where the person's previous involvement in these welfare organizations means that the person is considered socially problematic, which has the potential of being designated as a personal medical problem. For the individual administrative official, the difficulties that are regarded as being prevalent in the occupationally disabled can serve as a basis for explaining why a certain person applying for work has difficulty in getting or keeping a job.

The National Employment Office's view that the occupationally disabled have particular difficulties on the labor market is supported in recent government studies and reports. One such report states that 'the past few years have entailed an increase in pressure for transformation, where labor-intensive companies and subsequently even public service activities have tightened up their organizations with more technological solutions and fewer jobs. The organizations have also become "slimmer" or "leaner".' This is said to have affected people with functional disorders in particular. One administrative official at the National Employment Office explained:

> The requirements of employers have increased all the time, but the people who apply for work with us remain, they are linguistically weak, they are the middle-aged and older people who generally have a weaker position on the labor market...they are hopelessly out of it, they don't have a chance of asserting themselves.... Sweden has accepted an enormous amount of refugees, often these have a very poor basic education, many are illiterate and have worked within agriculture in their home countries, and that is all the difference in the world.

Another administrative official reported similar experiences in his fruitless efforts to obtain work for certain categories of job seekers: 'It can be about an immigrant who has been working as a cleaner for a number of years, has four years of schooling in his home country, speaks very bad Swedish. What do we do with this kind of person when employers can pick and choose?' This administrative official related that in conversations with employers he has often been confronted with the attitude 'we want the best, we don't accept second-raters.'

In some cases, there is no doubt that a jobseeker will be difficult to place on the labor market based on the experiences of the occupationally disabled as these are interpreted by the officers of the National Employment Office. However, there are certain cases, the so-called grey zone cases as they are called within the National Employment Office, that are more ambiguous. One of the administrative officials defined the grey zone cases as 'complex cases, psychologically deviant personalities, hidden addiction,

odd customers in general terms.' Another official emphasized that they are
'persons that you cannot point out as having anything physically or mentally wrong, but there is still some kind of disability at the basis of their
behavior.' Yet another administrative official implied the following for this
group:

> One cannot say they have a medical functional disorder, but that there
> are other causes and reasons. We all have our own different person-
> alities; one can be odd in different ways. One can have deficiencies in
> one's social ability, creating difficulties on the labor market resulting in
> long-term unemployment; it is our way of meeting with this type of job
> applicant where one cannot automatically point to a disorder.

The regular method for an administrative official to obtain confirmation
of the difficulties of a 'grey-zone case' is an 'in-depth investigation': 'If you
[the administrative official] are uncertain of the extent of the disorder, you
should call in an expert, for example a doctor, a psychologist or counselor,'
as stated in the National Employment Office's training materials. Thus,
some of the allegedly problematic job applicants are passed on internally
to special units for the occupationally disabled. In contrast to the service
provided by the ordinary offices of the National Employment Office, the
special units have a more all-round competence in inquiry issues, which is
considered to be especially important for some persons suspected of having an occupational disability. According to a document on these special
units, in general their clients are 'persons who are irresolute when it comes
to choice of profession, the so-called vocationally unsure, or those who feel
uncertain in the face of (re-) entry into working life. However, a considerable number of those looking for work have limited working capacity as a
result of an occupational disability or other problems with adjustment.'

According to an administrative official, the normal procedure is that
the jobseeker initially makes contact with a local employment office and
then staff there 'refer' the potentially occupationally disabled person to a
special examination unit. 'The person registers with us and we discover
that there are occupational hindrances that make it impossible to apply
[for a job] in the usual way.' An administrative official at one of the special
units explained that 'very difficult cases' that the ordinary employment
offices are not able to handle 'are referred to us, so-called grey zone areas,
cases for investigation.' Another official at a special unit pointed out that
they had 'very good resources' for identifying, mapping, and analyzing the
personal qualities of the jobseeker in order to explain the person's problem
with the labor market, especially in terms of 'hidden disabilities.' But even
'clear problem cases' are normally referred to the special units according to
an administrative official: 'As soon as they [ordinary national employment
offices] have an applicant that they discover has an occupational disability
by virtue of the applicant referring to a skin problem, or why he or she

cannot accept certain jobs, etc., we make sure they obtain a doctor's report confirming the medical problem and then the case is transferred here.'

Over a period of several weeks of focused investigation at special units within the National Employment Office, the jobseeker is examined for such things as 'ability to concentrate, perseverance, social ability,' as one administrative official explained. Another administrative official pointed out that by virtue of their skills in analyzing an occupational disability, they are good at discovering 'hidden disabilities,' limitations that previous investigations and interviews had not discovered. An administrative official observed that more medical problems could be discovered thanks to a certain methodology:

> The largest group was previously the intellectually disabled for they came directly from special secondary schools. However, the group that is continually on the increase is the group of occupationally disabled persons with mental health problems, and among others those that are called 'specific learning difficulties,' DAMP, ADHD, Asperger's.

A lot of the investigative work to establish whether or not a person 'suffers' from an occupational disability is based on the jobseeker undertaking various kinds of work. One administrative official stated that they had a 'practical department where you can use a lathe and do welding. Everyone doesn't need this, but for the group that is selected it can be a very good start.' In a document describing the operations of the special units, jobseekers are offered 'electrical and machine work with exercises in drawing and measuring, office work with computers, etc. The aim of the practical occupation experience is, in addition to providing the jobseeker with new experiences and insights, to investigate the prerequisites and suitability of the jobseeker for different types of work with regard to disability.' During the course of the investigation, there are also opportunities for jobseekers to have interviews with social workers, psychologists, and other experts in order for their backgrounds to be analyzed and their current (medical) status determined. One administrative official at a special unit noted:

> The staff has special competence within different areas of disability. We have skills in youth issues, in receiving young people where they are, and specifically for those that are disabled. Many perhaps haven't learned to stand on their own two legs being extremely well taken care of since they were little, perhaps very rightly so.

In some cases, medical exams, work training, and interviews with counselors and psychologists are used to confirm the jobseeker's difficulties, which have been noted by the administrative official over a shorter or longer period and which he or she sees as establishing why the applicant is difficult to place in the open labor market. One administrative official explained:

If we are dealing with a personality disorder and nothing has been documented, we can't just classify the person as occupationally disabled even though we experience him as such. Normally, it is our industrial psychologist who will carry out an industrial psychological investigation to confirm his status. We also have social advisory officers for those with a social problem, and this is so to speak what we discover.

If an administrative official suspects that a jobseeker has mental problems, he or she may be referred to professionals trained to diagnose such problems, as one might refer a person with bad hearing to an ear specialist. In general, the comprehensive investigation is about 'persons with functional disorders being able to take part based on their own ability,' as one administrative official put it. More specifically, 'help for the occupationally disabled' must 'place the individual in the center' as a person in charge of two government studies of occupational disability said in a radio interview. He continued:

> Before people get into different [social welfare] programs, a proper survey of personal prerequisites should be carried out; the persons in question should be able to select what they want to do with the rest of their working lives, and society should be there supporting this.

Supported by various studies and based on documentation from a doctor or other medical expert, the administrative official of the National Employment Office eventually makes a so-called *disability coding*. This coding is a formal and legal prerequisite for employment with Samhall. This is emphasized in the handbook *A Knowledge of Disability*, published by the National Labor Market Board in Sweden for use by administrative officials at the National Employment Office.

> It is important that you code occupational disabilities so that you can offer jobseekers special guidance or [direct them to] the labor market policy programs that are reserved for persons with a reduced working capacity.

As support for the practical coding procedure, this handbook is recommended 'as a crib.' It contains a general description of what an occupational disability entails: 'The concept of an occupational disability has been created to emphasize that a person with a functional disorder may be occupationally disabled for certain tasks or a certain working environment.' Essentially, it emphasizes that an occupational disability is linked to the ability to obtain and retain a job. Thus, the investigation that every administrative official has to carry out, as a basis for the disability coding, is intended to 'identify which *limitation* the functional disorder signifies in relation to the requirements of working life.'

The handbook describes that the disability coding is not only important from an administrative point of view for the National Employment Office, but also for the unemployed person, who via the coding will have significantly better opportunities for obtaining a job through a labor market policy program:

> Work for all is an important part of the labor market policy. In order to give those with an occupational disability the same possibilities as other jobseekers, there is the possibility of setting a disability code. The code allows access to more detailed service and/or access to the labor market policy programs.

In other words, the disability code is a medical certification that a person is entitled to welfare support, which is concretely brought about by the formal labor market policy efforts that are available, in this case Samhall.

In the current handbook, the types of disability that have been established in 14 codes (year 2005) are discussed in more detail, where the eight first codes are of somatic/physiological character and the final six are of a psychic/social nature. Concomitant with the growth of the number of occupationally disabled people in Sweden (the group has increased by about 350% during the last few years according to statistics from the National Employment Office), the number of codes for defining people as occupationally disabled has steadily grown, thus indicating that the more conceptual tools for targeting and classifying people as disabled, the more unemployed people can potentially be classified as occupationally disabled by the National Employment Office.

- Cardio, vascular, and/or lung disease (code 11)
- Childhood deafness (code 21)
- Hearing impairment (code 31)
- Serious visual impairment
- Poor eyesight (code 32)
- Motor-handicap requiring movement aids like a walking frame or wheelchair (code 41)
- Other motor handicaps (code 42)
- Other somatically related occupational disability (code 51)
- Mental occupational disability (code 61)
- Intellectual occupational disability (code 71)
- Social-medical occupational disability (code 81)
- Asthma/allergy/hypersensitivity (code 91)
- Dyslexia/ specific learning difficulties (code 92)
- Acquired brain damage (code 93)

Two to four pages in the handbook are dedicated to each type of disability, defining it in part based on a general description of the disability, and in part on the basis of a discussion about 'characteristics and extent.' There is even a discussion about 'things to think about,' which aims at making it easier for the administrative official to recognize the disability based on the available documentation and an interview with the jobseeker. The types of occupational disabilities and the descriptions of these,'medical indications of occupational disability,' enable administrative officials to confirm occupational disabilities in jobseekers through their interaction with the individuals themselves, as well as to help the jobseekers to recognize their disability by presenting medically objective arguments that a particular disability exists.

- For example, *code 31, Serious visual impairment,* is defined as 'an occupational limitation due to the lack of usable sight and which is compensated for with the use of other senses. It involves a visual acuity of 0.05 or less or a field of vision that amounts to 10 degrees or less from the center.' Under the heading 'characteristics and extent' it states, among other things, 'as *visually impaired* we count persons who have such bad vision that they have difficulty in reading normal writing or orientating themselves in an unfamiliar space with the help of their vision,' and that 'the visual impairment in itself is no hindrance for work. A visual occupational disability arises in the relationship between the faculty of vision and the requirements of the work.' Under the heading 'to think about,' it is ascertained, among other things, that 'persons with a visually impaired occupational disability do not constitute a homogenous group.... The only thing that connects them is that their occupational hindrance is sight-related.'
- *Code 71, Intellectual occupational disability* is defined as 'an occupational limitation caused by limited learning ability resources.' According to the document, these persons can be recognized by the fact that they have 'difficulty in carrying out assignments due to a deficiency in intellectual capacity'; for example, by virtue of 'insufficient ability for abstract thought' and 'a slow ability for processing.' In his or her contact with such persons, the administrative official is encouraged to think about 'taking time to listen...using simple, short sentences, giving one piece of information at a time, speaking in a steady tempo.'

The practical procedure of the coding itself should take place in consultation with the jobseeker. However, the process of arriving at an occupational disability is normally not transparent for them. One day, the administrative official presents the jobseeker with a suggestion of a code, which the jobseeker is to accept or not. In substance, the proposal to the occupationally disabled person is an individual decision by the administrative official, even if it was arrived at with the support of colleagues and medical experts. Consequently, it is the experience the administrative official has of the jobseeker as an occupationally disabled person and not the jobseeker's personal experience as being occupationally disabled that is the deciding factor.

The jobseeker must always confirm his or her new status as disabled by signing a document in which it is clearly stated that he or she 'agrees' with the coding and the suggested medical diagnosis. This signing verifies the jobseeker's personal responsibility for his or her occupationally disabled state, and that he or she accepts those measures that are considered as being necessary for employment at Samhall. 'You must never set a code without the agreement [of the jobseeker], you must always do this together with the jobseeker,' an administrative official at the National Employment Office pointed out. 'The jobseeker should be in agreement with being registered as an occupationally disabled person,' as it was stated in a government study. Another government study concluded, 'this implies that everyone who is assigned to Samhall should have an occupational disability and personally accept this.'

If the jobseeker does not personally regard him- or herself as occupationally disabled, the onus is on the administrative official to convince the jobseeker that he or she has a functional disorder that should be coded as an occupational disability. Normally, the administrative official has documentation from investigations with the National Employment Office, doctor's certificates, referrals from the social welfare service, and others to support his or her argumentation. For their part, job seekers must rely on their own experiences. Unquestionably, the person has difficulty in finding or retaining a job, which is often supported in the investigatory material, or by the simple fact that the individual is long-term unemployed or has moved in and out of various labor market policy programs as offered previously by the National Employment Office. One administrative official recounted that he always concentrates on 'what the person wants and what the person knows' but that for many groups 'will is often stronger than knowledge.'

The 'problem' with not being able to realize one's disabilities is common, one administrative official thought: 'You have to accept your problems if you are going to go on.' He gave as the example of a female jobseeker: 'She has great difficulty in realizing it. It is probably an experience that all the occupationally disabled have and which becomes difficult when you realize that you have limitations.'

Another administrative official recounted that a normal attitude among jobseekers when being informed about their disability code was, 'there isn't really anything drastically wrong with me and I want a job like anybody else out there.' One administrative official emphasized 'in my mind, having self-insight regarding one's disability is very important...many of these people are in a really difficult situation, they often end up in conflicts, they have never been able to keep a job, you must be able to take a look at yourself and ask "Where am I at now"?.' In this context, often the investigations that the National Employment Office has carried out with respect to the individual, such as practical training in certain activities or discussions with a psychologist, fill the function of being able to convince certain individuals that they *do have* personal problems that require actions. Administrative officials at the National Employment Office have access to information, which allows them to recognize occupational disability in people who do not necessarily experience themselves as occupationally disabled.

However, the situation can be the reverse. A man who worked as a cook at Samhall recounted that he had applied for work as a cook in restaurants for many years but had always 'been turned down' and that eventually he felt increasingly depressed:

> At the National Employment Office, they told me you had to be ill to work at Samhall. I wondered what I would do. Cut my arms? You have to hurt yourself, you have to make yourself ill.

Finding a job was more important than anything else he imagined, and over the years he had become convinced that Samhall was his only chance, without Samhall he would remain unemployed. Finally, the National Employment Office placed him in a queue to Samhall. The administrative official had then asked him if he felt bad or if he had problems, and when he said he was healthy and felt quite well, she still indicated that he had a disability, namely that he was overweight. Consequently he was asked to see a doctor who certified that he was overweight, which was the official explanation of his problem; and this enabled him to get a position as occupationally disabled at Samhall. His disability code became 'other motor handicap,' code 42.

An administrative official at the National Employment Office emphasized that 'you have to have a medical infirmity, you have to have a medical diagnosis, but we can't only rely on the basic medical data for the disability coding.' Another administrative official thought that many problems such as 'hidden abuse, problems with relationships, problems with cooperation, mentally deviating personalities,' are not noticed in doctors' examinations. As has already been said, a period of practice can therefore be of decisive significance for enacting of personal problems. An administrative official pointed out, 'we require basic data from a doctor, but doctors perhaps do not have a clear idea of the entire picture. The doctors who are asked to evaluate work capacity have no training in this.' Consequently, another administrative official was of the opinion that if 'we have a doctor stating that no problems exist, we can be presented with a veritable Catch 22. On those occasions, you must encourage the jobseeker to find another doctor who can be more responsive,' and verify that the person has certain medical problems. Furthermore, the doctor's certificates that are used as a basis for the disability coding do not always need to reflect the current medical condition of the person, but may describe an older sickness or injury. One administrative official at the National Employment Office explained:

I must admit that one of the good things with Samhall is that they have not always been so precise in requiring recently documented base data, they have roughly accepted what we have said. They have been generous in that way.... Similar things have happened here in Stockholm, although there have been doctors' reports that have been years old.

Naturally it may be equivocal which of the 14 possible codes should be applied to a particular jobseeker, not least because the codes themselves are ambiguous. In this respect, the coding system's 'unclear framework of rules' and 'subjective basis for forming a judgment' was criticized in a government study. It was observed that 'there are often circumstances like long-term unemployment and a relatively high age that can be behind the disability code' rather than any 'regular' bio-medical problems. The same study established the following:

> The majority of the occupationally disabled employees at Samhall have either no or only one functional disorder that has significance for their job. When it comes to the severity of the occupational disability, supervisors [at Samhall who were interviewed in the study] estimate that approx. 70% manage their jobs well and the functional disorders have only a marginal significance in these cases.

Thus, the medical problems and limitations that the unemployed are said to have and which one assumes are demonstrated by an inability to obtain or retain a job are not always synonymous with the formal disability codes. This was emphasized in another government study:

> Many people who obtained work at Samhall have a complex of problems of medical, social and personal conditions which are not so easy to translate and group as one number in the National Employment Office's categories of occupational disabilities.' It was observed, 'the codes applied by the National Employment Office do not always correspond with real occupational disorders. The possibilities of the National Employment Office to make medical assessments are entirely dependent on the doctors' reports. It can be difficult to gain access to these and they can even contain a description of only one injury or one illness for persons with more than one functional disorder.

As noted above, the disability coding and the medical diagnoses are necessary for the National Employment Office to be able to offer the welfare support measures that employment at Samhall can entail. After a person has been coded, according to one administrative official 'he or she may be entitled to some of our services, e.g., wage allowances and Samhall.' If a disability coding is not implemented before the question of employment at

Samhall arises, the official will risk being criticized. 'The code must always be used when we are going to apply a measure [wage allowance, Samhall etc.]. A person must not be uncoded for then our controllers will come and say naughty, naughty!.' Only when the jobseeker has been formally organized as an occupationally disabled person by designating him or her as medically problematic, can the person obtain welfare assistance.

According to an administrative official it was probable that among some people who were designated as occupationally disabled, there were those that had suffered serious illnesses which limited the chances of them competing successfully on the labor market. However, it was also probable according to him that there were some people who were considered to be occupationally disabled without being ill in a medical sense. This was also the point of departure in two recently completed government studies on immigrants, certain groups of young people, and those who lived in sparsely-populated areas of Sweden. One of these studies observed that 'persons with an immigrant background—especially in metropolitan areas—have been assigned sheltered work at Samhall more as a result of their language difficulties than that they—in a formal sense—have an occupational disability.' All in all, it is possible to observe, as it was formulated in a government study that 'in a labor market policy context, the decisive question is whether a person is occupationally disabled, i.e. has a functional impairment that also results in reduced working capacity. However, the extent to which working capacity is impaired cannot only be defined on the basis of the functional disorder, but actually involves the ability to carry out specific assignments.' Thus, it is the possibility of obtaining or retaining a job that is the decisive factor, rather than whether or not the person is ill or healthy in a medical sense. Therefore, the term 'occupational disability' should be seen from the point of view of the individual's ability to carry out certain jobs, where the disability itself is the limitation in work that is actually experienced.

Hence, occupational disability can be something medical, but in many cases it may instead be something that the National Employment Office experiences as involving the person's social or linguistic ability, or other kinds of human behaviors. For that reason, long-term unemployment can in practice be the reason for a position as occupationally disabled at Samhall, which can especially be the case in sparsely populated areas where in many places in Sweden, Samhall may be the only or the dominant employer. For example at a site in the County of Dalarna, some people working there had previously worked in the mining industry and even if a majority of them declared that they had pains in their backs and knees, they would probably not have been working at Samhall if the mines had still been open. One supervisor at Samhall in the County of Skåne, recounted that many of his employees had been unemployed for a long time 'and eventually they are entitled to work at Samhall.' Still they were all considered and classified as medically problematic cases. (Internal statistics from Samhall show that there are 16.6 Samhall employees per 1,000 inhabitants in the County of

Jämtland, which has suffered from steep unemployment for many years, as opposed to 2.9 in the vibrant County of Stockholm, Sweden's metropolitan area).

Certainly, one administrative official at the National Employment Office witnessed the following:

> Most jobseekers have an aversion to being coded…if it concerns intellectual difficulties, mental occupational disabilities. Very many who need a lot of support have stress-related symptoms, and to be branded with a mental occupational disability code isn't very amusing.

The very fact that they needed help from the National Employment Office may have embarrassed them. One administrative official said: 'Many people who come to the National Employment Office don't want to talk about this.' An administrative official witnessed that there are many who question whether they really 'need an allowance' in the form of a wage subsidy or employment at Samhall. Another official explained that some jobseekers think that 'it is somewhat unattractive to work at Samhall…generally speaking people think it is unattractive to be at Samhall.' In this respect, a government study reported, that 'coding an occupational disability is a sensitive issue. In itself, the coding can appear disparaging in terms of self-esteem and for the possibilities of mobilizing one's own resources.'

Despite these possibly negative implications for self-esteem, most people agree to be disability coded, since they eventually learn that this is the only reasonable option to get a 'normal life.' One administrative official explained: 'People [the jobseekers] are pragmatic…[if] it's about being able to pay the rent and buy food, they'll have to accept certain things' (i.e., being labeled as disabled). 'They get status, can take out loans, they can get an apartment, it brings with it many positive things.' A former Samhall employee wrote about Samhall in a book, stating 'the work at Samhall was the worst thing I have ever experienced: But I was forced to work there. I had bought a new house together with my significant other. Now, fortunately I have a disability pension.' An existing employee wrote the following:

> I have tried working in one of Samhall's factories. I felt so incredibly bad there that I would rather take my life than be stuck there. My goal is to get out into the ordinary labor market. For my own part, thanks to Samhall I have permanent employment, a stable income and an apartment of my own.

It is not the individual characteristics of the person with respect to his or her ability to speak a foreign language, be able to carry out welding operations, be a skilled cook, or have experience of construction work, that controls an eventual assignment to Samhall, but the individual occupational disability that has been ascertained as a result of previous assessment and codification by the National Employment Office. According to a government study, the idea behind Samhall is that 'Samhall should be a measure for the occupationally disabled persons who have the most difficult position on the labor market.' In this perspective, being assigned to this last straw on the labor market can appear problematic for a jobseeker, a former Senior Manager at Samhall thought:

> Nobody can apply for a job at Samhall. Instead, you are 'assigned' to a job there by the National Employment Office. In other words, a socially maladjusted person doesn't even have the right to apply for a job. Somebody else tells him or her that it is best if he or she begin working here or there. Anybody who has been excluded from working life on the open labor market, the disabled, is more subject to the arbitrariness of others than anyone else.

That it is expedient to accept a proposed assignment to Samhall is made clearer when one looks at the formal framework of rules surrounding unemployment benefits in Sweden. As a jobseeker in Sweden, you are formally 'at the disposal of the labor market' and normally receive unemployment benefits. Refusing an assignment for employment at Samhall requiring a disability coding is certainly possible 'but then the National Employment Office usually submits a report to the affected unemployment benefit fund to call into question unemployment benefits' as observed in a government study. Thus, usually people accept an assignment to Samhall, even if they experience it as 'a real come-down, of being set aside' as one administrative official at the National Employment Office said. Some people experience employment at Samhall as 'negative, the last chance,' another administrative official at the National Employment Office explained. Still, there are people who resist. An unemployed person wrote in a book about Samhall:

> I have read about Samhall, about how badly people are treated. I will soon begin there, but NO thanks!! Even if this means that the National Employment Office will exclude me [from unemployment benefits], and life becomes an economic hell.

Normally the assignment to Samhall starts when Samhall reports a need for a certain type of occupationally disabled manpower to the National Employment Office, much in the same way as other employers do with the exception, of course, that they would not experience a need for occupationally disabled persons. An agreement between the National Employment Office and Samhall constitutes a so-called quality assurance of the recruitment process to Samhall and includes, among other things, requirements for 'adequate documentation of the occupational disability to be submitted to Samhall by the National Employment Office before the recruiting process,' e.g., in the form of 'a doctor's report and other relevant documents showing that occupational disability exists.' Samhall can refuse an assignment from the National Employment Office on the grounds that 'the jobseeker [should] actively be able to function in a labor work organization and take part in a production process,' as it is stated in one Samhall document (i.e., the person must be the one that Samhall is competent to rehabilitate). A supervisor at Samhall explained that the National Employment Office sometimes 'tries to dump those that are the least equipped on us.' Another supervisor thought that in practice, 'a one-sided utilization' of the assignment right from the National Employment Office does not work since 'Samhall has a corporate organization that also has to function.' A supervisor pointed out that 'in our installation we have a need for certain occupational disability types; for instance, we can't have blind people here.'

Before recruitment, the administrative official of the National Employment Office should have completed a document specifying, among other things, the person's 'education,' 'previous jobs,' and 'possible support requirements' to provide Samhall with basic information about the occupationally disabled person in order for the organization to decide whether or not the person is sufficiently occupationally disabled to be assigned work at Samhall. 'Three-party cooperation' implies that a representative from Samhall and the National Employment Office respectively meet the jobseeker to go over his or her background and to discuss the possibilities of employment with Samhall. These interactions are typically focused on the person's problem status. When assigning a person to Samhall, it becomes necessary to confirm the medical problems that were established at the National Employment Office or to find further reasons for the person's presumed difficulties, which make them a more or less suitable recruit for Samhall. Statements by recruits to Samhall who maintain that they are not sick or handicapped must once again be called into question and refuted, as well as all notions that their problems are simple and therefore do not require extensive rehabilitation. Normally, this dialogue is preceded by contacts between the administrative official at the National Employment Office and supervisors at Samhall to establish if there exists a recruitment requirement for a certain occupationally disabled position. In an internal Samhall document the following was maintained:

> The National Employment Office and the Samhall Group have the common commitment to promote the possibilities of work for persons with occupational disabilities, but our areas of responsibility and our roles in this work are different. It is very important that the two organizations have close collaboration and a similar way of viewing things if we are to fulfill the mutual commitment in an effective manner.

A joint document from the National Employment Office and Samhall refers to the importance of three-party collaboration (i.e., collaboration between Samhall, the National Employment Office, and the jobseeker) because the occupationally disabled person should experience that he or she can affect the prevailing situation. Of course, the person has already accepted his or her coding as occupationally disabled (i.e., as medically problematic). In this phase it is a question of whether or not to accept a position at Samhall as occupationally disabled and in this process it is important that the concept 'The Individual at the Center' is observed: 'With the individual at the center, employment at Samhall should constitute a positive and goal-oriented opportunity for the jobseeker. This entails that the prerequisite, expectations, and needs of the individual for developmental and supportive efforts should serve as a guide during each employment situation.' Hence, during the assignment phase, the individual is someone to be taken into account and respected to the extent that he or she participates in the assessment by reporting existing limitations and problems to Samhall and the National Employment Office. To this extent, the individual is indeed 'at the center.' The assessment aims to reach a deeper understanding of the person's medical disorders over and above those that have emerged at the National Employment Office. In the process, the assessment requires cooperation on the part of the occupationally disabled so that Samhall can perform its task of assessing occupational disability, in the same way as a patient must 'work with their doctor' if an examination is to be performed in a satisfactory fashion.

As already observed, administrative officials at the National Employment Office witnessed that some jobseekers reacted in a negative way when Samhall was proposed. As one of them said:

> 'Is it one of those sheltered workshops,' they ask. 'I will never go to one of those and be with drips and the mentally retarded': The whole of society is still imbibed with, 'we don't want to have a sheltered workshop here,' it's a kind of proverbial phrase, it has a bad ring to it to say that.

Another administrative official at the National Employment Office said that she had discovered that if she or her colleague 'supplied information about Samhall in a "positive manner", then everything was okay.' In addition to providing the occupationally disabled with 'suitable' information about Samhall (which in written and spoken form are different variations of what Samhall has to offer in the form of 'developing and rehabilitative work'), administrative officials will accompany the occupationally disabled person on a visit to a Samhall site that has recruitment needs. These visits can result in mixed impressions, as witnessed by an administrative official of the National Employment Office:

I have been out with young people whose eyes were filled with terror, and actually in my opinion, in situations like that, they don't have to take it [i.e., accept employment]. On the other hand, I have been out with young people who have shouted with joy and thought that this was a dream job and needed such monotonous work assignments.

Consequently, not all occupationally disabled jobseekers are assigned employment at Samhall because they cannot be convinced that this is an attractive solution. An employment official working with Swedish-born, highly educated persons 'suffering from depression due to fatigue' as she chose to label them, did not even think that Samhall was an option for this group. 'It isn't reasonable, dignified' as she expressed it. Traditionally, Samhall has recruited blue-collar workers, and to the extent that the employees at Samhall have had a higher education and worked in high-income professions in their previous careers, they have often been immigrants.

One administrative official emphasized that the personal preferences of the occupationally disabled should decide if employment at Samhall is to be realized:

I have been out to places [at Samhall] where I have been so unpleasantly affected; e.g. they have garbage sorting where the young people are on an assembly line sorting plastic materials, there are sharp objects, a noisy working environment, filthy. I thought it was a terrible place to work. In the office, we had many discussions about whether we should assign people to a workplace that we ourselves are so unpleasantly affected by or couldn't even imagine working there ourselves. However, at the same time, we agreed that we should not apply our own values, and we took every young person who was interested with us so that they could form their own opinion.

Overall, administrative officials did not refrain from the possibility of assigning occupationally disabled persons to Samhall by referring to the 'individual's personal decision to accept employment' and by referring 'to the fact that they are disabled.' One administrative official declared: 'You see that they are desperate to get a job, training is unrealistic, no other employer wants them for they are odd in some way, for them the fact that Samhall exists is a great thing.' As an administrative official at the National Employment Office, you typically don't have anything else to offer when offering Samhall. As said earlier, Samhall is said to be the last welfare measure in a chain of support activities. Administrative officials inform the jobseekers of this idea, as well as the economic sanctions that can ensue as a result of refusing employment in Samhall in the form of the suspension of unemployment benefits. Confronted with these insights, usually most occupationally disabled people accept the situation that they find themselves in and accept employment at Samhall. This acceptance is taken as evidence by the National Employment Office that the jobseekers have eventually accepted their predicaments as occupationally disabled; that is, that they *are* occupationally disabled.

Before accepting someone for employment, Samhall requires that the person practice at the possible workplace for a period of six to eight weeks. A supervisor at Samhall explained that the trial period is intended to 'see what the individual is suitable for,' and to decide what assignments the job-seeker should work on at the local worksite. At Samhall, the trial period is called 'in-depth mapping.' It is aimed at the following:

> Ensuring that the right target group is recruited...it should complement the information received from the National Employment Office. The purpose of the mapping is to acquire a broader picture of the individual in order to find suitable opportunities for development within Samhall.

The reason why Samhall wants a trial period before employment is confirmed is that the disabilities that the National Employment Office have observed and confirmed via disability coding do not always comply with the experiences occupationally disabled persons have at Samhall. One supervisor at Samhall stressed: 'The *real problems* come to light during the period of practical occupational experience.' One of his work colleagues emphasized: 'The facts discovered at the National Employment Office are only the top of an iceberg; the situation is often much more complex, the difficulties much greater.' Another supervisor thought that the National Employment Office 'seldom writes down a proper diagnosis' about the person in the case records appended to the jobseeker's employment application, 'at least, not from our perspective...the injuries detected can only be seen during practical work, they are hidden for the National Employment Office.'

One supervisor related that she often asked herself the following with regard to an occupationally disabled person under consideration for possible employment:

> What has this person really applied for, what kind of problem are we talking about? Many people go to the doctor for problems with their back when they are really suffering from a psychosis.

Another supervisor pointed out that the disability codes specified in the employees' case histories from the National Employment Office 'often do not tally' and instead 'real problems crop up once they start work here.' Yet another supervisor related about a meeting with a jobseeker:

> He was clearly ill, he was schizophrenic, but this was nothing that the National Employment Office had detected—you understand, our

clients are very clever at manipulating and taming people. When he was here, we could clearly see that he was ill, but when he was at the doctor's he acted normal. Then he committed a violent act in town and subsequently the doctor pronounced him as sick, and now he is locked up undergoing treatment—there are a lot of hidden things that they [doctors and the National Employment Office] don't see but we do.' Consequently, one supervisor thought that 'sometimes you have to kind of be involved from the beginning in order to understand a person's real impairments.

Several supervisors referred to mental illnesses and other problems more difficult to diagnose that can 'lie just under the surface' as one of them declared, and which have not appeared in earlier investigations at the National Employment Office, since it 'lacks the proper routines for discovering those,' as the supervisor said. One supervisor assumed that people that say they have problems with their backs, difficulties with language, or dyslexia are hiding something more complex; for example, war phobias in refugees or mental illnesses among certain cases of long-term unemployment. A member of Samhall's corporate management explained: 'Many of our employees do not look as if they have a disability, when they in fact have mental, socio-medical problems.' One supervisor thought that 'especially among the immigrant group you find lots of people who talk about how much they know, despite the fact that they don't.' However, she implied that this 'is quickly revealed when they are put to work with us.'

The in-depth investigation at Samhall into the already established occupational disability at the National Employment Office can reveal other disabilities in addition to those already confirmed, or generate the experience among the staff that the disabilities that were previously ascertained do not constitute any limitations, but there are other much more significant problems. This is stressed in an internal 'visionary document' for Samhall where it is established that Samhall should focus on an extensive and systematic 'mapping undertaking' to carry out an in-depth analysis of the occupationally disabled. One experience that Samhall has discovered when mapping Samhall employees 'has been that the disability codes that existed at the time of employment do not provide a true picture of the person's actual prerequisites. After the more in-depth mapping, more codes would be available and would thus provide a more correct picture of the occupational disability.' That clients' problems are re-framed to match Samhall's routines is exemplified by the results from a project within Samhall:

Of sixteen people, six were judged to have double and triple disabilities. When assigning people to Samhall, the National Employment Office had indicated a double disability for two persons. Mental illness and motor disabilities were added after more in-depth mapping.

Thus, thanks to the in-depth investigation Samhall's supervisors were able to observe more disabilities than before, thus turning the disabled people into legitimate clients of Samhall. Consequently, a non-occupationally disabled person coded as occupationally disabled at the National Employment Office can be labeled with additional medical problems at Samhall concurrently with the establishment of more disabilities.

'Formal mapping' during the trial period entails that the client is in different work teams in the Samhall unit in question and tests different work assignments and meets other occupationally disabled individuals. One supervisor explained that 'they are able to test different work assignments and see if they can manage these whereupon an assessment is carried out.' During this period, a supervisor follows the person extra carefully and also has contact with the group leader in each work team who provides information about how the person 'fits into the team' and how he or she carries out the work. The trial period is documented on a form, 'In-Depth Mapping' and in the event of employment would be placed in the case history on file at the workplace (the file which has accompanied the jobseeker from the National Employment Office). Before possible employment, the person also goes through a medical examination at Samhall's Corporate Health Service, which is confirmed on the form 'Confirmation of Health Visit for New Employment' and which is placed together with other documents in the person's case file after the person has signed the form, and thereby accepted the problems and limitations that have emerged during the examination. A supervisor who had recently received a new employee, presented a case history where Samhall's corporate health service had observed that the person was 'sensitive to stress and suffered from heart problems,' which the supervisor thought was important information for him to be able to place the employee correctly from the very beginning. The content of the case history is filed under lock and key in the current workplace in the event of employment and the employee's immediate superior has access to it.

The assessment routines with respect to recruitment are directed towards the supervisors with the aim of getting them to act in a specific way; that is, what they should look for in the occupationally disabled person's behavior during the trial period. A document, 'Assessment of Work Requirements' consists of a number of 'factors' that focus on individual problems and limitations that the supervisor can use as a check list when assessing a jobseeker. Based on several parameters and questions, the occupationally disabled individual is also asked to pay attention to his or her behavior during the trial period. The person is given a form and is asked to fill it in. This form is presented to the prospective employee who is told that 'the aim of the mapping is for the company to get to know as much as possible about you in order to be able to find appropriate development possibilities for you within Samhall.' The mapping is fed back 'to the recruitment manager and is taken up during three-way discussions together with the National

Employment Office and forms the basis for your first development plan with us.'

This activity is largely based on earlier investigations of the individual, primarily by the National Employment Office. A supervisor talked about the difficulties he had experienced when such information about a person had not been communicated to him. 'I don't know what I'm dealing with, so I have to try and ferret out what problems they have. I'm always asking myself what he is classified as [i.e., what is his disability code] so that I will know how to deal with him. Another supervisor said that for many years she wasn't allowed to 'know the background' of jobseekers to Samhall, which made her 'wonder many times why they came there. I didn't always believe that they were disabled.' She explained:

> They didn't have to declare their background; if you were an epileptic, you didn't have to reveal that, and so you just stood there. We have to know how we are to deal with people. Now it's been a good thing that we have had investigations about what types of disabilities people have, often people themselves are quite forthcoming and tell us what their problems are, and when they come, their documents tell what disability code they have been assigned by the National Employment Office.

One supervisor argued that access to the information in the National Employment Office's case file of each occupationally disabled person provides a 'good guide, for then we know how we are to treat people from the very outset. There is information telling me that I can't place the individual on certain sites.' According to one supervisor, the case file helps him understand 'what the person is not able to handle.' Another supervisor explained: 'I get help in avoiding mistakes, such as asking him [the jobseeker] to read aloud at a meeting and he turns out to be dyslexic.' One supervisor explained that it is a good thing to have background information about the jobseeker's problems, for 'you get an idea of the angle of approach. If he has a problem with alcohol or drugs, he can't work with others who also have similar medical problems. They have a tendency to gather and find out that they like alcohol and the like. So it's great to have as much information as possible.' To this extent, it is essential that the supervisor has knowledge of the person's problems in order to be able to manage new employees as occupationally disabled and to serve as a legitimate starting point for an in-depth study where the point of departure is that the person *has* medical problems, but where probably all problems have not yet been discovered.

The fact that some of the occupationally disabled still at this stage of their careers as occupationally disabled can maintain that 'they are only here [at Samhall] because there was no work elsewhere' as one supervisor expressed it, or as an occupationally disabled employee at a Samhall worksite wrote in a book, 'I feel like I have been cajoled into Samhall. I only have a hearing impairment that I don't notice when I am wearing my hearing aid. I came to Samhall primarily because I was unemployed,' is regarded as problematic since you cannot officially get employment at Samhall solely based on unemployment. As a result, the trial period for employment at Samhall aims at influencing the individual to finally accept that he or she is occupationally disabled. Without this personal acceptance, fulfillment of the role of occupationally disabled becomes hard to accomplish, thus jeopardizing the larger enterprise through which Samhall secures its continued operations. According to one supervisor, discussions with the occupationally disabled individual are aimed at 'focusing on the disability, especially if it is not a visible disability.' In these discussions, it is important that the jobseeker is entirely open about his or her problems. 'It is about turning the problems inside out,' a supervisor implied, and of getting them to 'think about and realize why they have ended up here [at Samhall].'

The questions that supervisors at Samhall ask the individual and which are based on the inter-organizational routines established between the National Employment Office and Samhall regarding the recruitment of occupationally disabled people to Samhall, presuppose that the person *is* occupationally disabled, which he or she has agreed to earlier via the disability coding. Any other point of departure for discussions would not be feasible. When the individual begins at a worksite at Samhall, it is 'important to be open with your problems, for then you are accepted by the work group, otherwise people just go around wondering and there is an uneasy atmosphere,' one supervisor explained. Thus, another supervisor used to encourage the occupationally disabled person during the trial period to 'be honest and tell me what's wrong with you!.' Information that has not come out during earlier discussions and practice will come out then, a supervisor emphasized, 'especially things like addiction problems that people can often conceal.' The emphasis on the idea that the person is 'needy' is further stressed by the introductory routines which give the recruit an idea of how Samhall will look upon him or her in the future. A supervisor asked a person who was practicing at one of Samhall's workplaces, 'if you think you are so terrific, why then do you think you are here?'

Another supervisor explained that many of the jobseekers lack 'insight into their problems' when they come to Samhall despite the earlier efforts of the National Employment Office to convince them of the existence of their disability:

> Many do not realize their limitations, they are often very verbal so they can deceive most people; however, they don't know as much as they think they do, which becomes clear pretty quickly—a lot of them have an inadequate knowledge of themselves.

Yet another supervisor explained that 'many have the will but can't assess what is feasible. They can't do what they want to do, they don't understand, e.g. they can't count or write...it isn't always that easy for them to understand what is happening around them, they have a long way to go.' One supervisor related that some of his personnel 'don't understand normal instructions' pointing out a group of 'mentally retarded individuals' who sat working with a packaging job. 'They don't understand, the point doesn't always get home to them, such things are normal at a workplace, but the most difficult thing for them is realizing that they don't understand.'

As already said, being able to determine and diagnose a picture of the medical problem in the new employee that he or she eventually must come to embrace is an important part of the Samhall recruiting process and is ultimately about creating prerequisites for suitable assignments within the company. If an employee 'does not understand that he is occupationally disabled' as one of the supervisors put it, the supervisor can have problems placing the person 'in the right place.' One supervisor explained that some occupationally disabled persons say 'there's nothing wrong with me' when they come here. It is easier for us when they have an insight into their problems at an early stage.' Another supervisor took the example of the visually impaired:

> I have worked with blind people. It's about getting them to accept that they have quite a lot to work with. Many of them do not have a knowledge of their illness when they start with us.

A supervisor working in a cleaning unit who has often had to receive many new personnel during recent years related that recruits to Samhall often 'say that they are healthy, but they do not understand that they are sick and have problems.' One supervisor thought it was important for her 'to persuade people to understand that they are sick and have problems' already before employment became a reality. This self-knowledge is of pivotal importance for the person 'being able to work for us.' A colleague of hers explained, 'many people come here believing that they can manage all kinds of things, but that isn't the case.' She thought that this was a result of inadequate self-knowledge and 'is typical for new occupationally disabled employees,' those that have recently received an occupational disability code from the National Employment Office. Only when individuals have accepted their problems, is it possible to assume that they will be able to function well in their jobs at Samhall: 'Alcoholics are so clever and industrious in their work when they have realized that they are alcoholics' one supervisor concluded.

On the whole, supervisors at Samhall feel that the company has become better these days in determining problems and limitations in the form of occupational disability at an early stage, before the person has been employed, not least thanks to the fact that supervisors have been trained in interpreting behavior as an 'indicator' of different illnesses or disabilities.

One supervisor related that a nation-wide training course in disability studies that all supervisors complete has helped her and her colleagues in dealing with occupationally disabled persons by helping them understand how a typical occupationally disabled person behaves. Other supervisors thought that they had become better at creating a trusting relationship with the client in an effort to induce the applicant to be more open about his or her problems. One supervisor exemplified:

> Sometimes people are not open about their problems and we only discover with time that they do not know certain things or that they don't understand but just take chances. Thus, it is important that we gain their trust at an early stage.

7   Development

When an agreement about sheltered employment for an individual as occupationally disabled has been reached between Samhall and the National Employment Office, Samhall takes over 'the responsibility for the personal and professional development of the employee,' as agreed between the organizations. This is confirmed by the client, the administrative official of the National Employment Office, and the Samhall representative all signing the 'Agreement about Employment at Samhall.' Once again in writing the individual confirms that he or she is in need of this kind of social welfare. The document is placed in the person's file.

The entry to Samhall implies that the newly employed person moves to an environment different from the one to which most people are accustomed. Several of Samhall's workplaces are located in industrial areas or similar kinds of labor-intensive environments, separated from the rest of society. In exceptional cases, there is no sign outside the Samhall workplaces. Approximately 30 Samhall employees worked at a private company in the basement of a large industrial plant, but there was no sign to indicate that this section only housed Samhall employees. In another staffing assignment in a hospital, 10 or so Samhall employees worked in their own area, but similarly, there was no Samhall sign to indicate that.

Often the Samhall workplaces are close to hospitals or other welfare institutions, such as a clinic for back injuries or a psychiatric emergency clinic. A Samhall workshop where a packing operation is carried out is located on 'Institution Road,' which, according to a supervisor there, is 'an unfortunate name with respect to our employees.' Another workplace is close to a psychiatric clinic for young people and a number of other care institutions, which according to one of the occupationally disabled employees at Samhall, is called 'the village of idiots' by people in the surrounding residential district. A newly employed occupationally disabled person at a Samhall workplace that was located in an industrial area surrounded by other companies said that she initially felt uneasy about going there: 'When you drive past here, you can see that the people are disabled, some have difficulty in walking, some use walking frames, I thought that all of them were idiots here.' One supervisor related that 'many are ashamed that they are working at Samhall...they get off the bus one stop early so as not to disclose where they work; we supervisors probably do that as well, we know what people think of Samhall.'

In some external workplaces where Samhall personnel are hired, the Samhall employees choose to dress in their own clothes, despite the fact that they have access to Samhall work clothes. Others who wear these clothes, rip off the Samhall patch. One employee explained that 'we just want to be like everyone else.' At a worksite in a hospital where Samhall employees had various administrative assignments, some of them had chosen to wear white coats like the rest of the hospital personnel in the department in order not to be differentiated from them. An occupationally disabled person working at one of the Samhall factories related that when she met acquaintances, she said that she was a welder, and 'if they then ask more questions, I say that I weld bathroom cabinets,' and 'more reluctantly I say that I work at Samhall.' One supervisor explained that when he was among friends and colleagues at previous worksites, he felt that 'they look down on me a little now, they are probably wondering why I can't cope with a job in a normal company with normal employees.' One of the occupationally disabled employees wrote in a book about Samhall:

> I have not told anyone except my mother that I am working there as I know what people think who don't know the company. And I know that I am not the only one who avoids talking about it.

As a new employee at Samhall, you usually encounter a workplace with extensive 'adaptation for disabled persons' in the form of such equipment as toilets for the disabled, elevators that have space for wheelchairs or power-operated chairs, wheelchair ramps, ergonomically designed tools, chairs that can be raised and lowered. One employee declared: 'Samhall is good when it comes to physical aides, it has always been so.' Some employees need aides to find their way around the premises and visitors to Samhall workplaces may encounter people in wheelchairs, people using walking sticks, and people who are blind or deaf. A human engineer employed at Samhall's Corporate Health Service and who often visited the worksites to 'check on disability adaptation' as she put it, inspected operating positions, work materials, giving advice and tips to personnel about how they could avoid injuries or better manage their work. These 'adaptations for persons with disabilities' are based on the idea that the employees, once it is clear that they have one or several disabilities, require a particular environment that is adapted for persons *with* disabilities in order for them to develop *as* occupationally disabled. According to a pamphlet addressed to Samhall supervisors: 'Since the majority of Samhall's employees are persons with a variety of disabilities, higher requirements are set for the working environment.'

During the first week of work, the new employee usually receives information about work assignments and work accessories, working hours, routines when reporting in sick,and general regulations. The information is 'adapted to the occupationally disabled's needs' when it is presented to the individual, as one supervisor put it; for example, by handing out pamphlets written in a 'simple and straightforward way.' Often individuals have already come into contact with these materials during the orientation period preceding employment, but people are only given more specific information about what they will be working with after they have formally been employed.

The fact that the individual is legally and formally *employed* as occupationally disabled is manifest in several ways during the first week of work. For example, the employees are assigned work clothes with the Samhall logotype often printed or sewn on the chest or back, they receive a locker with a padlock where personal belongings can be stored before the working day begins; in some cases, they are assigned their own workplace with different types of tools, and they receive miscellaneous work materials. The work clothes are called 'profile clothes.' According to one supervisor, the idea behind these is to help workers 'experience a feeling of belonging' as well as to show uniformity with respect to such people as customers and supervisors who are not occupationally disabled Samhall employees..

Perhaps the most important manifestation of employment as an occupationally disabled worker is that henceforth verbally and in writing both within and outside of Samhall the person is termed 'occupationally disabled' and a systematic distinction is made between employees in the regular labor market or 'personnel in normal companies,' as one supervisor put it, and partly between other personnel within Samhall, such as supervisors and other managers. One of the Samhall's economic reports noted:

> All employees are important for Samhall's activities, but the terms of employment differ. The National Employment Office assigns unemployed jobseekers with occupational disabilities to employment at Samhall. This entails that these jobseekers have access to a position that is reserved for this target group. The labor law conditions differ for supervisors and managers in Samhall that are not recruited by assignment from the National Employment Office.

As a rule, the organized introduction at the workplace for the occupationally disabled implies that the new employee obtains information about Samhall and the activities of the local workplace. Even if most employees at Samhall have a basic idea about the company and the working conditions that prevail there, they seldom have a deeper knowledge of the direction of activity, and what is specifically expected of them as occupationally disabled employees. 'I didn't know very much about this...no more than what there is in the newspapers,' one woman related. A colleague of hers said: 'I didn't know much, no more than I knew that it was for the sick and the occupationally disabled.' During the introductory period, the new employee usually receives information about the history of Samhall that stresses Samhall's mission to rehabilitate occupationally disabled persons. For example, an article in the company magazine was handed out to new employees with a reflection on the theme, 'From Lunatic to Functionally Disordered,' which, using sketches of people screaming and wearing jesters' caps, described a development in the perception of the occupationally disabled over time, and where the origins of mental hospitals and the existence of forced sterilization were discussed. This framing of Samhall employees and Samhall in a historical perspective is complemented during the introduction with more up-to-date verbal and written information about the company, where it is stated that Samhall is 'unique' thanks to 'its ability to offer varying work environments for people with different functional disorders and to allow employees to develop and grow based on their individual pre-requisites.'

Often, the supervisor will choose a mentor from among the occupationally disabled workers in order to facilitate the introduction of the new employee into the workplace. Workers can become a mentor after internal training, and a supervisor said that she chose those that were 'experienced' to be mentors. One assignment for the mentor is to introduce the individual to other fellow workers and especially to those fellow workers that belong to the work group in which the new employee has been placed. As one worksite supervisor explained, 'it [mentoring] can be necessary since it is difficult to learn things in the work team; you have to fit in and comply with whatever is applicable.' Another supervisor pointed out, 'as a new employee it always takes a little time until you have gotten into the group feeling and can begin relying on the group. The mentor can help with this.' The mentor is the one who has most contact with the new employee during the initial stages and apart from introducing the individual to the workplace, the mentor shows the newcomer where to shop for lunch, how to go to and from work using public transportation, and where, if necessary, to change to work clothes. One supervisor described it as if the mentor were constantly accompanying the individual so that he or she 'doesn't feel lost' or is confused when faced with new situations. Another supervisor said that the mentor 'takes care of the new employee, you always have someone around you and someone with whom you eat breakfast and lunch.' A mentor on a warehouse work team introduced new employees in both the practical work and such things as lunch and coffee breaks. She said to one of them: 'Now it's time for a smoke and here [in the group] we say that everyone doesn't need to smoke, but everyone needs a break, so you just follow the crowd,' whereupon they all went together to a coffee room.

During the first week at a worksite, a new employee was included in work team discussions, which often dealt with team members injuries and problems, and there the new employee was encouraged to talk about his or her problems. A mentor, who during recent times had been on the sick-list due to his 'not feeling well' as his supervisor explained it, told a new employee that the personnel at the workplace were often on the sick-list because of their problems, but the mentor was there for 'those that were sick most often and had the most problems.' (The new employee had previously said that he 'wasn't sick, only unemployed.') Especially for those that had 'inadequate understanding of their illnesses,' as one supervisor put it, it is important that they 'get the support of their mentors in talking about their problems' in order to 'be accepted in the work group and to develop properly.' According to one supervisor, some new employees can feel 'shy' and 'one trick I have is to tell them all about my limitations; for instance, that I only went to elementary school for eight years.' Another supervisor said that it was important to be open 'to gain their [the occupationally disabled's] confidence. Usually I am a little more personal with the new occupationally disabled in order to demonstrate that we can talk about anything here.'

Apart from the practical introduction at the workplace, another assignment for the mentor is to serve as a source of information for the supervisor regarding the 'condition' of the new employee. This is said to be crucial in order to provide the person with 'an individually-based development.' One mentor pointed out that an important part of her work was about 'trying to see if the individual feels okay, some are open, others are shy.' The first week's experiences with the new employee are reported to the supervisor, which adds to the previous information about the person in his or her case file from the National Employment Office. In addition, the person's behavior is noted by the supervisor during the new employee's initial period at the workplace and during the previous recruiting process. In training material for mentors, it is stressed that 'a mentor supports the supervisor in question to *facilitate* and *guide* new personnel during that time in a new workplace. The cooperation with a supervisor is fundamental.'

The introduction of the new employee usually also includes a personal discussion with the supervisor, in which they go through the person's social situation (marital status, previous occupations, general family situation) and medical status, unless this has not already emerged during previous discussions or during the compulsory health inspection at Samhall's Corporate Health Service (e.g. alcoholism, epilepsy, dyslexia, diabetes, allergies, back pains, ulcers, social phobias or other problems that are said to explain their occupational disabilities).

The central idea of 'adapting work to the occupationally disabled's individual requirement based on a mapping of their needs and conditions,' was translated by a supervisor to 'setting the right person at the right place from the outset based on his disability.' To that extent, individual adaptation is about adaptation based on type of disability according to the disability codes. According to another supervisor, the trial period at Samhall that the new employee goes through is about 'ascertaining what the individual can tackle successfully' (e.g. 'can he cope with cleaning stairs, can he cope with external property maintenance'). As has already been mentioned, the suitability of the individual for different types of work at Samhall is based on the person's occupational disability code, and not on professional background, education, personal preferences, or similar qualifications. Samhall can offer different types of occupations adapted to different groups of disabilities, such as suitable work for the visually impaired or those with motor disabilities.

Thus, Samhall's rehabilitation activities are built up around the organizational idea of occupational disability. If a person has a social phobia, the company does not subject him or her to a lot of people; a visually impaired person can work in a dark room but not with soldering electronic components, where vision is essential; and a person with a motor disability is presumed not to be able to work with the cleaning of stairs. One supervisor related that at his workplace the distribution of work was arranged 'on the basis of stress level' where different phases of work were regarded as being stressful in different ways and that 'the stronger ones' amongst the occupationally disabled workers, could work with more stressful jobs and 'the weaker ones' with less stressful assignments.

Different work teams usually carry out different tasks based on the disabilities that the individual members are said to have, which in concrete terms implies that the existing established occupational disabilities form the basis for the practical placement in a work group. The reason why a new employee has even been assigned to a specific workplace can be that he or she already has certain established limitations that make that person suitable for the work carried out there and this division usually continues at the workplace in question. If you are declared to have 'a low intellect' you will be considered suitable for performing assignments offered at certain Samhall workplaces. If you are dyslectic, you will be considered for specific assignments at specific workplaces. Your initial behavior as a person of low intelligence or a dyslectic must subsequently be developed further in the work itself, in the same way that an individual that has newly passed an examination in economics develops his or her professional career as a company economist. Thus within Samhall, there is an expectation that employees will develop *as occupationally disabled* in order to skillfully reproduce Samhall's basic goal of 'providing meaningful and developing jobs for the occupationally disabled.'

Certainly, Samhall's personnel have varying personal backgrounds, but as a result of the disability coding, they are in different personnel categories, which create those work groups that are out in the different workplaces. This division between groups of the disabled, which entails working at different workplaces or changing occupation within the same workplace, is in keeping with the disability-adapted environment that Samhall wishes to achieve, and when the work is group-based, this adaptation will be group-oriented. Hence, a necessary conclusion for disabled employees at Samhall is that their disability is 'their qualification' as in other welfare benefits: the established disability is what justifies employment at Samhall and the fact that the individual is considered for certain jobs *for the disabled* made it reasonable for a supervisor to say, 'We have great diversity here, here you will find all kinds of disabilities.' As noted, the designated disability, not previous experience as a successful dentist, carpenter, cook, or met-alworker is what governs the placement of people in work teams and the assignment of work tasks. The ability to act in a disabled manner affects the individual's career in Samhall and in the larger welfare system of which the individual as Samhall employee is a part.

The placement based on the type of occupational disability that prevails within Samhall workplaces also exists in a similar way between units within the company where different kinds of operations are directed towards differ-ent activities such as cleaning, elder care, carpentry, riding schools, farms, restaurants, hotels, large-scale kitchens, auto repair workshops. The name of the work group or workplace indicates the disabilities that the employees can be perceived to have, For example, the general internal feeling in the company seems to be that packaging assignments are among the simplest and most basic jobs and that only 'people with minimal talents and people otherwise limited' would do that type of work, explained a supervisor. Other groups or activities indicate other qualities in employees. Often, 'the mentally unstable' work within home-help service groups, another supervi-sor related. They were deemed suitable to take care of demented old people who were said to require 'a kind of slow-motion environment in order to feel really good.' This supervisor thought that 'there I believe they [Samhall employees] have a sureness in aim,' especially since he thought that people with an occupational disability could be presumed to find it easier to enter into older people's situation. According to the supervisor, 'many older peo-ple and in particular the demented also have a "functional disorder when it comes to intellect".' Hence, 'disabled people have been able to help other disabled people.' A psychologist hired by Samhall, who was in charge of a training course for a group of occupationally disabled employees about 'encounters in institutional care' with old people in a service home for the elderly, believed that 'many elderly people have a disruption in communica-tion, which also applies to Samhall's personnel, and that is why they suit each other so well.' In a Samhall document, it was maintained that work with the elderly was appropriate for the occupationally disabled:

> Employees at Samhall work with assignments that are adapted to each individual's functional disorder. Within the elder care [area] it is by no means a disadvantage to have a slow work pace, especially when it comes to contacts with the elderly. In this way, work with elder care suits so many of Samhall's employees very well.

As a leading subcontractor to private and public organizations in Sweden, Samhall has to have a wide range of occupational disabilities to be able to operate as comprehensive an organization as possible, where specific occupationally disabled employees can be matched to specific jobs. For this reason, 'we want to have a variety of jobs in order to be able to achieve adaptation for the individual...people have different handicaps,' explained a leading Samhall manager. Persons that have been classified as of low intellect, are said to have minimal talent and to be allegedly mentally retarded, are regarded as suitable for certain tasks, while people with social phobias, addictions, or other asocial behavior are considered as being suitable for other jobs. The CEO for Samhall explained: 'If we are to successfully tackle assignments...we must have a mixture of different functional disorders and different impairments. We can't only have people with grave disabilities, we need support there. We are trying to run this like any other workplace.'

One supervisor further explained: 'We have learned that some occupationally disabled people are good at certain things, for example, installing chassis, nobody can do everything, some groups have become very clever at certain kind of fixtures, we can't just move people around, for then we will come up against problems with quality.' A colleague of his at a laundry facility where employees with 'low intellect' worked, observed: 'The personnel that we have here at the laundry, can *only* work in the laundry.' Similar work that particularly suited those with low intellect could be found at several other workplaces. One supervisor called them 'idiotically simple jobs for a normal person' but it 'makes them happy, at least they have something to do.'

Samhall emphasizes that rehabilitation to a 'normal life' is best accomplished through work activities that are adapted to occupationally disabled clients' individual requirements. There is a prevailing expectation within and outside of Samhall that the company should offer work that is 'adapted to the specific needs of the occupationally disabled,' regardless of whether or not these are carried out internally at Samhall's own workshops or at external workplaces via staffing assignments. Hence, Samhall offers an environment sheltered from many of the demands and complex situations that can arise on the open labor market and which it can be assumed the employees will not be able to tackle successfully. In a Samhall document it is formulated, 'Work at Samhall should be *available and adapted* to people with functional disorders.' In reality, this often means that the job must not be too demanding; and this is presumed to benefit the development of the employee.

A supervisor for some of the Samhall employees working on a staffing assignment explained that Samhall's niche 'for managing both business and personal development requirements for the occupationally disabled' was to concentrate on simple assignments: 'We take the simpler assignments so that they [the company at which they had a staffing assignment] can take the more difficult ones.' A member of Samhall's corporate management team meant that more and more people in Sweden 'are becoming educated, that's quite true, but there are an awful lot of assignments in this country that are simple in nature, but there are not many people wanting to tackle them.' Here he saw an important future market where Samhall could expand and grow concomitant with the growth of more people in Sweden needing their services. 'In California, there are many illegal immigrants from Mexico who have the labor-intensive jobs [we can offer].' Another manager explained, 'Samhall can compete on the market for unskilled personnel.'

One of Samhall's former press relations officers, who after her employment there wrote a book about her time at Samhall, described her impressions after a visit to a workplace:

> The occupationally disabled each sit at an individual worktable, which in turn make up parts of a large common worktable. On the common worktable, there is a large carton with nails. The occupationally disabled employees pick nails from the box and place these nails in smaller packages. I assume that I have been unlucky and contact the regional CEO immediately. 'Surely, this is not meaningful work.' Inside me, I just want him to tell me that it is a mistake. However, he smiles at me in a friendly manner. 'These are only temporary work assignments while waiting for other assignments to come in.' Back at the corporate head office, I tell people about my visit during a mutual coffee break with a few fellow colleagues with many years at Samhall. I'm still waiting for a reassuring answer. However, one of the branch-hardened employees answers, 'Well, if you've seen one workshop, you've seen them all.' The others nod in agreement.

It is not surprising that a government study concluded that occupationally disabled persons have monotonous and simple jobs. That is what is regarded as appropriate for them, given their needs *as occupationally disabled*. In a CD ROM distributed by Samhall, it is pointed out that the labor market, 'is often more stressful for people with functional disorders than for others. Persons with functional disorders often specify that they work with monotonous assignments, in noisy environments, and think that work is stressful and monotonous. They also have less influence over their work.' Further, it was ascertained that outside of Samhall, 'employees with occupational disabilities get poorer jobs, they are often underemployed, are not allowed to do themselves justice, have limited social contacts' and that 'others make the decisions regarding employees with occupational disabilities; they themselves are accustomed to not complaining about unsatisfactory conditions.'

Still, various representatives from Samhall emphasize that work at Samhall should not be perceived as 'ordinary' just because it is simple and repetitive. One supervisor at a unit where documents were sorted and archived explained: 'The job sets great demands on accuracy. It's not just about sitting gluing and taping documents, but also about checking that the civic registration number tallies on each form.' One supervisor of a cleaning unit stressed: 'Cleaning is not a simple job, there are aids and other things. The cleaning system we have today is not at all like what we had before; we keep a constant check on developments and change appliances and methods and the like.' Often, the company magazine has reports about individual occupationally disabled employees who declare that the work is 'full of variety,' 'requires great accuracy,' provides opportunities for 'working at one's own pace,' and that Samhall's customers are satisfied and request Samhall's products and services. For example, in one report there was a story about a person who worked with packaging thousands of May-Day flowers each day. The employee said that she 'thinks that the job with May-Day flowers feels meaningful.' Another article had several photographs where the personnel used clothes similar to hospital scrubs: green, with a cap and plastic gloves. There was an emphasis on the work being advanced, that the personnel went through a formal control procedure with regard to hygiene, that the work 'requires manual dexterity and precision,' and that one always has to 'be concentrated and efficient in one's work.' In accordance with this picture, Samhall's publications usually contain many photos of smiling and happy occupationally disabled employees.

Despite the general emphasis on the significance of offering Samhall employees 'meaningful and developing work for the occupationally disabled,' one supervisor declared: 'I have people here with a university education that sit placing nails into plastic bags. I can think of it sometimes, but most often I dismiss it because it becomes troubling to me.' One problem in this context, as one of his colleagues pointed out, is that 'Samhall's jobs are intended for the weakest people,' but that 'even the strongest people have to perform these.' He described a department at one workplace where a group of occupationally disabled employees sat assembling paint rollers, which entailed taking the roller holders from a carton, installing the rollers and then placing the finished product in another carton. 'The work is perfect for several people in the group, but for others it is just too simple,' the supervisor said. A salesman at Samhall said:

> What I have experienced many times during all these years is *one* we don't believe that our employees can do as much as they can since they are occupationally disabled, *two* that we demand too little of our employees. We have a huge differentiation when it comes to the work capacity of our employees compared to that of a normal company, and thus we must be good at making demands on those that *can* produce a lot, *can* do a lot theoretically, but we have been a little stupid in that respect. We start at the lowest common denominator for our employees.

A member of Samhall's management team pointed out that 'one shouldn't underestimate the ability of our employees. Many times *we* place limiting factors on them by deciding how things are.' Another Samhall manager stated: 'Many are actually quite good at working.' In this context, an occupationally disabled employee ascertained, 'There is a lot of prejudice about us among the supervisors,' and another occupationally disabled person explained: 'Many times I have said to the boss, "I would be able to do that and that too", but each time I've had to hear, "You wouldn't be able to do that; it demands speed" or "this is probably not for you; you have to be able to tolerate stress to do that".' A manager at Samhall noted in the company magazine that there is 'a lot of prejudice about Samhall's personnel and great ignorance about what our employees are able to tackle successfully.'

One supervisor meant that on the whole, the occupationally disabled do not appreciate 'the idea of job rotation, they feel safe with what they have, of knowing what they have to do in the morning.' Another supervisor related, 'many of our employees have failures behind them which makes them fearful of failing again.' Yet another supervisor stressed the following:

> There mustn't be that much variation in the work. It is important that they [the occupationally disabled] can do the same thing for a long time so that they can learn it and feel safe with it.

This consideration is not only communicated directly via supervisors but also in the company magazine and video, where the positive sides of working with repetitive assignments in the work teams is often maintained. In a report in the company magazine, there is a story about one of the employees who worked with changing covers on video cassettes day after day: 'This is a great job, exactly the kind of job I like most of all. Others may think that it seems monotonous, but that is what suits me. My head spins when there is too much variation, or when I have to tackle several things at the same time.' One supervisor thought that the reason that his employees invariably work with the same thing each day for long periods is that 'most of them are mentally frail; as soon as something happens outside the standard framework, things don't go well. This is the way our employees function.'

Most supervisors did not organize recurrent changes in work because they wanted to safeguard the development and rehabilitation of the occupationally disabled. It was generally assumed that since the employees were occupationally disabled, they had need of a relatively constant work environment. But there was also a need for guaranteeing Samhall's production based on standard economic principles. This was stressed as being important in a CD ROM for supervisors at Samhall:

> By alternating between work assignments, it is possible for a person to develop and learn new things. From the point of view of health, this is

generally advantageous. However, for people with functional disorders, it can sometimes imply an obstruction. Instead of having to specially adapt a single operation, perhaps several operations must be adapted in order for them to work for an occupationally disabled employee, etc. This investment may be judged as being too great for the unit.

One supervisor emphasized the value of the routine nature of the work which could help employees to cope with personal and social problems:

> If you take those that are not mentally retarded but perhaps have a criminal background or [a history of] other asocial behavior, they often come here to learn how to be punctual, learn how to get on in a group, learn how to deal with one's feelings. Sometimes they can have a fit of rage so they have to learn how to handle all of these things.

Another supervisor talked about one of his employees who was 'world champion at screwing things up' when he started at Samhall and spread 'chaos around him; there was no order at all.' After many long discussions, 'nag, nag, nag,' and first and foremost by working in a storeroom where the demands for being systematic and for order prevailed, his behavior changed. 'Now there is fantastic order; he was "converted",' the supervisor declared. A book about Samhall's personnel development concepts notes that 'unlike many of the environments which people frequent during the hours of the day, the workplace has a strict *structure*. A well-structured environment like a workplace can contribute towards making a person with mental and social problems feel so much better that a positive process is initiated.' Since most of the work is highly repetitive, one of the occupationally disabled employees experienced that she had even 'brought order in her private life' thanks to her employment. She related that her job at Samhall was about weighing raw materials for food production, which requires 'precision and a feeling for numbers.' She said, 'I have become much more precise at home after working with this.' In this context, a government study about vocational rehabilitation listed a number of indicators in people who required rehabilitation via participation in a structured working life, such as 'lack of focus; insufficient ability to prioritize; lack of vision or future prospects; insufficient project and action planning; insufficient participation,' which were all factors that implied organization through work.

Even if the work content at Samhall workplaces usually changes, the actual character of the work remains unchanged; for example, one day an employee at a restaurant is packaging hundreds of portions of pancakes and thick pea soup, and the next day hundreds of portions of fish with mashed potatoes; or at a site where 'books are converted,' one week the employee is ripping off the covers from fictional works and textbooks the following week; or at one packaging facility, one month condoms are packaged, while next month lip balsam is being packaged. Repetition and reiteration are the response to the alleged individual needs of the occupationally disabled to work with simple assignments in a repetitive way. One of Samhall's cleaners expressed it as: 'each day is like any other; I know this job by heart.' Another employee distributing food by car each morning according to an established schedule observed as he put the key in the ignition, 'I can do this job in my sleep.' Or as a third employee explained: 'I don't think about what I'm doing; it all goes automatically.' One occupationally disabled employee who worked with soldering components declared: 'Soldering is soldering; it's the same thing all the time regardless of what you are soldering.' A supervisor at a warehouse for lamps explained, 'the object of the job is to pick, pack, and sort, but naturally, it doesn't matter if the products are light bulbs for cars or light bulbs [for home use].'

Neither does the repetitive element in the job differ between groups or between work units. The soldering of components, the packaging of frozen food, the preparing of journals for microfilming or scanning, or the cleaning of stairwells imply no great variations in the collective supply of work at Samhall. A unit head at a packaging industry plant explained: 'People learn things when they repeat the same thing over and over again; we have the same routines, or similar routines. If we package electric light bulbs for Osram [a customer], the routine for this job is similar to packaging for another customer.' One supervisor complemented this by saying, 'each product has its own routines, but in some way they are quite similar.'

The fact that people with different personal backgrounds basically perform the same work assignments is of less significance. 'It doesn't really matter what type of job it is, the occupationally disabled function in the same way,' a supervisor explained. Regardless of whether the employee is a highly educated academic who has previously worked with administrative assignments, or if he or she is a former miner, Samhall offers a similar working environment founded on a concept of an 'adapted working environment for the occupationally disabled.' One supervisor explained: 'The work suits most of them; we have standardized and simplified most processes.' One of the employees commented on this by saying, 'we are different; we function differently, but we are not treated differently.'

The result of these and similar attitudes is that not only the content of work (i.e., a focus on repetition and the carrying out of simple tasks) but also the work time for the execution of different jobs is 'adapted to the limitations of the employees,' as one supervisor put it. For instance in Samhall's external staffing assignments, Samhall's personnel 'do not have stress in the same way' as other personnel, according to one supervisor. At an external workplace consisting of a storeroom, Samhall's personnel were allowed to do lesser quantities of work than non-disabled workers, and had several breaks. A newly employed supervisor at a Samhall industry remembered that he often became 'frustrated' about the working pace when he was new, but with time 'I have become more a part of this Samhall spirit; it is calmer and steadier, so now I feel a lot better.' One of the occupationally disabled employees, a former cook who had a completely different assignment at Samhall, said: 'When I came here, I almost burst out laughing. When I was a cook, almost every minute was booked, but things are completely different here.' One supervisor thought that the overall atmosphere was 'apathetic' and that 'everything here takes such a long time, but one will have to adapt oneself to this; there is a reason for the existence of Samhall, our personnel has certain handicaps.'

A newly employed manager (who had previously worked as a manager at another company) had often posed the question of whether it is legitimate to make the same demands on occupationally disabled employees as for employees at other workplaces. He meant, 'I have really had to adapt my style of leadership' and that he had 'to be much more careful since I am dealing with fragile individuals. What I regard as trivialities can be immense for them.' One site manager declared that at the beginning of his career, he 'tried to make normal demands on the employees' but several of his subordinate supervisors, who had worked there for several years, had told him 'you can't do this, for they are disabled.' At this unit, they had 'a major problem with drugs' and despite the objections of his fellow employees, he chose 'to come to grips with this' where previously 'things had previously been swept under the carpet.' He took the example of one of the employees who he 'had managed to get into a treatment center,' but 'a lot of people here were against me for that.' In his opinion, 'managers at Samhall are not encouraged to make normal demands on the employees since we regard them as disabled; we have a lower standard here than at other companies.'

According to Samhall's Manager of Personnel, supervisors at Samhall 'have a particular responsibility for carrying out Samhall's program of rehabilitating the occupationally disabled,' Typically, supervisors perceive their work at Samhall as something unique compared with other companies, especially since they experience that the employees are 'in need of their support' and require a different kind of treatment. As it was expressed in a government study:

> The job of supervisor at Samhall entails responsibility for the social development of the occupationally disabled. This 'curative' role entails that the job as supervisor at Samhall is decidedly different from supervisor jobs at other workplaces.

One supervisor pointed out that as 'supervisor you can't be too quick or too tough, you have to adjust your style to the occupationally disabled.' One of her fellow supervisors who had previously worked in the private industry believed, 'Samhall is vastly different compared to other companies, you don't think along the same lines; there is another mentality. Samhall accepts that it's okay to go with a loss. 'We have people with problems,' they say.' An 'important difference to other companies,' another supervisor thought, is that at Samhall you need 'a lot of patience with people; our personnel do not work like most people.' He went on to say that sometimes there could be 'serious conflicts and quarrels within the work groups' and 'at such times it is important to be calm and try to direct the discussion.'

In their role as formally appointed leaders, some supervisors assume that occupationally disabled people need to be confronted in a particular way. One supervisor said: 'You can't talk to these people like you can to ordinary workers; you can't be a boor, you have to take it easy, people are very sheltered here; in a normal company you can push people in another way.' Another supervisor criticized a group leader in a work team at an external employer because he had 'pushed too much work' onto two of the occupationally disabled in the group. 'You have to remember that they are impaired.' Several supervisors experienced that 'you can't demand as much of them as you can in normal companies,' as one of them put it, since 'many of our employees are limited by knowing that they aren't able; they can't see, they can't walk properly, they don't comprehend, they've heard all their lives about what they *can't* do.' The CEO of Samhall explained:

> I usually say at employment interviews with [prospective] new managers, 'if you haven't bought Samhall's business concept, you shouldn't start here, for you will never be happy, you will always be confronted with situations where rational decisions are not possible; you must get the idea that Samhall is different. I have seen a lot of people who have come to us who have been really successful outside of Samhall but have been terribly frustrated when rational decisions have not been possible; you have to employ other dimensions when making decisions.

One supervisor thought that is was 'the human dimension' that drove him in his work: 'You get so much in return. I'm the kind of person who protects people. If they [the occupationally disabled] are ill, I send them a card; I send them Christmas cards, listen to how they feel, and we should do this when they are ill. We show that we are thinking of them, that they haven't been forgotten.' Often, this care for occupationally disabled employees transcends the limitations of the workplace and working hours: 'My supervisor has visited me at home and met my friends here. I think this is nice,' one of the employees recounts in an interview in the company magazine. Several supervisors in an industrial facility said how they sometimes had gone downtown looking for personnel that had not been at work, but who had instead 'been sitting drinking on a bench' as one of them put it. Others had helped employees to arrange for an apartment, have contacts with the social welfare authorities, the police, and the Regional Social Insurance Office. These more 'personal' dimensions of relations with employees make 'many supervisors feel that they are carrying out very important and significant work. One motivating factor is the sympathy supervisors say that they feel for the occupationally disabled, a government study ascertained. The study went on to say: 'A driving force [for supervisors] is that they experience that it is very rewarding working with the occupationally disabled on a personal and emotional plane.' One supervisor pointed out that his job was of extra importance since 'managers in other companies tell me that 'we don't have the energy to serve as daddies for the disabled'.' To be a successful supervisor within Samhall requires 'a strong psyche: there are problems in all workplaces, but here there are personal problems all the time, e.g. with economy; many of the employees have the bailiffs after them due to addiction problems,' alleged one supervisor. One Samhall publication maintained 'that being a department head and manager at Samhall is a challenge out of the ordinary.'

Some supervisors experienced it as their duty to be present during the workday for 'personnel development,' one of them explained. A part of the job is to 'be out and make sure that the personnel feel okay,' said another supervisor. Several of them have previously worked at companies other than Samhall. 'Compared to being a supervisor out there [i.e., in other companies], here we have to be more of a support person; I have to be something of a father, a mother, a psychologist, a man Friday,' said one. A supervisor expressed the following in a government study:

> Before I came here I was a supervisor at an industrial facility. There my work was to check on which order was to be dealt with and then organize and distribute work assignments for the day. My work here is more comprehensive. Apart from supervisory assignments, I am father, priest, and counselor for those working on my team.

More often than not, this is manifested in physical contacts in the form of hugs and sometimes kisses: 'You can understand the feeling when you come to work in the morning and get hugged by your fellow workers [the occupationally disabled],' another supervisor explained in the same study. In that respect, one supervisor meant that it was important for the occupationally disabled to 'be seen and confirmed' and exemplified this with a woman 'whose day is spoiled if she doesn't get a hug in the morning.'

The ideal supervisor at Samhall is a person who not only has a 'humanistic basic outlook' but also 'a businesslike way of thinking,' as one member of Samhall's corporate management put it. Or as the CEO for Samhall stressed: 'You can be both rational and a humanist, you don't have to be either the one or the other.' A desired 'profile' for a supervisor is empathy 'for the special needs' that occupationally disabled workers are presumed to have. A manager for a wood industry which employs five supervisors said: 'My supervisors must have an interest in the employees, an empathetic feeling.' The corresponding qualifications as a manager were also emphasized by the Samhall CEO, who thought that it was important 'to be a humanist, I wasn't a humanist when I began at Samhall, but have become one for I have met so many of our employees, especially since I worked in a smaller town, then you meet many of the employees in the town and then you realize just how much the job means.'

One supervisor implied that, on the whole, the occupationally disabled employees 'need control personnel,' especially for new types of work (e.g. when a new packaging job arrives in a packaging workshop). Another supervisor pointed out that a new assignment was never handed over to the work team 'in a democratic manner, which would have resulted in chaos.' Thus, some supervisors were of the opinion that it was necessary for them to be 'firm in their direction of the employees.' One supervisor thought that this stemmed from employees' 'occupational disabilities and poor self-confidence.' Another supervisor explained: 'Since many [the occupationally disabled] are apprehensive, clear guidelines are necessary.' In this context, a head of an industrial unit emphasized, 'supervisors are needed; we need them to set the bar so that we don't have to discuss what applies.' A supervisor who had worked for several other companies before coming to Samhall noted:

> Outside of Samhall you can hand out a job and know that it will be fixed, but I can never know if X here will do the same tomorrow as he did today, even if we are talking about carrying out the same job. They [the occupationally disabled] forget things, they can get things into their heads...you have to keep a constant check, participate in the process itself.

Some supervisors said that at the beginning of their Samhall careers they had felt confused in their meetings with the occupationally disabled. However, it had become easier to relate to them after obtaining information about these persons' problems, either via information from other supervisors about specific personal difficulties in the form of alcoholism, dyslexia, mental illness, or other medical problems, or thanks to their own investigations into these alleged personal disorders. One supervisor related that 'in the beginning I thought like this: I won't enquire into their occupational disabilities, why they are here, but after a while I discovered that it's initially better to go through their files to see what kind of occupational disability they have in order to encounter them as occupationally disabled.' The CEO for Samhall thought that today 'disabilities are not visible' compared to earlier when Samhall primarily employed 'the motor disabled and mentally retarded.' The CEO explained that 'an addiction is invisible, and consequently many people may think that "these people are healthy" and this is clearly a dilemma for us.' A member of Samhall's corporate management related about his own confused experiences of a visit to a workplace when he was a new employee:

> I was talking to a guy, and then asked a supervisor, 'What does he do here?' it was as if I had been talking to someone who was on an entirely

equal footing with me. Then he [the supervisor] told me that this was a guy who had been involved in a terrible car accident; he couldn't function properly.

A behavioral scientist who trained supervisors in 'communication with the disabled' said that she had met many supervisors 'who are really bewildered when it comes to dealing with situations' and took the example of the relatively large group of 'disabled immigrants' working at Samhall 'where it can be difficult to imagine what they have experienced and consequently they do not know how to treat those that have experienced torture and other things.' Thus, at some workplaces medical experts were sometimes hired who gave information about different kinds of disabilities, such as epilepsy, a social phobia, ADHD, and how these disabilities can be recognized in employees' behavior. A supervisor related, 'We [supervisors] try to learn about disabilities; experts come here and inform us and we go on courses, you have to learn to recognize the symptoms, otherwise we don't recognize their individual needs.'

In order to 'better recognize disabilities,' as one supervisor expressed it, all supervisors at Samhall complete a training course on occupational disability. The course is arranged by Samhall's Corporate Health Service and aims to help 'new supervisors [to] quickly familiarize themselves with the conditions of those with functional disorders.' The course is made up of various case studies on different types of occupational disabilities. Each case study has a formal description of what a specific type of occupationally disabled person looks like in terms of their behavior (e.g., a 'dyslectic' or a 'mentally retarded'). A newly employed supervisor, who had previously never worked with the occupationally disabled, declared that when he came to Samhall, he was 'received really well' and was impressed by the comprehensive introductory training courses offered him and other newly employed supervisors. In contrast to other companies that he had worked for where 'the introduction was completed within a matter of hours,' 'several weeks' were devoted 'towards entering into this special world, the world of Samhall.' He thought that the courses he attended, 'straightened out a load of questions regarding the disabled.'

After having participated in the introductory training courses, several supervisors experienced some of the occupationally disabled employees as 'obviously needy' in relation to themselves in the sense that they were considered to be sick, whether in physical or mental terms, functionally disordered or suffering from other medical problems according to the case studies' descriptions. After having attended the courses, a number of supervisors started addressing individuals or groups of individuals from the point of view of their medical problem, which was also a normal occurrence in Samhall's company magazine and other Samhall publications. One supervisor worded it as follows: 'The personnel force consists of mentally retarded individuals, alcoholics, the physically disabled.' Some supervisors pointed out that a disability code was needed for employment at Samhall; that is, only established medically-problematic people were employed at Samhall, and thus it was only logical to 'regard the employees as disabled.' A fellow worker clarified: 'Employment at Samhall is based on the fact that you *have* a disability, a sickness, or another medical problem.' Consequently, another supervisor thought that if a person is employed at Samhall, this is 'evidence' that there are *needs*; thus 'the question about what is wrong with you "is in the air".' This opinion was shared by a fellow supervisor at another workplace, who said, 'all those working at Samhall have problems; that's why they are here.'

In order to better understand the employees' bio-medical needs and requirements as occupationally disabled, several supervisors encouraged members of work groups to 'talk about their problems.' At a workplace meeting, one supervisor suggested that each working week commence with a 10-minute discussion about 'the difficulties you are carrying around with you' and that the work for the day be distributed based on this discussion, so that 'those that don't feel all that bad this week can do a little more than those that feel worse.' This focus on health or non-health in addressing the disabled was already a routine at another workplace and the supervisor declared, 'Several people need someone to talk to in the mornings when they have problems.' Some supervisors took part in the discussions and one of them told a person who was sad about a personal issue; 'You are really good' and 'I know you can do this,' thus encouraging the person to reveal her problems. Another supervisor implied that regular meetings of this kind were important to bring out 'if there is anything that doesn't feel right' for any of the personnel. He linked this to the individual's private life during one of these meetings:

> If you don't feel well here and are unhappy, it will affect your families. Therefore it is important that everyone talks out about why they are here and what problems are behind this.

A supervisor emphasized how important it is for occupationally disabled employees to be 'honest about their problems' in front of each other, declaring that 'the most difficult thing is our obligation to secrecy. We [supervisors] cannot openly talk about the problems of colleagues [the occupationally disabled].' However, in order to circumvent this rule, 'We try to encourage our employees to be open with each other; we have mutually decided that we should not conceal our problems,' as one of the supervisors put it. At one workplace, one of the occupationally disabled employees related: 'We are used to talking about how we feel. If I feel bad, I say so and then the others know that it's OK to take a break.' Another employee declared: 'We are open with our problems in the work team; we have to be; we are talking about complete trust.'

One supervisor related that employees often 'voluntarily tell me about their problems and this demonstrates their trust for me as their boss.' Another supervisor explained that the knowledge acquired from the employees' case files is complemented via ongoing discussions at work about the individual's situation at work and in life. She believed that to be a good supervisor who can contribute to the development of the disabled employees 'it is important to acquire a fundamental knowledge of the personnel, which requires that I work with them for a long time; you have to get a handle on the personnel.' She exemplified this with one of her employees who 'she talked with a lot' since 'she had problems with her son and other things.' Most work days they sat down at the coffee table together with the other personnel to 'talk through what has happened,' as the supervisor explained it, and it was concluded with the supervisor giving the employee a hug.

In a number of meetings in which the members of the work groups were encouraged to talk about their individual problems and limitations that were assumed to exist, sometimes a member of Samhall's Corporate Health Service took part. A nurse at this unit explained:

> Many times I have been surprised that people [the occupationally disabled] are not more afraid about their privacy...they talk openly about their problems. I think they should maintain a certain degree of privacy. Naturally, some people should know, but not everyone should know what has happened in my life, about how terrible things have been.

The focusing on problems in work groups and between fellow workers during coffee breaks and at lunchtime is said not only to be about creating a forum for the exchange of experiences between the occupationally disabled, but also about creating an arena for increased understanding for their respective situation as disabled due to various medical problems. One supervisor explained that it is very important for the personnel to 'understand each other's problems and disabilities' and to 'learn to take these into consideration.' Another supervisor thought that the personnel 'must think disability' when they interact with each other and 'adapt their behavior for everyone who has a disability.' In this context, one supervisor said that it is important to 'teach people to understand each other's problems if they are to succeed in their own rehabilitation.'

In these contexts occupationally disabled employees often refer to illnesses and other problems when talking about themselves, such as by introducing themselves with, 'I'm dyslectic,' 'I have a problem with my back,' 'I have an ulcer'; 'I have heel spurs.' A highly educated immigrant suffering from MS and who now worked at one of Samhall's factories with packaging assignments, said, 'This sickness has destroyed my life, my dreams, my career.' Another of the employees, who had difficulties in speaking, used to hand over a copy of a magazine report to visitors at the workplace where he worked. The report had the heading 'This is how my life was changed. All my dreams about my future were wiped out in a second!.' Not all clients were, however, convinced of their alleged medically problematic status, but rather took a pragmatic stance. A newly employed occupationally employee declared the following:

> In the beginning, I tried to be normal, but in time you start to act stupid in order to be able to cope; it's kind of like a game for each other. I often have to sink to the level of others in order to be able to work with them; you have to be able to express yourself in their way. There is a risk that you can switch over; that some day you have become like them yourself.

An occupationally disabled man working in a packaging workshop was critical about 'mixing different personnel groups.' He said that 'they mix us up with mentally retarded,' which, according to him entails that 'we that are not so sick must adapt to those that are really sick; eventually we may also become sick.' One of his colleagues, recently employed, claimed that 'not only supervisors address you as if you were sick, the colleagues do that as well. Perhaps I am disabled after all.'

Of course, in Samhall there are individuals that try to resist the claims made about them; as already reported in the previous chapter on Samhall's recruitment, these persons are commonly seen as 'lacking insight into their illnesses.' Several of the occupationally disabled clients felt that the idea of them being disabled prevented them from acting 'normally' in their respective workplaces; for example, taking initiatives for improvement. 'Being disabled assumes helplessness and dependency' as one of them put it. In a book about Samhall, one of the clients said: 'If you come with your own ideas, these are quickly brushed aside.' Another employee argued:

> After so many years within the company, I've learned exactly how the ideal Samhall worker should be constituted: You shouldn't object, not think at all, accept everything corporate management devises and even be glad and thankful for the great honor of working there.

A colleague of his explained that he had pointed out that there were 'problems and deficiencies in the job, that there is too little variation' and that subsequently he encountered 'freezing out and victimization from the supervisors; one of them said to me that I could just as well stay at home.' He concluded, 'We are not the ones who have mental problems, it's the supervisors who do.' Another client emphasized:

> My belief when I began there [was] that this should be rehabilitation, but if anything, the opposite was true. Many don't feel well, but unfor-

tunately too few dare to say anything. The fear for countermeasures from corporate management is great, which I have personally experienced via relocation.

One of the occupationally disabled employees who was suspended from his job, claimed that Samhall has 'become a territorial-minded colossus that has outlived its day, in my mind primarily because of incompetent supervisors who are so jealous of their meal ticket that they kick at everything and everyone including those that exhibit good judgement, civil courage, and to top that: Personal initiative!.' Yet another employee argued:

> Beginning at Samhall results in complete loss of one's human dignity. At this workplace the occupationally disabled employees are subjected to different types of abuse by the so-called labor management if they exhibit the least suspicion of personal initiative or individual thought.

An occupationally disabled person said that during lunchtime he used to work on private things, 'To keep my brain working' and showed a little room where he was busy building model aircraft and cars from drawings he had downloaded from the Internet. This was his 'safety zone' as he expressed it; 'Here I can get away from my colleagues and supervisors.' One of the employees related that when he was new, 'I thought a lot about the question of mental retardation and Samhall' and 'thought about what this kind of environment could do with me,' but 'now I only try to switch myself off.'

Despite these critical accounts by a minority of Samhall's 22,000 employees,[1] individual occupationally disabled persons testified that they seldom persisted with presenting their criticism: 'Eventually you lose interest and give up; nobody listens to us,' one of them explained. Another employee said, 'I've been criticized a lot for my criticism; it's just not worth it.' In one of the contributions in a book about Samhall, one of the employees who remained anonymous said that the following

> [Samhall] influences 'uncomfortable' employees to resign or take out a disability pension.... There have even been uncomfortable persons who have said what they think that have been subjected to a campaign directed at getting them to give notice to quit.

One of her colleagues said that 'the supervisor claimed that I had talked badly about the company. I got no help from the union. More likely they have taken part in the victimization. The union is part of the tragic story with Samhall.' Another employee argued: 'It's strange that just because the state is the owner, this treatment can continue, and also with the acceptance of the union.'

As a rule, most union representatives, supervisors, and leading managers of Samhall do not provide any criticism of Samhall. Instead, they emphasize how important it is that a company like Samhall exists to 'help the neediest in society.' To the extent that criticism has been ventilated by supervisors and other leading officials at Samhall, this criticism is from former employees. For example, one former Samhall public relations officer wrote:

> My own reflection is that generally speaking, the first impression of Samhall is very positive among all those that come into contact with the enterprise. Criticism of the enterprise comes concurrently with increased knowledge about the reality that hides behind the facade.

Another former public relations official at Samhall stated in a magazine:

> Already after a few months I began to ponder about what I was actually doing. I was out and about in the country meeting many people, both on the shop floor and at the director level. I began to acquire impressions. I was really shaken up. Basically speaking, walking around in work premises built for so-called sick or disabled people is an abnormal experience.

8 Transition

The ultimate goal of Samhall employment is to make the transition to employment with a regular organization, and according to Samhall, the ultimate proof that the organization's rehabilitation works in terms of making people less dependent on welfare support. According to an agreement with the Swedish State, Samhall should yearly be able to achieve transitions of 5% of existing staff. 'The organized transition process,' as it is called at Samhall, includes a number of practices, ceremonies, and procedures aimed at 'guaranteeing the same individually-based approach at the termination of employment as at its beginning.' The formal responsibility for transitions lies with the employee's supervisor at Samhall and the National Employment Office:

> Our organizations have mutual responsibility for providing the Samhall employee with opportunities for a transition to employment with another employer. On the part of the Samhall company, this is about everything from preparatory and motivation augmenting measures to supporting and following up the employee after the transition to another employer. When the efforts and forms of support provided by the National Employment Office are deemed necessary, the National Employment Office is also afforded a responsibility for contributing towards bringing about a transition. An important point of departure is then that all employees that are prepared for a transition are reported and registered as applicants for an exchange at the National Employment Office.

The Samhall supervisor is the one who decides if a person is 'mature for a transition,' based on his or her experience of the development of the occupationally disabled person. The supervisor then contacts the National Employment Office so that together they can decide on a suitable workplace. A government study that carried out an interview survey among Samhall's occupationally disabled employees with the aim of mapping Samhall's transition work, posed the question, 'Have you ever during recent years talked to your immediate superior about what will happen with you in the future?' This hinted at the significance of the supervisor for the realization of transitions. An administrative official at the National Employment Office was of the opinion that 'those people who succeed in transitions' are those that had 'been observed' by their supervisor at Samhall 'for a long time.' A Samhall document described that the process was initiated when 'the employee and his or her immediate superior are in agreement that the employee is *prepared for a transition* (both can and wants to).' Among other things, the responsibility of the National Employment Office for transitions involves offering a new employer on the regular labor market a wage subsidy during the first year of employment, which usually amounts to between 50 and 70%. One supervisor at Samhall emphasized that 'we are forced to pay out wage allowances since they [the occupationally disabled] do not have the same capacity as healthy people.' Consequently, 'wage allowance are central for our transitions' another supervisor at Samhall pointed out, which was confirmed by an administrative official at the National Employment Office who thought, 'There is a difference between working in a sheltered workplace [Samhall] and at a normal workplace. He [the occupationally disabled person] may need extra instruction and the like,' which would thus motivate a wage allowance. A wage allowance presupposes that the person continues to be coded as occupationally disabled, which is an administrative requirement for granting a wage allowance within the National Employment Office. Thus, even if a person leaves Samhall as an occupationally disabled employee, he or she typically continues to be occupationally disabled in the wider welfare system of which Samhall is a part.

An administrative official at the National Employment Office declared that good collaboration with supervisors at Samhall is essential for succeeding with transitions. She was of the opinion that the supervisor at Samhall is 'the person with the best knowledge' and 'knows what the employee is like.' For this reason it is 'the supervisor who has the primary responsibility for the transition process,' which is also established in the above quoted cooperation document between Samhall and the National Employment Office. Another administrative official at the National Employment Office related how during the course of the years he had 'become friends with the supervisors at the different workshops [at Samhall]. We have become more and more intimate as time goes by, I have been out with the supervisors a lot, we have lunched together.' Essentially, staff members at the two organizations decide on the future of the occupationally disabled person; in this case whether or not he or she is to exit from Samhall.

During 'transition conversations' in which occupationally disabled employees take part, the employees are expected to talk about their view of themselves and what kind of work they would like outside of Samhall. 'The person tells me he would rather work with cleaning, storeroom work, or in a restaurant,' an administrative official at the National Employment Office in charge of accommodating ex-Samhall employees related; but, according to him, most often 'there is nothing written down about how they function in the different kinds of work and we would really like to know this when trying to place these people.' Another administrative official of the National Employment Office was of the opinion that 'it's not serious' to rely on what the employee expresses regarding 'his or her dreams' and therefore implied that the supervisor at Samhall is a more reliable indicator of the person's 'real needs.'

Indeed theoretically, it would be possible for an occupationally disabled employee at Samhall to look for a job outside of Samhall on his or her own, without the involvement of the National Employment Office and Samhall, and eventually find employment outside of Samhall. In practice, this is probably not realistic because predictably a potential employer will require a wage supplement in order to hire a former Samhall employee, whom he would assume is disabled, injured, or has particular needs, or that the employer would simply not wish to miss out on a wage allowance. One of the occupationally disabled employees believed that she could understand that employers were skeptical about employing personnel from Samhall: 'A position at Samhall implies that you have a problem and so it is only logical that they [employers] think, "Will he stay at home and be sick a lot?"' In a magazine report about employees at one of Samhall's workplaces, one of the employees declared, 'You can hardly get another job after working here; nobody wants you when you have worked at Samhall.'

Furthermore, a Samhall employee cannot personally hand in his or her notice, just as he or she could not with any company, authority, or similar in Sweden, and expect economic support from the unemployment benefit fund, which only applies to people who are involuntarily laid off. Redundancy due to lack of work is something a Samhall employee does not have to reckon with since up to now the organization has never applied this. Not making people with occupational disabilities redundant when there is a lack of work at Samhall is something of a 'sacred calf' and is thought to create a good base for the rehabilitation of the employees by offering them a secure and stable work environment. Thus, in reality, the Samhall employee enjoys lifetime employment in the form of a post with tenure where redundancy due to lack of work is not practiced. In a government study it was observed that 'since 1980 [i.e., when Samhall was founded] no employee with an occupational disability has been made redundant due to lack of work,' even if this is formally possible. This possibility 'is simply not *used*,' the study pointed out. For this reason, you are 'almost a serf at Samhall,' one of the occupationally disabled employees declared.

Despite the supervisor's formal responsibility for 'assessing transition maturity,' as one of them called it, the real responsibility for transitions lies with the occupationally disabled themselves. One supervisor declared that the occupationally disabled must 'be ready with their rehabilitation process' and that they must arrive at 'what they want to do outside of Samhall.' She related that during the personal development discussions with the clients, she used to ask, 'What do you want to do after Samhall?,' but also emphasized that 'you [the employee] have to give me the assignment, you are the one who should know what you want and which companies you would like me to contact.' In other words, the occupationally disabled employee must convince the supervisor that he or she is no longer occupationally disabled before the supervisor will arrange a transition.

At a meeting with around 40 employees, one supervisor said: 'I promise that I will never force you to do anything, for example, transitions. The initiative must come from you.' This is in line with the perception marketed in an information CD for supervisors at Samhall: 'There are no simple shortcuts to successful transitions. Fundamental is the idea that each employee plays "the starring role in his or her own life" and in supporting the person to take personal responsibility for their own development.' An occupationally disabled employee said: 'You have to take your own initiative to leave; you have to put your foot down; convince the boss that it's time.' At a workplace with around 50 employees, one of the employees said, 'Some of us must go on and want to leave this place. There are seven of us who have decided that we have to get out, but quiet! Don't say anything!' In a group of occupationally disabled, there was talk about leaving the company and different ideas for leaving were discussed, such as getting together and starting a business. The supervisor at the workplace in question, who was very aware of the employees' wishes, commented, 'Many of them want to do so much, but they can't.'

Several supervisors did not believe that the employees would be able to cope with the demands of the external labor market, given their experiences of the occupationally disabled as helpless and in need of much assistance. An employee related that he had provided several suggestions of companies that might be interested in accepting him, but 'the supervisor said that things weren't just right at the moment.' One of the employees pointed out that it might be problematic to make contact with external employers during working hours as 'you have to leave your job [to do this], and this isn't always so easy.' Another employee explained that it was difficult to apply for work during working hours for practical reasons since there was only one telephone for the 100 or so employees working there(and the phone was located in a corridor with heavy employee traffic), as well as only one terminal for Internet searches that was limited to 15 minutes a day. One employee wrote in a book about Samhall, 'If we are going to the National Employment Office or doing something else, to seek a job or training, we have to sign out. I have not received any help from Samhall to seek any other "normal" job.'

One supervisor experienced that partly there are 'those who want to leave; they do everything to leave; but then there are those who want to leave, but who don't have the ability; they haven't understood; they believe they can do it, but I know that they won't be able to.' Another supervisor thought:

The persons who have worked here a long time; I don't think we can get those to leave, that we can pass them on to the open market. They are so terribly secure; they know how things function at Samhall; they are completely destroyed if you talk to them about life outside of Samhall. Then there are those that have great self-confidence, who believe that they can cope with most things, which they can't. Then you have to stop that person and teach him this thing first before you continue.

One of the employees, a man of around 25, related that when he was new at Samhall, he was optimistic about being able to leave the company soon, 'It would only be temporary,' but that now after six years at Samhall, 'I don't care anymore.' A newly employed occupationally disabled person emphasized, 'I want to leave. At least I am not going to stay here all of my life.' In 2003, another person, who had previously worked as a car mechanic said, 'The idea was that I would be here for a year; I have been here since 1985' and a colleague of his who had worked in Samhall for 12 years, declared: 'I never thought I would be here so long.' A woman related about herself and a colleague, 'We have worked at Samhall for 15 and 17 years respectively, and for 15 and 17 years respectively we have wanted to leave.'

One of the employees at another workplace emphasized that it was important not to stay at Samhall too long, for 'if you have been here too long, you give up, you lose your initiative.' One supervisor argued: 'You shouldn't be here [at Samhall] too long!...the older employees [become] mother and father figures and take care of the younger employees.' One of the occupationally disabled employees pointed out that he believed that 'self-confidence' did not improve but got worse from working at Samhall, because 'they force you to carry out simple therapeutic jobs so that eventually you believe you can't do anything.' Another of the employees said, 'If your self-confidence is good, it gets worse here. After a time you feel worthless. Then it is not so easy to leave Samhall.' And a third person thought, 'You are oppressed here...and then they get the idea that you will have to leave when you have been floored. If you aren't crazy when you begin here, you'll become crazy eventually.' Yet another employee said, 'First you are broken, and then you lose your power of initiative, and then you get to hear that you yourself have the solution to your problem by them [supervisors] saying that the initiative to transition should come from me.' Thus, several occupationally disabled were generally disappointed that 'Samhall has not managed to arrange a job for me,' as one of them put it; or that 'Samhall doesn't take any responsibility for me,' as another employee said.

At a workshop, a young man said, 'It's important not to stay too long here for then you easily become permanent.' He thought that the job was monotonous and 'you are locked to certain assignments, eventually you become fixed in your mind.' An administrative official at the National

Employment Office related that many of the younger new employees at Samhall 'have a strong belief in their own ability, so there you almost have to apply the brakes for they don't know their capacity.' The administrative official could observe that the younger people she had recruited to Samhall during the course of the years still worked there, which she believed was due to 'security—and if you work with these kind of monotonous assignments, you automatically get stuck, you lose faith in learning anything new. Finally you don't believe in your own ability.'

A woman of around 60 who had worked at Samhall for 20 years thought that the company must 'go in for getting the young to leave; we older people are a lost cause. Many young people establish roots easily; it's easy to remain at Samhall.' A colleague of hers explained: 'When I was new here, I believed that I would soon leave; I was active and applied for other jobs, had plans, but after a while I gave up.' Several younger men at one of Samhall's workplaces testified that when they began at Samhall, 'I heard several times that Samhall was only something temporary, a step along the way,' as one of them declared. One supervisor thought, 'Most people who have been at Samhall for more than three to four years are very difficult to get out. It [transition] should happen during the first year.'

A government study recently ascertained that

> Today, of Samhall's employees with an occupational disability, almost 40% have been employed in the company for more than 10 years. After this long period at Samhall, most of them have come to regard their employment at Samhall as a secure position. The longer employment at Samhall lasts, the less the possibility of leaving Samhall.

Under the heading, 'locking-in effects,' another government study about Samhall stated: 'Persons with a long period of employment [at Samhall] to a lesser degree are apt to go over to a job on the regular labor market.' A nurse at Samhall's Corporate Health Service believed, 'We have many that have worked here for many years and they have become adapted to Samhall and find it difficult to imagine anything else.' An administrative official, who had worked at the National Employment Officefor several years with transitions of Samhall employees,, explained, 'Our clients eventually stop thinking about normal jobs in the future.'

Some supervisors argued that another reason for the problems with realizing transitions can be found in demands for the maintenance of good businesslike production by Samhall that relies on a certain amount of occupationally disabled manpower. One of them said that it is 'mostly the middle layer that will have to go, not the most able,' one supervisor explained. Another supervisor said, 'The unit has its mainstays and I don't try pass on these people in the first place but the middle register who are weaker.' An administrative official at the National Employment Office thought that it was a dilemma for those at Samhall who are 'too capable' since 'they keep production going.' He believed that the most appropriate persons for a transition 'are seldom identified as ready for a transition.' Another administrative official at the National Employment Office observed: 'There are people that they [Samhall] need to cope with for production...who are very capable and who could very well hold their own on the labor market as we see it.' A supervisor was interviewed in the staff magazine, and said, 'We supervisors are in breach of our duty if we organize work so that everything depends on certain key persons. This would put a brake on transition work.' A government study implied that there was a tendency among supervisors to keep 'the most able and most productive personnel.' A radio report pointed out that 'production at Samhall should be carried out on businesslike grounds, but at the same time the state demands that the company should stimulate employees to seek work on the open labor market. Having to always get rid of competence is a problematic goal for a company.' This was also ascertained in a government study that emphasized the following:

> If the employee during his or her time at Samhall has gained experience and become skilled and thus obviously contributes towards the economic goals, there is no motive for the local management at Samhall—which also has to comply with economic requirements—to contribute towards a transition to the regular labor market.

Of the few transitions that are realized, around 40% fail and the individual returns to Samhall. One Samhall document emphasizes that all occupationally disabled employees leaving Samhall through transitions 'have the right to return to Samhall up to a period of 12 months (so-called return). This 'right to re-employment' was introduced in 1983 to make it easier for people to dare to take the step and try other jobs on the regular labor market. This possibility is important, especially for the employee who would otherwise never dare to give it a try.' Some supervisors at Samhall and administrative officials at the National Employment Office were of the opinion that it is the occupationally disabled employees, rather than the external employers that cause returns: 'It can be really stressful out there,' declared one supervisor. A supervisor, who worked with arranging transitions at the request of several Samhall units, believed that the returns depended on the fact that the occupationally disabled employees 'did not fit in':

> You become isolated at the new workplace; you are different, perhaps you experience that you can't manage the job so well. I also think that they feel that others know that they are receiving allowances, that they are not like the others.

He also believed that insecurity in the new employment compared to the Samhall position with regard to the risk of termination could play a role. 'Often they ask, what if the company were to become bankrupt a year from now. I believe one has a great need for security when one has a disability.' Of the few individuals that do not return to Samhall, around 90% of them continue to rely on welfare support through wage allowances, thus remaining codified as occupationally disabled. In essence, few people who enter this system leave their formal welfare identity as occupationally disabled.

An administrative official at the National Employment Office with long experience of transition work from Samhall to other employers thought that the returns were due to the following reasons:

> There is too great a difference between outside and inside of Samhall. Persons can often be unprepared for what it can be like to work outside Samhall. One has become used to a specific environment, and sometimes there is quite a large difference between the environment at Samhall and a corresponding environment at another company. Not only with regard to production requirements, but even other, social requirements, all kinds of things you have to take into account in the working situation. People don't look at you in the same way at a workplace outside of Samhall.

One supervisor believed that the most common reason for an employer not wanting to retain the Samhall employee, was that the person was often 'sick and didn't come to work, perhaps come for a week and then be at home the following week without saying anything. There are demands on them that they should be present.' Thus an administrative official at the National Employment Office implied that returns 'are more likely to depend on the employee' than the employer.

In general, supervisors believed that transitions are difficult to realize because the employees do not even want to finish at Samhall. A supervisor said, 'As soon as I submit a suggestion for a job [outside Samhall], they answer that it wasn't [the type of job] they were thinking about, too far to travel etc.' Another supervisor thought:

> They [the occupationally disabled] don't want to; they are uncertain, many are afraid, many have perhaps been out and been laid off and consequently lost their self-confidence. When they go outside of Samhall, they are confronted by uncertainty; they can be afraid, be terminated; the company can close down. You often hear this, 'What shall we do if they close down' and they are right to do so. I believe they feel assurance at Samhall, great assurance, plus they have so many [coworkers] they know here, a feeling of fellowship among the disabled; the social bit; you are not left out here.

One supervisor related: 'During our counseling of employees, most people say "I am so happy; everything's great; I have really good friends" and if things are so satisfactory, then we shouldn't do so much; they just don't want to do anything else. Plus they know that perhaps they wouldn't have been able to do anything else outside of Samhall; this is their life, their world, these are their friends.' A government study concluded the following after having interviewed a number of occupationally disabled employees:

> The interviewed occupationally disabled declare that they feel a strong social security in the relationship they have developed to fellow workers and management personnel at Samhall. The occupationally disabled conveyed the impression that it was difficult to imagine finding similar security elsewhere.

An administrative official at the National Employment Office was of the opinion that 'many people within Samhall have real fellowship; they meet at weekends and in the evenings, and they can be difficult to get out onto the open labor market.' A colleague of his commented that at a workplace at Samhall, the employees were 'really difficult to get out anyway for they were so terribly happy at work.' A government study ascertained:

> A factor reported to give positive motivation and driving force is the we-feeling that people more or less strongly experience within the Samhall companies that were examined. A factor that contributes to that we-feeling is that people are assembled round a common value-system that occurs as an effect of working at Samhall and not out 'on the open market.' In this case, 'we' are the Samhall employees, 'they' are the people outside.

For this reason, one manager of a Samhall workplace believed, 'Many people feel, "I see, you want to get rid of us in order to achieve your goals [with transition], you want us out just so you will get so and so many pegs". That's the way many react.' An administrative official at the National Employment Office believed that many Samhall employees thought in the following way:

> Why should I venture out into uncertainty and the cold; Samhall says that they can't fire us due to the lack of work, and if you come from another country and all that involves in the form of terror experiences, then you don't want to move. Then there are many other groups with intellectual disabilities that have tried jobs on the open labor market; been treated badly. You feel secure there [at Samhall]; you have your friends there. Security is preferred to development. If you are badly treated, the primary thing is not to develop and be like everyone else; the primary thing is 'I'm not treated badly here.'

Samhall's CEO believed, 'For our employees, this [Samhall] is their backbone in life. Many of our employees have been excluded, not only from working life, but even from social life and this means that one doesn't have the security outside of the job that we [the non-occupationally disabled] have.' One supervisor declared, 'Our employees often lack social contacts; they are lonely.' Another supervisor continued: 'Many have been unemployed for several years. They have perhaps failed all their lives, they have been excluded at many companies; there hasn't been a place for them on the team. Many have poor self-confidence.' A colleague at another workplace thought: 'For many people here, this [Samhall] is the only thing they have and there is an immense difference compared to other companies, they have no social network at home, they have no family or children, when they come home, they sit down and watch TV. Work is then very important for they have their friends and acquaintances here.' Thus, according to another supervisor, 'The unique thing with Samhall is that there is a job for the disabled; they feel there is meaning in going to a workplace. I believe that the social bit means a lot to them, they have fellowship.'

A government study observed, 'The work with transitions is rendered more difficult by the fact that the occupationally disabled lack sufficient incentives to leave Samhall. For many occupationally disabled employees, security of employment is valuable.' Based on an interview study, it was also ascertained:

> In the first place, the majority of the interviewed occupationally disabled imply that they value the fact that their job at Samhall is secure. In many cases it is about persons who, prior to employment at Samhall, had been in working life for many years but who had been laid off due to lack of work or illness and because of this had been unemployed for a longer period. Normally, the work rate is lower at Samhall and the company has substantial job security.

Another study concluded, 'The picture of the occupationally disabled as having little motivation to leave is confirmed in the interviews carried out in the group of occupationally disabled. Only one of those interviewed indicates that he/she was interested in a job outside of Samhall.' A person working with transitions and training posts at Samhall was of the opinion that when there are problems before and after a practice or transition, this was because 'we have not succeeded in motivating our employees. You have to show how positive it will be for the employees to leave.' In that respect, a supervisor said, 'Often people are not motivated to get away; they are afraid' and one of her colleagues related, 'If you bring up the issue of transition, they stay at home for a week.'

According to several supervisors, an important reason for difficulties with transitions is a harsh labor market for the occupationally disabled, for whom continued employment at Samhall seems to be the only realistic alternative. A government study established, 'The supervisors point out two partial explanations for the problem of bringing about transitions. The one partial explanation exists externally and constitutes the harsh climate on the labor market. The other partial explanation exists internally and is made up of the fact that the occupationally disabled in general have low motivation or a great resistance to finding their way out onto the open labor market.' A supervisor explained, 'A prerequisite for being able to leave for another job is that there is a job to go to.' One of his colleagues meant, 'It is impossible to effect transitions as long as the labor market is the way it is.'

This opinion is also marketed repeatedly within Samhall via the company magazine, information videos, and discussion themes that are directed at occupationally disabled employees during workplace meetings. A Samhall brochure that was available at different Samhall workplaces stated: 'Unemployment is higher among persons with functional disorders than among others. Therefore, Samhall plays an important role on the current and future labor market.' In an article, Samhall's CEO said the following:

> The current labor market is characterized by structural changes and closures. At the same time, the demands for competence and flexibility are increasing. Long-term sick-listings and disability pensions are on the increase. This development clearly shows that in the foreseeable future there will be a need for a number of different labor market efforts [such as Samhall] to safeguard the possibilities for work for the functionally disabled with several exposed groups in working life. I am convinced that Samhall will play an important role as one of these efforts.

Ideas about the difficult labor market for the occupationally disabled are based on the special needs of the occupationally disabled due to their medical problems that are assumed in Samhall's methodology for rehabilitating the occupationally disabled. For example, in a letter to the Ministry of Industry, Employment and Communications, Samhall's CEO wrote:

> Today's working life is far from being available for persons with comprehensive and lasting functional disorders. Many are simply not employed since they are not able to enter the existing production processes with the demands imposed there on work pace, communication, flexibility, professional competence, etc. A new type of employment is needed for this target group with lasting support and fundamental adaptation of the job and work environment that Samhall can offer.

An article in the company magazine, 'We Are Playing an Increasingly Important Role,' which was written by Samhall's personnel manager noted:

In the future, Samhall will play an increasingly important role. The obvious exclusion from working life, the increasing number of sick-listings, and the difference in competence among the unemployed and those that industry is calling for, will make it more and more difficult for the functionally disabled to get work.

To the extent that one defines oneself as occupationally disabled, the message is clear: the labor market *is* more or less hopeless, implying that Samhall is the only feasible option.

In their interviews with the occupationally disabled, the authors of a government study established, 'The occupationally disabled express resignation at the thought of obtaining and coping with a job outside of Samhall,' which was based on the notion that their injuries, disabilities, and other medical problems created limitations for them on the open labor market. One of the employees said in an interview: 'I wouldn't be able to cope with a job out there' and another said, 'There are no jobs to get; it feels meaningless to try.' One of the younger employees who had previously worked in a food store was convinced after six years at Samhall that working in food stores was not the thing for him any longer. 'The job is too much; too much responsibility,' he stated. 'I need peace and quiet, otherwise I feel bad.'

Several occupationally disabled employees at Samhall related that they needed to work under the sheltered conditions offered by Samhall that they had come to appreciate and demand after some time of employment. Echoing some of Samhall's own theses, one of them explained, 'It's harder out there [at external workplaces], but on the other hand, people there are healthy. Samhall is calmer and more secure.' A colleague of his thought that it was important to 'work at one's own pace if one's ill,' and another employee explained, 'Here things are adapted to my capability; that's good because my body is the worse for wear.' Another occupationally disabled employee said that it was important not to have to work in a 'hectic and stressful environment, for I can't cope with that. Then I feel bad, and that's why I am here.' A woman explained that previously she had worked in a food store and there 'I sustained repetitive strain injuries.' At Samhall, where she worked with filing activities, she thought, 'the stress isn't as apparent as in normal workplaces.' A colleague of hers said, 'You are able to work; you don't have stress. At a normal company, you have to be healthy to keep up,' and a person at another workplace thought, 'You can't demand that sick people should work so quickly.'

One of the employees, an immigrant from the former Yugoslavia who was a graduate engineer but who worked as a cleaner at Samhall said in a radio report that personally he had been forced to take responsibility and 'fight' and that he used to be 'best'; best at the university, best in his previous jobs, and the best cleaner at Samhall. 'I have thought a lot about leaving Samhall, of finding something for a normal person, but unfortunately I can't count on finding something tomorrow.' Two former miners in the

County of Dalarna, who came to Samhall when their mines were closed, did not see any alternative to Samhall, especially in and around the community in which they lived. 'What can you do when there is only Samhall for people like me, old and worn-out,' one of them said. An immigrant, a woman around 50 years of age who spoke poor Swedish and who worked at a Samhall workplace in which there were other women in the same age bracket and from the same language area as she was, saw few opportunities for work outside of Samhall due to 'injuries, age, language.'

An employee at another Samhall workplace believed, 'Because of the state of the labor market, the only chance for me is to work here; I have no chance anywhere else. The National Employment Office has also informed me of this.' A middle-aged man asked, 'What chances are there for jobs outside when even young people can't get jobs?' One of the occupationally disabled employees pointed out the special needs that he had as a sick and disabled person: 'In comparison with other workplaces, the benefit here is that I can take my problems into consideration'; and another of the employees thought that he could imagine working outside of Samhall, but only if he obtained a wage allowance so that 'I can be at home a few days when I don't feel that well, or work at a more steady pace if I need to.' A colleague of his said that he knew that they did not take his problems and injuries into consideration at other workplaces: 'It's difficult to get anything else, it's not worth making the same effort as we did when we were younger; nowadays we have our injuries.'

The fact that many clients at Samhall after a period of employment feel occupationally disabled and cannot work 'in the normal fashion' is first and foremost evidenced by the fact that few persons who enter the formally organized welfare system of occupational disability eventually leave it. By becoming convinced that they suffer from the problems that the organization proposes, namely occupational disability, exit becomes hard by referring to one's functional disorders. The experience of occupational disability can also be illustrated with sick-listing statistics. At Samhall, on average, sick-listing numbers are at 20% and in certain units they can amount to 30%. This should be compared with the average of 2 to 3% for other work organizations in Sweden. Likewise, Samhall employees incur the most injuries at any work organization in Sweden. In the annual reports the relatively high sick list numbers at Samhall are said to be the result of 'Samhall employees hav[ing] functional disorders that can increase sensitivity for different kinds of stresses in and outside of the job,' thus pointing out that 'as in previous years, employees at Samhall report more occupational injuries than employees in other companies. Labor-related illnesses have increased in recent years and are at a higher level than in the rest of industry.' On the whole, supervisors did not feel that the high sick-listing figures at Samhall were anything out of the ordinary, which was explained by the fact that Samhall personnel were sick and disabled. 'That is why they are here,' as one supervisor put it. Generally, there is an attitude among the supervisors that it is impossible to affect the problems and limitations the personnel are said to suffer from. 'Sick-listings are around 20% and we can't do anything about that,' one of them said.

An occupationally disabled employee said:

> They say that Samhall is for rehabilitation, but you don't get better here. I have never been rehabilitated and I've worked at Samhall for 15 years now.

One of her colleagues related that earlier in her professional career, she had seldom been on the sick-list but since coming to Samhall she 'often felt bad and was home a lot.' Another employee wrote in a contribution to a book about Samhall, 'I have more pain now than I had when I began [at Samhall].' A relative of a Samhall employee wrote in the same book that Samhall recruits 'completely healthy people' who 'have to work themselves to the bone in a mass of meaningless monotonous jobs which the open market automated a long time ago.... My relative has pains in his arms and shoulders since he came to Samhall. They weren't there before.'

As a result of most Samhall clients becoming convinced that they are disabled, asis proved by their behavior as occupationally disabled, most of them eventually express strong commitment to the organized welfare system of occupational disability. An occupationally disabled employee at Samhall who was interviewed in the company magazine and who like his colleagues did not risk being laid off due to lack of work, said, 'It's difficult not knowing what will happen in the future,' but that 'it's nice to know that we have a guaranteed job in the future [at Samhall].... To be sure, not many people have this kind of security.' One person experienced great anxiety that Samhall would not be there in the future. 'If Samhall were to disappear, where would we turn, who would take care of us? Samhall must remain.' In a book about Samhall, with regard to a proposition regarding reduced government grants to Samhall, one of the employees wrote: 'Where will all the occupationally disabled go in the end? Who will take care of them?'

9 Medicalizing Management
Diagnosis

Samhall's recruitment, development, and transition constitute familiar human resource management practices of recruitment and selection, examination and documentation, training and development, testing, exiting, and so on. These common observations can fruitfully be explored by interpreting them according to my framework of 'Medicalizing Management' as a central idea for explaining the institutionalization of social welfare. To Samhall, medical ideas are relevant to its management of its clients; its management is also a medically conditioned phenomenon. Samhall draws on a standard medical model's activities of managing humans through diagnosis, classification, rehabilitation, treatment, and therapy, which become critical mechanisms for its institutionalization. In all, Samhall's management practices enact its most important environment through medicalization that subsequently becomes the focus of the organization's medicalized adaptation to its environment.

Chapters 9 and 10 revolve around an analysis of two main medicalizing management activities: *Diagnosis* (i.e., the identification of an individual's alleged disorder, in this case occupational disability), and *Treatment* (i.e. the rehabilitation of the client by resolving his or her problems).

Medicalizing management practices of diagnosis consist of (1) the effective *selection* of whom to serve based on medical assessments and examination of individuals' conditions; (2) the rational *classification* of individuals as medically problematic in terms of occupational disability; and (3) the organized *confirmation* of clients as occupationally disabled when entering Samhall.

SELECTION OF UNEMPLOYED INDIVIDUALS AS DISABLED

When a person registers with the National Employment Office as unemployed, the organization's interpretational analysis swings into action, whereby registration with the National Employment Office is taken as prima facie evidence that the individual is the sort of person that it is the organization's aim to assist. The empirical world for both the administrative official at the National Employment Office and for the job applicant is ambiguous and uncertain to a degree, and the case is considered on the basis of a problematic and confused situation in relation to certain organizational norms of occupational disability at the National Employment Office, which justify various assessment measures. Organizationally driven enquiries and searches are problemized (i.e., driven by the existence of an identified problem). Without an organizationally enacted experience by which to proceed, the administrative official at the National Employment Office would be groping in the dark. The initial formulation of the problem has implications for the targeting of the organized process that follows, which is adapted to the original organizational problem that the administrative official encountered from the outset; namely, the person's inability to find or keep a job.

Based on a social, political, and administrative decision to offer welfare support to people that are considered 'disabled,' the social deviation in the form of unemployment, especially lengthy unemployment, implies that the person concerned *has* some more or less obvious personal problems that can be discovered, diagnosed, and treated on medical grounds; whereas the 'normal' is defined as the ability to find and keep a job. Identification of the problem influences the questions that are asked by the administrative official, what aspects of the job applicant's conduct the administrative official notes and which are ignored, as well as which of the statements made by the applicant will be regarded as relevant or or otherwise. The National Employment Office's environment in terms of 'hard to employ' people is largely the result of its own assessment routines and standard operating procedures at the point when the applicant is first interviewed. This is largely the result of organizational learning where the National Employment Office acquires experiences of its environment that are continuously retrieved in organizational rules and routines and that guide its current operations. The collection of data on and information about clients is rule-driven, the product of earlier experience stored in the organization's 'memory.'

In determining the 'status' of a job applicant, the National Employment Office organizes and sorts, on the basis of certain implicit theories as to what the 'problem' consists of, in the stream of experience that each interaction with the job applicant involves. The National Employment Office must know what to 'look out for' in order to reach the 'right' experience; that is, the correct interpretation in relation to its existing norms and routines. In the main, the National Employment Office operates on uncertain, ambiguous, and equivocal behavioral input which is made more manageable through acts of interpretation, sense-making, and organizing. In managing this uncertainty it may be essential to gain an insight into the job applicant's self-image, his or her soul, and the most private side of the individual's personality, which becomes a critical prerequisite for the ensuing attempts to normalize his or her behavior in relation to the organization's dominant rules and norms. As already noted, this assessment is largely organizational by relying on certain formal practices and routines as enacted by the National Employment Office. Experience *as* occupationally disabled is not something given as the outcome of pure receptivity, neither for the job applicant nor for the administrative official: Each individual has experienced a variety of situations which have provided a great deal of experience without the person necessarily thinking of him- or herself in a specific fashion.

Those experiences that are significant for a person, that have some meaning, are those that they choose to take into account and in so doing they select from the general chaos of experience that is present at all times. If experiences are not sorted and organized, they cannot result in experience of any kind whatever; and this sorting and organizing is largely an organizationally rule-driven affair from which the National Employment Office learns. It follows that the formally organized process of inquiry used by the National Employment Office and directed towards the unemployed, is crucial in creating the experience of occupational disability; that is, of enacting the environment in accordance with rules and routines of disability. The experience of being occupationally disabled is established through the unemployed being given help, guidance, and direction to help them identify behavior in their previous life that may be categorized as expressions of occupational disability. Focusing attention on the stream of ongoing experience is key in generating certain experiences, which in the case of the National Employment Office is accomplished through retrieved experiences of the past relating to occupational disability.

In targeting occupationally disabled persons, the National Employment Office influences the individuals to experience certain needs and wants by participating in certain organizational assessment activities, not least at the special units. If eventually the individual experiences occupational disability, he or she can become a productive and rational organizational player which the reproduction of the National Employment Office's routines and standard operating procedures cannot do without. Only by certain unemployed persons behaving as occupationally disabled, can the organization fulfill its ambition to assist occupationally disabled persons; that is, unemployed individuals that are said to suffer from various medical disorders. The idea of influencing people is core to organizational functioning: by acquiring certain experiences, thus learning behavioral skills, individuals may eventually come to act as instruments to organizations.

For a person who potentially has an occupational disability, to be invited to undergo assessment at the National Employment Office involves the organized and controlled transformation of an ambiguous situation into a less ambiguous one, thus making the National Employment Office's environment more 'manageable,' which is beneficial to its operations. By influencing the job applicant to reflect on hitherto non-medical experiences, an experience forming the basis of an occupational disability can be constructed in the interaction between the National Employment Office and the client. A specific experience in the person's memory can be generated as a part of his or her conception of self. It may be necessary to combine many previous experiences, weaving them together to form a uniform experience as blind, deaf, or some other form of bio-medical disorder building on conscious attention being paid to previous experience in life, that can now be given the status of an organizational explanation of current behavior (such as why a person has failed to get a job). For the administrative official at the National Employment Office who suspects that the applicant is occupationally disabled by enacting organizational routines and standard operating procedures for targeting potentially occupationally disabled persons, it may be necessary to persuade the job applicant to think deeply so as to induce them to become aware of their alleged medically problematic situation.

In this process, the administrative official from the National Employment Office can be regarded as both prosecuting attorney in the form of the manager of the preliminary assessment and as judge who delivers judgment in the form of an action plan. Job applicants, in the light of their demonstrably problematic behavior, have either to defend themselves by attempting to refute the assumptions about medical problems that exist, or to accept immediately or at a later date the existence of the problems that have been attributed to them. This formal authoritarian relationship is indispensable to the efficiency, speed, and reliability by which occupational disability can be enacted in the National Employment Office's environment. Indeed a key idea in theories of formal organization is the formal superior–subordinate relationship that acts to make any human bargaining and interaction less volatile, insecure, and ambiguous, thus generating overall efficiency and rationality in human interaction. The ability to impose a particular worldview stems from a belief in the legitimacy of authority, which in the case of the National Employment Office is taken for granted by its staff given the medical frame of reference it is using. Any attempts at questioning the validity in the claims made regarding the clients' conditions can be seen as pathologies and evidence of the original (medical) diagnosis. The superior-subordinate relationship between clients and administrative officials is contingent on the formal setting of the National Employment Office. Acceptance of this asymmetry is confirmed by the client when he or she contacts the organization in the first instance, much in the same way as an employee accepts, within limits as defined by the particular social context, an employer's formal authority by it being grounded in certain formal and legal rules.

The process at the National Employment Office can be seen as an organizational procedure where the individual is to be molded so that they admit 'with insight,' that is to say, to take responsibility for their medical problems and limitations. These may thereafter be given as explanations for their inability to get or hold down a job. This is a process of both making the individual an object of organizational influence and control; and a subject as occupationally disabled by acquiring experience of how to act and behave as occupationally disabled (i.e., as bio-medically problematic). By learning what it means to be an occupationally disabled person, the client becomes a legitimate player in the organized efforts by the National Employment Office to manage unemployed persons. If the client accepts this role, ceases to be an ambiguous and complicated case, and becomes instead a distinct actor that can contribute to the National Employment Office's operations in a positive way by accepting its assistance, he or she participates in some of the organization's norms and routines. By eventually presenting herself as 'occupationally disabled' she can finally be managed as an individual case to which certain organized welfare operations are appropriate. Only then can she become a case that the National Employment Office can help, given the medically-oriented routines it has at its disposal. Indeed, the routines make the organization necessarily myopic by limiting the type of problem that can be experienced and thus treated. This is not due to lack of intelligence but to learning where the National Employment Office continually generates feedback between its experience and competence.

Overall, the organization of the occupationally disabled at the National Employment Office is dependent upon particular ways of knowing. These particular ways stem from the organization's existing routines that act to interpret an ambiguous and uncertain environment. Clients are to be transformed from individuals with heterogeneous wants, preferences, and beliefs into homogenous actors in the shape of occupationally disabled persons. This medicalization of unemployment requires vocabularies and ways of representing what is to be administered, and which is proposed in various activities in which both clients and representatives of the organization find themselves. These practices are both examples of authority and ways of 'knowing.' They act as sense-makers to the administrative officials of the National Employment Office and the clients, and include various methods of documentation, assessment, calculation, observation, and so on. It is crucial to make people visible, and this is accomplished by reducing the equivocal elements present in raw and chaotic experience, which can be achieved by applying a certain formal organization to those elements.

The knowledge, experience, and resulting authority in this process is neither cognitive nor is it stored in written forms; it is contingent upon the acting out of certain routines and practices. It is only by beginning to practice the idea of occupational disability in certain organizationally monitored activities that the experience of occupational disability can be generated. In that regard 'organization' is relational; it is exercised rather than existing by itself. If the National Employment Office is to maintain and develop itself it must induce unemployed people to act as occupationally disabled so that the organization can propose its solutions to them. Hence the National Employment Office is not an external something that operates on someone; it *creates* people, such as the occupationally disabled. Being occupationally disabled is not a self-evident phenomenon, something that can be observed, assessed, and examined. The label of occupationally disabled is developed in various formally managed relationships, discourses, and practices. It is not a bio-medical entity; it is the result of organization; hence of medicalization.

By being preliminarily constituted as an object (occupationally disabled) it becomes the subject of certain activities (examinations and assessments) that the National Employment Office is offering. To 'constitute oneself' as occupationally disabled through certain organizational practices is indispensable—no individual can become occupationally disabled by herself without the formal organization of the National Employment Office. Why? Individuals have cognitive limitations in learning specific skills and behaviors of any kind and need organization to acquire any rationality in their development, including that of becoming occupationally disabled. It is the formal setting of the National Employment Office that can provide the appropriate educative context for developing a person as occupationally disabled. Organizations provide rules of interpretation based on experience that enact situations. The assessment routines create a degree of certainty in the interpretation of the stream of varying and ambiguous experiences that the National Employment Office can experience in its contacts with job applicants and makes it possible to identify certain job applicants as *something*, that is, as potentially occupationally disabled, who as a rule the National Employment Office assumes are a group of people who have really major problems that can explain their lack of success in the labor market. Likewise these organizational practices potentially confirm the job applicants' interpretation of themselves as something, in this case as occupationally disabled.

Without the organizational interpretation routines practiced by the National Employment Office when the job applicant is selected, the experiences of the job applicant's problems would be uncertain and the object of continual questioning and speculation. The principle of analogy is central to these routines; that is, that certain job applicants, irrespective of personal characteristics, display certain common behavioral attributes that can be recognized and perceived as something (in this case as occupational disability), based on the observation that the applicants have significant difficulties in finding or holding down a job. It is the analogies themselves that permit the identification, through organized and systematized observation, of certain modes of behavior as occupational disabilities. Defined as 'interlocked human behaviors' an organization needs to foster behavioral homogeneity among its members in order to reproduce its norms and routines.

The National Employment Office's medically-oriented assessment procedures in which the presumptively occupationally disabled applicant participates, effectively limit the experiences that the job applicant generates about him- or herself. The organizational environment offered by the National Employment Office in general and its special agencies for the occupationally disabled in particular, which are adapted in the light of the belief about job applicants' potential occupational disability, may engender in job applicants certain experiences about themselves, such as feelings that they are, or are not, occupationally disabled. Both alternatives function as a model for the administrative officials at the National Employment Office in their conclusion that the job applicants are or are not occupationally disabled. In their assessment of the job applicants, the administrative officials and the experts whom they consult, start from certain organizational preconceptions that exist about occupationally disability and judge the job-seekers' statements and behavior with these as background.

On the whole, the assessments serve as tests of the theories and preconceptions that the National Employment Office has about the behavior of the occupationally disabled. The purpose of the assessments, however, is not to demonstrate any theory or other preconception as 'false' or 'mistaken.' On the contrary they are the fundamental mechanisms that give rise to familiarity with occupational disability. Staff at the National Employment Office tends to see what they have been trained to see by enacting organizational routines and the reality that they experience of people with occupational disabilities is constructed by the organizational practices in which they are engaged. By no means is it pathological, nor does it make the administrative official 'simple-minded' and 'myopic'; it is central for the National Employment Office to be able to carry out its routines in an organizationally rational and legitimate way. Since the administrative officials act in accordance with the National Employment Office's routines for the investigation and observation of the occupationally disabled job applicant, they are also, like their clients, steered towards discovering occupational disability. As noted earlier, without these routines, they would be groping in the dark when interpreting their own experience of the job applicants' behavior.

Administrative officials at the National Employment Office have a specific structure for the interpretation of the world around them or *gestalt* that selectively determines the character of the job applicant. This cognitive capacity, which is coupled to their work role as administrative officials, determines their experience of the job applicant's behavior. It is not, therefore, the case that stimuli from the job applicant can in themselves be understood as illustrating an occupational disability, that it is the occupational disability itself, so to say, where behavior is generated by the stimuli that precede it and where it is constructed and shaped by the reinforced stimuli that follow thereafter. The behavior is certainly real to the extent that it creates the conditions for a particular line of action; for example, the disabled person's use of a wheelchair. But with the exception of very simple cases of reflex action, external stimuli do not give rise to a specific reaction, such as interpreting the person as occupationally disabled. The reality that the administrative officials at the National Employment Office live in is not given to them as passive onlookers where, in their assessment of a job applicant's behavior they simply 'check' a list of behaviors that either does or does not tally with a certain theory. Instead, it is formed by the organizational actions that they reproduce in their roles as administrative officials.

Consequently there is no primary direct experience of the outside world in the form of occupational disability as the administrative official 'finds it' through sensory impression—all 'direct experience' is a completely private feeling. To the extent that a common conception of 'an occupationally disabled person' exists at the National Employment Office, it is the result of the administrative officials there experiencing certain job applicants in a collective fashion by enacting the same organizational rules. The administrative officials' experiences of job applicants are not copies of certain objective conditions that are of a permanent nature irrespective of their impressions. An individual administrative official can be led astray by his or her experiences and can misinterpret the reality to whose construction they have contributed.

Naturally this construction of reality is not a solitary act, but takes place instead from the standpoint of interaction with the job applicant, where the job applicant through his or her unique behavior and actions can influence the administrative official in a given social negotiation. But since the interaction is typically asymmetrical, not least because the administrative official has access to significant resources, it tends not to generate a fully developed, reciprocally constructive experience. Instead it asymmetrically reflects the expected preconception that the administrative official already has about occupational disability by acting according to formal organizational rules of occupational disability, where the job applicant's problematic behavior functions as the central symptom of occupational disability. It is not possible to generate occupational disability as a specific experience without this unique interaction: the surrounding world in the form of the job applicants are in this case the 'thing' that interacts with the administrative official's organizationally enacted preferences and competence so as to create the organizational experience that results.

The administrative official's knowledge of occupational disability is in this case something that has been experienced at first hand and involves both a 'passive and active element' in bringing out experience. When administrative officials experience a job applicant as occupationally disabled they react on the basis of certain pre-determined organizational routines that constitute the core of *their* organizational roles that in turn lead to certain behavioral results. The administrative official does something to the job applicant, such as asking him or her to participate in work training, and the applicant does something to the administrative official. Simply acting 'spontaneously' does not mean that the administrative official has an experience of occupational disability; it only leads to ambiguous and indefinable results. The action must be associated with certain preconceptions that the administrative official has about the occupationally disabled in working life, which are intimately bound up with the organizational roles that administrative officials fill within the National Employment Office. Only in this way can certain procedures taken in the job applicant's case come to imply that they can be regarded as potentially occupationally disabled, to whom specific welfare benefits can be applied. The National Employment Office's routines and rules as to how the occupationally disabled are to be managed (i.e., as medical cases) reduce a complex situation to one that is more easily handled through the objectification of the individuals to disability types to which certain lines of actions are linked.

Hence, the experience of functional disorder that must lie behind the conclusion of occupational disability arises in the interaction between the applicant and the administrative official and the reality that is generated by this is not something that has an independent existence. Nor is it an entirely private experience; it is 'intersubjectively real,' constituted as a result of certain formally organized procedures. The experience is not simply based on personal, subjective experience; it forms an organized reality not only for the job applicant but also for the administrative official with whom the interaction takes place so as to form an experience of the person in question. That occupational disability is experience-based does not, of course, mean that functional impairment due to, for example, illness or bodily defect, is imagined. The fact that a person lacks an arm or has diabetes is a fact not amenable to interpretation and is based fundamentally on the physiological ability that everyone possesses to see and understand certain things in common. If objective facts were to be isolated from the experiences through which they function, all experience would simply be reduced to no more than a process of experiencing—the result would be an experience that simply necessitates itself instead of real things in nature, such as brain damage, birds, or cars. As a result, some people can be distressed, while others are glad on the basis of real events and not simply from the standpoint of their experiences. If people were not certain that things such as other people have a separate existence independent of themselves, it would mean that every person's reality was nothing more than a dream, and there is no reason to believe that this is so.

Other people, in the form of job applicants with specific requirements and values, exist for the administrative officials at the National Employment Office. They are not just caught in their own organizationally enacted thoughts where they are only able to understand that which their organizational identity has prepared them for. This is why certain people are regarded as having a 'clear occupational disability,' often with regard to motor difficulties or partial sight, while other people instead are perceived as ambiguous 'gray zone' cases. Anything else would lead to an unreasonable tautology. That some job applicants are recognized by the administrative officials at the National Employment Office as occupationally disabled is, however, a result of the applicant's behavior *as occupationally disabled*, which is a result of their behavior being medicalized by the National Employment Office as occupationally disabled.

MEDICAL CLASSIFICATION OF DISABILITY

The formal disability coding of the occupationally disabled can be understood as the organized classification that the National Employment Office assumes in certain situations, making possible the 'secure' interpretation of previously insecure, raw, chaotic experiences as an expression of occupational disability, and which can therefore come to substantiate the obvious in what previously were ambiguous (or non-existent) experiences of occupational disability. To this extent, disability coding is an administrative rationalization and legitimization of a 'difficult to employ' person's case. When both the job applicants themselves and the administrative officials at the National Employment Office use as their starting point the organizational category (in the form of administrative codes of occupational disability and formal definitions of the occupationally disabled person's character), it becomes easier to generate specific experiences of interaction that correspond with the organizational categorization. However, the behavioral rules for the occupationally disabled in the National Employment Office's coding system mean that the job applicant is also invited to join a procedure that can easily be developed into a self-fulfilling prophecy. Starting from an initial vague suspicion regarding occupational disability, the administrative officials at the National Employment Office adapt themselves to their codified experience of the occupationally disabled. This in turn influences their interaction with the job applicant. The job applicants for their part are influenced to make an equivalent adjustment and a self-reinforcing spiral of occupationally disabled behavior can be established.

What the administrative official and perhaps others 'have known' all the time can eventually be established 'with medical certainty'; that is, in relation to certain organizational norms, on the grounds that the job applicant's behavior matches the administrative categories around which the coding system of occupational disability has been built. Ambiguity in the earlier decision-making process as to how a specific job applicant should be dealt with ceases and the job applicant takes on a formal and legitimate organizational role on the basis of which all future adaptation takes place. Henceforth the client *is* occupationally disabled, possessing certain needs and requirements which the organization is competent to understand and respond to. As noted above, the experience of someone as occupationally disabled is not engendered through stimuli in the form of occupational disability 'dropping' on the administrative official. Experience of occupational disability originates instead in an interaction between the job applicant and the National Employment Office that follows on from the organizational routines that are enacted, where it is less a question of matching a welfare solution to a given personal problem and more of matching constructed personal problems to given welfare solutions. It is only in certain organizationally enacted processes that certain experiences of self become possible. By individuals (prospective and existing clients and administrative officials) practicing occupationally disabled routines, the formal organization of occupational disability is being reproduced. That the number of codes of occupational disability has increased over the years is a nice illustration of the two facets of medicalizing management: By medicalizing individuals' behavior through coding them as disabled, the management activity behind this transformation must adapt to increased medical problems among individuals by further extending its medicalizing management.

The National Employment Office's ability to experience occupational disability in its environment is not a matter of its competence in discovering disability, but of its ability to enact it through organized observation on the basis of certain organizational practices made possible by the coding system. The administrative officials form an initial suspicion that a client has one or more forms of occupational disability by interpreting the job applicant's behavior, partly on the basis of some general ideas about which behavior is successful and which is unsuccessful in the labor market, and partly on specific types of disability that are given in the coding system, such as, for instance, socio-medical occupational disability (Code 81) for which certain kinds of activities are given. When the subsequent assessment has started, the previous experiences create the basis for new experiences and the occupationally disabled can spin a net of behavior that is perfected by means of the formal disability coding. The classification rules formed by the disability codes constitute a fundamental instrument with which the National Employment Office can confirm its experience of occupational disability in the behavior of the job applicant, in the same way as a doctor starts out with codified categories when identifying illness. The disability codes are similar to one another to the extent that they are different variations on the same theme of occupational disability and therefore permit the generation of common experiences of occupational disability for the administrative officials, which are thus not connected with the individual administrative official's personal experiences but are generated through the organizational routines that they instigate in their daily work. At the same time they create the necessary limitation on the administrative official's experiences: all behavior that does not fall within the framework of these practices is not occupational disability and hence is to be dealt with in a different manner.

People who are disability coded naturally exhibit a high degree of variation in their personal characteristics that perhaps can be used by both experts and non-professionals to explain why they have found it difficult to get or keep a job. But since they all are subject to a standardized coding process, they are confronted by essentially the same experience. These common experiences are engendered through their behaving according to certain organizational routines and rules that are coupled to the National Employment Office's program on the suitable organization of the occupationally disabled. Because these similarities of experiences and their response to them do not come from their personal condition, they seem to have arisen despite their condition. Thus they can be said to stem from the organizational practices that arise from the fact that occupational disability has a uniform social status, to which is attached a common fate and finally a common personal mentality.

In order to establish *an* experience of occupational disability among potential Samhall clients, a unitary interpretation as a basis for selecting people as occupationally disabled, it is necessary, as said previously, for the job applicant to be capable of seeing him- or herself anew, to observe previously experienced events in a new fashion, to interpret previous actions as a result of the occupational disability that he or she is assumed to have. An experience of occupational disability is constructed in this respect on events already experienced, not on those that are in the present: All organizational experience is based on 'already had.' In a similar way, as the administrative official goes back through a person's history in order to build a case for occupational disability on circumstantial evidence, job applicants must begin to look at themselves in a new light. In this respect, the 'organizational memory' in the form of theories of occupational disability that the administrative official implicitly and explicitly enacts is an invaluable mechanism for actually confirming an 'occupationally disabled's' behavior. Rules and routines are retrieved and encoded as experience; lessons from the past make any situation of choice, interpretation, and sense-making 'ordered' and 'rational,' hence 'secure.'

Disability coding and the process that lies behind it is perhaps the clearest example in Swedish welfare society of how individuals' behavior is medicalized. Simply put, the National Employment Office creates the occupationally disabled. People who are understood as deviant by the National Employment Office by their failure to find work on the open labor market, run a risk that, in time, they will be experienced as functionally impaired and ultimately will be coded as occupationally disabled. Clearly there is no desire on the part of the organization to stigmatize the unemployed as medically problematic, which for people in general implies various types of physical and mental limitation. The organization's intentions are appropriate in the sense of creating rational and legal conditions for its activities. Disability coding is based instead on a notion in society that functional impairments exist as personal bio-medical problems, are recognizable and require separate solutions; for example, labor market and other policy measures, which are different variations on the theme of welfare.

As already suggested, the disability coding aims at reducing the National Employment Office's initial ambiguous experience of its environment (i.e., of the unemployed) when meeting its clients, which is a standard operating procedure among organizations to buffer their core technologies. In order to give its interaction with its environment the necessary authority and legitimacy, it is made with the assistance of medical experts such as doctors and psychologists. The job applicant is rewarded for showing insights into the complex of medical problems that are said to exist and punished subtly if he or she persists in maintaining their personal views regarding their condition. This normalization is done by labeling the person 'unreasonable' or 'lacking in insight,' where the person is said to 'block or resist the truth.' The evaluation of the job applicant made by the experts progresses by drawing attention to previous personal experiences, which are given a meaning by describing them as an occupational disability. The particular medical experience *occupational disability* like all other experience, is something that has already been experienced but which needs to be articulated and brought into focus through medicalizing assessments and examinations so that it takes shape and thereby becomes manifest in the consciousness. As said above, experiences are something that are 'already had' but that are made meaningful as a result of the National Employment Office's procedures for attending to certain experiences.

A central task for the professionals surrounding the job applicant relates in this way to the applicant's acceptance of the medical difficulties and problems that the professionals themselves have identified based on their organizational procedures and routines that focus their attention on specific issues. Job applicants must show that they understand their alleged medical problem as others have formulated it before any further steps can be taken in the shape of collective action. By agreeing to be coded as disabled and signing a document in which the specific disability code is presented, the applicant ultimately confirms this as analogous to an employment contract, where the individual agrees to act organizationally within certain limits as specified according to that contract. It may well be the case that job applicants in their initial contact with the National Employment Office have referred to various personal problems as reasons for the failure *they* have experienced in the labor market, such as lack of relevant skills or job experience, a stomach ulcer or diabetes, problems which can be presented to make the National Employment Office understand that the person requires extra help. But these problems must still be questioned unless the National Employment Office experiences that they do not correspond to the formal conception of medical problems as proposed by the 14 disability codes. Only then can the person be organized and helped as occupationally disabled. It follows that job applicants are induced to learn to 'show insight'; that is, to behave as the National Employment Office expects them to behave if it has proved very difficult for the applicant to get or keep a job, irrespective of the reasons that the applicant is able to suggest.

Organizational discrediting based on 'objective medical evidence' is not simply a matter of transforming an individual from a human being into an organizational object in the form of a disability code that can easily be matched against the administrative apparatus that has been constructed around social welfare services. It is also a fundamental prerequisite that enables the person to give up their previous self-image and to learn a new one. Discrediting is therefore central for re-socialization to a new social role, that is, the role of an occupationally disabled person. As soon as the job applicant learns what it means to be defined by welfare society as unfit for work for medical reasons, handicapped, and functionally impaired for working life, the potentially threatening definition (a threat that facilitates the applicant's association with the self-image that society gives them) is weakened. In many respects, it is therefore a question of re-defining experiences so as to make the person's new experience of themselves as occupationally disabled less frightening and unpleasant than it appeared to be when first presented. The element that initially was something that the applicant most probably avoided can, after a time, therefore become something that is, if not desirable, then something that nevertheless is acceptable.

Generally speaking, administrative officials at the National Employment Office must assume that the clients who are disability coded are medically problematic; what other reason could there be for their coding? The disability codes serve as a preliminary confirmation for the person of his or her new condition as occupationally disabled. Through disability coding, job applicants can recognize themselves as objectively handicapped, which has a major advantage in that those around them no longer need to convince them of their condition. If a client has problems with reading and writing, it is reasonable that they are dyslectic (Code 92); if they have a rash, that they are allergic (Code 91). The coding is central for the continued establishment of a self-image as occupationally disabled: the individual can only make contact with their earlier diffuse experiences through the coding that others have attributed to them; that is, they can only get in touch with the 'deeper self' as an object, not as a subject isolated from social organization. This takes place on the basis of social relationships and interactions in an organized reality.

As a rule people experience only those things that they have learnt to pay attention to because someone around them has pointed out these things for them, acting as 'competent models.' People typically understand things that as a rule they have a prior understanding of and those entities they have a prior understanding of are those that have been categorized and suggested to them. There are therefore no *a priori* theoretical, logical, or practical grounds that are of use as a basis for coding certain people as occupationally disabled. The current administrative definitions of occupational disability are quite simply an imprecise method for categorizing people who have found it difficult to get or hold down a job, but that are necessary for the National Employment Office to carry out its mission in a legally rational way. In substance, an occupational disability is something that one experiences in social interaction with others and where the disability can undoubtedly be objectified through a process of verbalization and analysis.

Disability coding, from the standpoint of the different disability types that are based on it, is invaluable in the process that the job applicants undergo so that they can come to regard themselves as occupationally disabled and therefore can sort themselves out from the group 'fully occupationally fit.' The bewildering stream of experiences that earlier can be assumed previously to have marked the job applicant's self-image as a result of the difficulties that they have met in the labor market, can now be enacted through the organized attention paid to their own behavior by means of specific typical behavior. That which was previously difficult to understand becomes easier to explain by referring to the fact that one is dyslectic, allergic or 'suffers' from other medical problems. The organizational language that the disability code constitutes is in this case already articulated experiences of handicapped behavior that the job applicant can learn for the purpose of adapting him- or herself to the role designated for them by the National Employment Office.

Like most other medical diagnosis, the codified experiences of occupational disability have undoubtedly an objective character that can be sensed as something external to which a job applicant can relate intellectually and thereby can have an effect on the job applicant's self-image by defining certain norms of behavior that the person can recognize as their own, disabled behavior. To begin thinking and talking in terms of disability on the basis of the formally organized code system is therefore important for the client to be able to 'act organizationally'; that is, as productive *de facto* members of the National Employment Office organization, and hence no longer constituting an uncertain external source of variety. By becoming an efficient practitioner as occupationally disabled, the individual learns what is expected from him or her as a member of a certain social organization. Unless the job applicant can assimilate the new vocabulary, continued communication can be problematic and the National Employment Office's assessment of the person as lacking insight into his or her own complex of problem is strengthened.

The codes therefore give both the job applicant and the administrative officials of the National Employment Office a ready-made scheme for interpreting behavior as objective signs of occupational disability to which both the administrative official and the job applicant must adapt themselves in their continuous interlocking of behaviors. From experience, the code system has also an expanding function that makes possible the 'objectification' and thus interpretation of experiences in the applicant's previous working life as signifying occupational disability An important aim of the code system is that the typing of individual experiences in a previously established norm of interpretation makes their previous behavior in the labor market *meaningful*: When all is said and done, it was the occupational disability and not any irrational and indefinable activities that lay behind the previously futile efforts to get a job, in the same way as an apparent 'act of madness' is given a meaning when the person on trial is classified as mentally ill.

Of course, the process of people beginning to identify themselves as occupationally disabled is not self-evident. There are people who try to resist it and insist that they are fully fit for work, but these people are in general not believed. The social expectation that the job applicant will, so to speak, enjoy things as they are, is reinforced by the fact that applicants who refuse to be disability coded risk losing their unemployment benefit or can be regarded as even more of a problem because of their 'lack of insight.' Once an applicant has agreed to be organized as having a potential occupational disability, it is even more difficult for the applicant to claim that he or she is not occupationally disabled.

Accepting a disability coding at the National Employment Office (and with it the formal classification as occupationally disabled), confirms the National Employment Office's initial enactment that the person is potentially occupationally disabled and should in future be treated as such: whenever a person has been classified as medically deviating in the sense of *having* a disability, all his or her future behavior and personal characteristics risk being colored by this label. Everything that the person does in future is taken as an expression of his or her occupational disability. It follows that in the continued management of the case, it is the person's occupational disability and not the person's relative working capacity that steers the process. From having been a person with a broad palette of behavior that can be used in different situations, the person is reduced by means of a disability coding to a behaviorally integrated unit with certain specific needs, all more or less clearly related to his or her organizational role of occupationally disabled.

To accept a disability coding is to accept the social role as occupationally disabled, which takes for granted that a person is medically problematic and should be treated as such. But most of all it implies that a person is in need of assistance. It is in the nature of the process that if a person has accepted a disability coding, he or she requires the help that the National Employment Office is competent to provide. The medical concept of 'rehabilitation' in welfare activity involves measures taken by the National Employment Office that aim to strengthen a person's ability to get or keep a job in the labor market. The circle is thus closed for the job applicant: they turn to the National Employment Office to find a job, which later on is established as the best medicine for coming to terms with their personal problems. Looked at in this way, the process involves identifying job applicants as occupationally disabled based on medical grounds, of redefining their view of themselves from that of being fully capable of work to being of only limited ability, and of seeing their alleged problem not as one of individual competence but rather as a social welfare issue that requires an extensive input from the social welfare authorities. This phenomenon is accompanied by an expectation from those around them that the person will present themselves as occupationally disabled and thereby demand the services that are available for the occupationally disabled. The 'maturity' of the occupationally disabled for the services that can be made available to them is measured by their motivation to acknowledge the reason for their problematic situation, and to understand who can help them with their difficulties. Once a person has been disability coded and become legally, organizationally, and officially occupationally disabled, their situation changes from that of a personal problem to one of social welfare for which certain labor market policy measures are available.

CONFIRMATION OF CLIENTS AS DISABLED

The focus during the individual's introduction to Samhall lies with persuading the person to confirm his or her medical problems, which is the only way for the person to become a 'legitimate' and 'manageable' employee within the particular social context of Samhall, since Samhall exists only for the occupationally disabled. The purpose of the examinations is to persuade the occupationally disabled to remember specific events and activities that can explain the occupationally-disabled condition that is expected of them, by focusing attention on the flood of experiences that exists stored, consciously or unconsciously, in their individual memories. The occupationally disabled can thus develop according to an organizational idea that they *are* occupationally disabled by becoming aware of their previous behavior in a specific, organized fashion. Previously diffuse or unidentified experience that constitutes a source of 'external uncertainty' for the rational operations of Samhall become clearer and new employees' doubts, if any, about themselves as occupationally disabled can be effectively limited. The logic behind this activity stems from the notion that people more or less unconsciously experience themselves as others experience them, which happens through a process of organized reflection in the form of a 'reconsideration' of their own experience of themselves. Each person, when interacting with his or her surroundings, generates something in the surroundings that they also engender in themselves, which unconsciously leads to their taking on the attitudes of their surroundings toward themselves. This process is central for the development of a specific self-image, irrespective of whether it is concerned with occupational disability or not, where the self-image is composed as a result of an organized admission of the occupationally disabled into Samhall.

By asking a person to talk about their occupational disability as was established earlier in his or her career, there is an expectation that a problem *exists*; and if the client looks upon the person they are talking to as a legitimate authority, this will influence the client's interpretation of his or her experiences as fully 'healthy' or 'occupationally disabled.' For instance, in the case of dyslexia, a person's experience of reading and writing difficulties as a diffuse and confusing problem is given meaning and structure by being connected with specific tasks *for dyslectics* that can be carried out at Samhall. In addition, the employee and also those around him or her who have become aware of the problem, find it easier to deal with the continuing relationship on the basis of an ongoing *adaptation to the occupational disability* rather than to the client as a person.

Meaningful experience is intimately connected with the organizational context in which the actor finds him- or herself: the administrative officials at the National Employment Office and the supervisors at Samhall take for granted an organizational conception that 'development' deals with the confirmation of a previously determined occupational disability and perhaps even the identification of a new one, and they behave therefore in an organizationally 'appropriate' fashion by fixing their attention on the person's occupational disability and on nothing else. The organizational rules for interaction that these individuals enact in organizational practices are of great significance for the generation of personal experiences. If the client is not able to experience occupational disability, this can be taken as evidence for the fact that there really *is* something wrong with that person. But if the person in question applies the interpretive rules as practiced by the organization, then they will 'with insight' be able to experience that which the organization already experiences, namely that they *are* occupationally disabled.

Many interactions of this kind can be defined as 'problematic,' 'equivocal,' and 'uncertain' since they are indefinite and since it can take time to 'reach the correct status' of the person. The uncertain experiences by some supervisors at Samhall of new employees' occupational disability, is taken as a justification for making a detailed assessment in connection with an appointment as occupationally disabled with Samhall. To experience a situation as problematic is, however, just a first step towards a formulation of *an* experience of a person's presumed problems, where an organizational assessment transforms an unclear situation into something more evident to the organization. The problems in terms of diffuse and ambiguous experiences of clients' preferences and needs are minimized by enacting an organizational interpretation of the situation.

Hence, Samhall does not adapt to an 'objective' environment through assignment by the National Employment Office; but to a 'socially negotiated' one. In this connection, it is more important for both the administrative official at the National Employment Office and the supervisor at Samhall to be able to claim that there is a genuine problem that justifies a weightier inquiry into the recruits' situation, namely the person's difficulties in finding or keeping a job due to functional disorders; that is, medical problems. Without finding such a problem, the whole process would seem illegitimate. The basic medicalized problem creates a platform from which all continued interaction takes place and which continually reminds those involved that all that is needed is to refine and complement the experiences of this basic problem to produce a more specific diagnosis (e.g., in terms of more disability codes).

The way in which *the problem* is understood in terms of organizational rules and routines influences which experiences are observed and which are ignored during the interaction, which focuses throughout on finding an explanation for a person's 'evident problems' in the labor market. This is the basis for the attitude of a *prima facie* character that Samhall holds towards the occupationally disabled and by which meaning is successively generated in the assessment; that is, the more the individuals are participating in Samhall's assessment routines and ceremonies, the more obvious it becomes that they *are* occupationally disabled. The inquiry stops when *an* experience of the person as physically disabled is determined in a satisfactory fashion. It will be reopened only if new ambiguities in the person's behavior were to be experienced in a later phase of his or her career. This demonstrates the reason why environmental insecurity is a key mechanism of organizational enactment.

The assessment that the recruits to Samhall undergo, as well as the other previous and later assessments made at stages during the Samhall career, are thus limited and take place on the basis of the preconceptions about occupational disability held by those who are running the assessments. The organizational rules and routines limit which activities are possible and thereby limit the experiences that can be generated. During the trial period at Samhall it is certainly not a question of turning the recruit's personality inside out, but of associating certain experiences of the person into meaningful already codified experiences of occupational disability. The limited process of searching for experiences is necessary in order to reach a conclusion and a basis for a decision on the person's status. Through this limited inquiry, rationality in the process is constructed, but at the price of possibly reaching the wrong conclusions. The ongoing assessments that are made of new employees at Samhall, based on various records that function as guidelines for the questions that are put to the person, allow the occupationally disabled to 'objectify themselves' so as to gain an insight into their 'real character'; namely, being occupationally disabled. Because certain questions are asked in a particular, organizational way, certain experiences are highlighted that previously were simply 'lived through' but which can be essential indications of an organizational idea of occupational disability. This consciousness-raising is important so that the occupationally disabled themselves can be convinced about their occupational disability and thereby can function in their future role as occupationally disabled employees of Samhall.

On the whole, these analyses, as well as the documentation and assessments carried out later on in the Samhall employee's career, are concerned with persuading the occupationally disabled to articulate previous experiences in life as an explanation of current medically problematic behavior. In working to persuade the employees to regard themselves as occupationally disabled in order to become targets of assignment, it is essential for representatives of Samhall to refer to previous behavior by drawing attention to specific experiences in their previous lives that can be associated with typical occupationally-disabled behavior, such as war psychosis, antisocial behavior, or difficulties in hearing or seeing. Without the ability to remember, one cannot experience—it is *lived experiences,* not current or future experiences that lie behind everyone's self-image and behavior and thereby make possible a separate working life as occupationally disabled.

Previous experience, conscious or unconscious, steers a person's attention in a selective fashion in different situations and thus permits certain experiences; for example, as occupationally disabled. In order to understand who one is today, one must understand one's previous behavior. The assessment performed for each potential Samhall employee is a question of paying attention to behavior earlier in life that can be interpreted as variations of an occupationally disabled behavior, that add to the self-image of the occupationally disabled that is necessary for employment with Samhall. In all, this learning process is an organizational affair where the National Employment Office and Samhall collectively enact an environment of experiences by inviting individuals into certain ceremonies and practices.

Here, the memory that each person has can make it both simpler and more difficult for him or her to perform effectively certain expected forms of behavior. To look at oneself afresh is therefore an important result of the segregation that takes place before and during employment with Samhall. By segmenting attention through formal organizing, specific (i.e., appropriate) experiences are enacted. Experiencing new situations in the same way as they have previously been experienced, for example, as an economist, a welder, a plumber, a dentist,, is as a rule dysfunctional with regard to employment with Samhall. Instead, experience of new situations must be based on the role as occupationally disabled. This occurs when previously lived-through experiences are associated as handicap behavior on the basis of occupationally-disabled behavior that has already been 'objectified as typical.' Previous experience that can be understood differently or completely ignored, is brought into focus with the help of the two organizations that operate on the basis of joint routines of occupational disability creates a basis for the enactment of experiences they are learning as occupationally disabled.

Each test of a theory on occupational disability that lies behind Samhall's assessment, as well as for the self-perception of the person under assessment, must finish at some point in the form of a decision, otherwise the test in the form of the assessment has not led anywhere. Obviously, this process does not have a 'natural' finish, but builds on the authority of the parties involved to claim that it is finished. To confirm finally that a person is occupationally disabled on the basis of an assessment thus takes place from the standpoint of the implicit and explicit theories and ideas that exist on occupational disability, where as soon as a match can be made between a person's behavior, statements, or attitude, and the theory, the conclusion is drawn that the person *is* occupationally disabled in the world of Samhall; that is, in relation to *its* norms. Consequently, individual skills are the analogue of organizational routines. The supervisors and others at Samhall do not recognize the occupationally disabled inductively from pure and uninterpreted data, but from deductive ones; that is to say, based on previous experience that is stored in formal routines, rules, and other theories on occupational disability that become activated in certain practices, such as when assessing persons as occupationally disabled.

Hence, supervisors at Samhall do not just 'fall over' experiences of occupational disability in their interactions with occupationally-disabled recruits for Samhall; instead, through their organized activities they largely *create* them in order to experience that problems abound and that Samhall is the most feasible solution in society to deal with them. Clients participate in this bargaining as the weaker party learning to play the role that has been designated for them. This learning loop of reacting based on the same routines on which acting is carried out is a standard feature of most organizational activity, known as a 'closed learning cycle,' where eventually a self-fulfilling prophecy may come true. For the occupationally disabled who at this stage can be expected to be aware of many contradictory experiences about themselves, this means an effective individual sorting of these ambiguous experiences, unless they have previously fully accepted their occupational disability. The organizational segregation that a job with Samhall involves contributes to creating the experience of occupational disability, in the same way as university entrance may be necessary for a person to begin looking upon him- or herself as a student.

The infirmity label in the form of disability codes and other descriptions of problems are certainly necessary for Samhall to be able to recruit personnel for their productive activities; but without confirmation through the behavior and attitude of the new employee that he or she *is* occupationally disabled, it is nonetheless difficult to implement an employment. It is therefore important that in those cases where a person 'does not have insight' into the problems that Samhall or the National Employment Office maintain that the person should have, to form this insight at an early stage. This is the only way that employment with Samhall can appear as reasonable for the client and for the larger society of which the organization is a part.

The starting point in a Samhall employee's career is that those seeking employment with Samhall have a medical problem since they are disability coded by the National Employment Office, and that thereafter it is necessary on the part of Samhall to narrow down the problem further, and to supplement it, as it were, with a range of other problems, so as to match the specific workforce needs existing within Samhall. The disability codes and other descriptions of the person's limitations, which are documented on each person's record, can in this respect require adaptation to the category of disability that Samhall is seeking. That is, if Samhall has certain jobs for which they want to recruit occupationally disabled persons, those so recruited must have a suitable occupational disability. If they do not already have this disability, such problems must be constructed so that they can develop 'normally' in Samhall and as welfare clients in general. The significant point is that by having defined a problem for the job applicant that is administratively legitimate, help by society is made possible in a rational and legal way.

In all, Samhall's introductory routines create the foundations for an 'effective' Samhall employment, where the person in question can function in the firm's administrative and business-like machinery by forgetting earlier self–images of themselves which are seen as really problematic (for example, that they are *not* occupationally disabled), and, so to speak, to begin their employment as a occupationally disabled *tabula rasa*. To enable Samhall to rehabilitate their employees *as* occupationally disabled and to be able to claim that the occupationally disabled have developed since they were employed, an initial immaturity must first be established. To be able to appreciate themselves as different, which is consistent with the new role as occupationally disabled that each new employee meets, it is necessary to alter a new employee's attention on their own lived experiences, so that the person, so to speak, begins again from zero in their career, and consequently starts demanding the services for the disabled that only Samhall can provide.

This organizationally framed individual focus has naturally already begun during the procedures that took place at the National Employment Office, but is given extra consideration during the introduction at Samhall where the attitudes of colleagues and supervisors about who one is, as well as participation in certain activities adapted for the occupationally disabled, make the new employee think about their behavior in earlier periods of their lives that was perhaps ignored but which can now explain their status as occupationally disabled. Changes in the attention paid to one's experiences can in this case lead to changes in the view taken of previously experienced events so that something that was previously understood as unproblematic can now be regarded as problematic. This is based on the assumption that every person through his or her experiences is a source of handicap behavior, but that there must be a change in 'self-awareness' to understand that one *is* occupationally disabled, and therefore needs help by social welfare organizations in order to live 'normally.'

The introductory routines at Samhall, which take as their starting point the offer to every employee of a 'disability-adapted employment' thereby create the organizational preconditions for each novice to begin to understand themselves as occupationally disabled, as part of a larger enterprise of Samhall enacting its environment. By following the organizational routines, the preconditions are generated for enacting experiences in line with the purpose of the medicalizing management routines: By highlighting previous experiences through the new role as an occupationally disabled employee at Samhall, the client finds it easier 'insightfully' to be able to understand the Samhall appointment as reasonable and necessary just for them.

10 Medicalizing Management
Treatment

In this chapter I continue my conceptual analysis of Samhall. Medicalizing management practices of treatment consist of (1) the structured *training* of clients through work adapted to occupationally disabled people's presumed needs; (2) the rational *counseling* as occupationally disabled by supervisors and colleagues; and (3) the *discharging* of clients as disabled from Samhall.

TRAINING OF CLIENTS AS DISABLED

The practical work that the occupationally disabled perform is central to their rehabilitation as occupationally disabled individuals. So long as a person has not seen, felt, or heard something, he or she is unable to experience it. The occupationally disabled learn the meaning of the concept 'occupationally disabled' by practicing occupational disability, that is performing certain forms of behavior coupled to work organized *for* the occupationally disabled, much in the same way as, for example, a pilot learns what it means to be a pilot by behaving in accordance with certain rules on how to fly an airplane and in that way acquires the experiences that are retrieved from the rules of commanding an aircraft. It is only after the employee has acted as occupationally disabled that the individual can understand who he or she is. All meaningful experience of occupational disability, which is essential if the employees are to make progress in the 'normal fashion' at Samhall, is experienced in the work that is performed. Each person is the source of a variety of experiences: this variation must be limited so that specific experiences can come into existence, which in turn can motivate certain activities that can be interpreted as an expression of occupational disability. The employees at Samhall constantly produce experiences about themselves in their practical interactions with their colleagues, supervisors, and objects, which can be interpreted in many different ways. The actual interaction between the occupationally disabled and their surroundings at work is, in this respect, central for the experiences that are generated when the employee enacts certain organizational practices, procedures, and ceremonies.

Samhall, as with other organizations, offers a limited cognitive environment that confronts the individual with given rules of behavior and regulates the person's freedom of choice in every possible situation. By behaving in accordance with the organizational roles and thereby in accordance with the work rules that are considered legitimate, certain specific experiences can be created for individual employees in a repetitive way that is in accordance with the roles that they are expected to perform. This is partly an individual question where people choose to locate themselves in an environment where they will generate certain experiences through the organizational practices in which they participate; partly it is an organizational question in that the organization offers, out of a complex reality, a simplified and specialized environment and therefore does not expose individuals to an unorganized number of experiences which they otherwise would only have lived through. Organizational routines create to this extent possibilities for people to learn socially accepted, that is, 'normal' behavior in a relatively focused and concentrated manner, rather that trying to get there on their own through a complicated individual process of trial and -error.

Work at Samhall, because of its limited and hence specialized character, to a degree relieves Samhall employees of their freedom to interpret independently their personally acquired experiences of themselves and others, which can form the basis of the confused concept of reality that the administrative officials at the National Employment Office and supervisors at Samhall feel that Samhall's recruits sometimes have. By means of the formally managed socialization involved in a job as occupationally disabled with Samhall, structure and order is created in the employees' experiences, where certain experiences are encouraged and others discredited or ignored. The role as occupationally disabled implies certain specific actions during the working day that create specific experiences for the employee and which are added to his or her self-image. To this extent Samhall influences the self-image that its employees generate as a result of the organized work in which they participate. The work enables the employees to concentrate on certain experiences that conform to the organizational role as occupationally disabled; for example, not having the ability to work with complex tasks or at a higher work pace. As occupationally disabled employees, they perform certain tasks that are adapted for the occupationally disabled, which in turn generate certain specific experiences that are different variations on the notion of occupational disability and which form the foundation of a distinctive competence *as* occupationally disabled.

It is true that in most of Samhall's workplaces, employees come from a great variety of personal backgrounds. But the clients are categorized on the basis of general disability types, which in turn are considered more or less suited to different work-related tasks. The specialization in specific 'disability-adapted' tasks generates a growing competence in the performance of just such tasks—an occupationally disabled employee who performs tasks adapted for those with occupational disability eventually *becomes* more occupationally disabled by performing these tasks because of the positive feedback generated between experience and competence—the more experience one has of something, the more 'skillful' one becomes. In this regard the practical work activities in which the occupationally disabled find themselves contribute to producing and reproducing Samhall as an organization of interlocked human behaviors. Behaving in accordance with the organizational rules and routines that define the unique organization Samhall, which are different variations on the idea that the occupationally disabled need sheltered employment, and that the working environment in general should be 'handicap adapted,' creates the conditions for the employees to begin to regard themselves as occupationally disabled and eventually start asking for a work environment adapted to their needs *as occupationally disabled*. This is the crux of the organized medicalization that takes place in Samhall. People find a meaning by reacting with the framework of a *particular* social experience, in this case, of disability. If a person has learned that he or she is occupationally disabled as a result of previous socialization, the person 'enrolls' in the situation with a different perspective from a person who has no experience as occupationally disabled. Through previous learning, the employee builds up a memory bank of experiences that helps the individual sort out the immediate impressions generated in each situation. This is why the initial assessment processes in the role as occupationally disabled at the National Employment Office and during the introductory period at Samhall is central for the learning that the occupationally disabled can generate during the rest of their career with Samhall. In each concrete work situation, the employees have to interpret different tasks in an interaction between themselves, their colleagues, the machines, instructions, supervisors, and anything else that forms their social environment.

By means of the previous experiences, this interpretation is managed to the degree that previous occurrences function as interpretive rules for the new occurrences; that is, the situations that are dealt with today are interpreted from previous experiences. In most cases, the interpretive rules are collective, where previously-shared experiences with colleagues influence how a new situation is enacted. Each and everyone has personal experiences that meet head-on with those of their colleagues in a daily negotiation, and result in the perpetual generation of a specific outlook that forms the foundation for the personal experiences from which each Samhall employee learns an organizational identity. This occurs primarily in the practical tasks where, for example, the new employees try to imitate the experienced workers whom they see as 'competent models.'

The competence shown by colleagues and supervisors as to suitable behavior is not, however, stored in their individual memories, but in the work practices in which they all participate and is managed on the basis of the medically-oriented organizational principles that are laid down as to the 'development of the occupationally disabled.' For employees themselves to try to arrive at an insight as to how they should act in this role at Samhall is too much to ask, in the same way as it would be too much to expect of a doctor to work out for him- or herself how to be a doctor. The rules of interpretation are not only collective, but are also formally organized, where the employees interpret their experiences in different situations on the basis of the organizational rules and routines that they have learned, which they reproduce through the legitimacy that they attach to them. The organizational rules, by means of the members' behavior, therefore generate certain situations to which the employees in turn adapt themselves. By behaving in a certain organized fashion, such as by performing tasks in a special way, unique experiences are created that can confirm or challenge the person's self-image as occupationally disabled. Work, adapted in a specific way, thus understood as a set of rules of organizational behavior and routines, is therefore to a great extent an 'attention-steering mechanism' of personally generated experiences.

By acting on the 'quality-assured routines' relating to the rehabilitation methodology and development of the occupationally disabled that exist within Samhall, it is possible to develop each employee in an occupationally disabled fashion, thus enacting a significant part of Samhall's environment through a managed process of medicalization. The work routines, which manage each employee's attention to their own experiences in their daily Samhall tasks, thus transfer potentially important residual experience of occupational disability to the individual employees so that they can function as legitimate employees. By learning these, they acquire relatively quickly a suitable norm of behavior and can as a result look forward to a good career within the organization on the basis of the norms and values that exist. Organizational rules and routines ensure that experiences of the older clients are transferred to the new, thus guaranteeing a uniform interpretation of the members' experiences.

Humans have developed an advanced ability to learn through observing others in their environment and this certainly encourages a relatively quick acquisition of social competence of distinctive behavior, by comparison with a relatively slow, individual process. By acquiring ideas and attitudes that are symbolically represented in people's gestures and statements, clients can learn the rules for the production of specific behavior norms without excessive personal exertion. To this extent, the implicit and explicit supervision and guidance of others in their environment connects with that of their own immediate environment and allows the transference of experiences that they personally have not generated. Thus, one does not need to be Caesar to understand Caesar; nor does a new employee of Samhall have to go through generations of learning as occupationally disabled to become specialized in that role. By observing others, behavioral rules are formed and in future situations the coded information is used for the steering of common activities *as occupationally disabled*. A symbol in the form of a behavior is in this respect the stimulus whose ensuing behavior is regulated.

The basic social control exists in the practical work situations, adapted to people's presumed medical problems as welfare beneficiaries, and in which the employee participates. Clients must continually refer their own actions to those of others so as to fit in and so that their own actions will appear as meaningful for themselves and for those around them. As already noted, the management of human behavior in organizations takes place not by specific people but by the specific relationships in which organization members join. This motivates the employees to act so as to reach a common result and consequently generates common, meaningful experiences in the form of occupational disability. Most *mean* the same thing, even if different conduct is activated, where all human experience ultimately is social. In this respect, a human being's behavior can only be understood on the basis of the behavior that characterizes the social organizations to which he or she belongs.

The organizational socialization that takes place through each individual's interplay with the environment, such as with coworkers, is in this respect one of the most significant mechanisms for transferring values, attitudes, and norms in terms of thoughts and behavior that form the basis of all human development. In order for a coherent, integrated self-image as occupationally disabled to be developed, a person must be a member of a specific organization where that self-image can be enacted: and an individual *becomes* to that extent occupationally disabled by acquiring the organization's norms. The organizational rule system creates a meaning that is supported by such phenomena as myths, symbols, rituals, and stories, but also of explicit and formal rules and procedures. From experience, an occupationally disabled person's self therefore becomes clear as his or her 'organizational self' as a part of the occupationally disabled brotherhood. People look at themselves from the perspective of the starting point of others as members of the organization and only then can the unique experience of occupationally disabled be generated. By means of the organizational practices that the occupationally disabled perform, they can behave in an equivalent, organized fashion. Without these organizational practices, they would have remained different in character and behavior with, for example, the complications that this entails in communication and collaboration *as* occupationally disabled.

As in other organizations, the practical work at Samhall is organized by formal and informal working routines. The most significant aspects of the work are regulated partly through the division of labor that exists between different tasks, partly through the rules governing specific tasks. In this respect, Samhall's unique experience of the occupationally disabled is entrenched as noted above, in the work routines. Every individual employee certainly possesses knowledge on how to behave as occupationally disabled, but there exists 'meta-knowledge' in the common routines that are practiced, which is based on concepts and ideas of what is a suitable working environment for the occupationally disabled. This knowledge cannot be articulated in its entirety (written or spoken) but exists ensconced in distinctive organizational practices. To this extent, it is not possible to reduce the occupationally disableds' experience of occupational disability to their combined knowledge. This would be to ignore the unique system of rules and routines that enables coordination of the employees' behavior *as* occupationally disabled. That which is learned is therefore intimately connected with the specific conditions under which the learning takes place, where learning is not concerned mainly with learning a task, but rather as learning to *become* a member of an organization *by acting organizationally*. In this respect, the organization and arrangement of tasks are of central importance for which experiences of self are generated. Work 'adapted to occupational disability' has the potential to generate among people an appropriate context for learning to act as occupationally disabled.

Employment with Samhall means that an employee is expected to develop as occupationally disabled through the personnel development routines that are activated by the firm. The organization of the occupationally disableds' working day, which stems from certain rules and routines, influences which experiences are produced socially between the occupationally disabled and Samhall. During the practical work, it is a question of behaving oneself according to the organizational rules and routines, which provides the foundation for certain experiences which, in time, the employees learn to interpret. The message from Samhall is that work in itself is the method of development for the occupationally disabled. But the reverse situation is just as obvious; in which the occupationally disableds' ability to improve as occupationally disabled maintains a certain level of activity by Samhall, in the same way as a medical student's progress towards becoming a doctor makes it possible to maintain a certain level of medical production in society. If the employees did not learn their organizational role as occupationally disabled in Samhall, the institution as a social welfare organization would not survive—Samhall's basic identity and *raison d'être*, its 'domain' and 'core technology' is to *provide work for the occupationally disabled*. It is therefore central for Samhall to develop its employees *as* occupationally disabled; that is, as persons in need of the work environment that Samhall can offer.

COUNSELING DISABLED CLIENTS

All organization is built on a social dynamic where people observe their surroundings so as to interpret the experiences that are generated in different situations and where more experienced, and 'competent actors' function as counselors and in that way make it easier for novices to learn a certain attitude about themselves. By associating the experiences that the supervisors have of their employees with typical organizationally derived images of disability, a connection between a person's unique behavior and a general type of behavior can be generated and clarity in the supervisor's experience of the person *as* occupationally disabled can be constructed that contributes to his or her guidance of the individual in that specific role. Largely, this is accomplished by following organizational rules; the activity thereby adds to Samhall's overall enactment of its environment. Supervisors cannot control or even recognize an occupationally disabled person by studying the specific person's individual qualities unless these individual qualities are associated to a greater whole, no more than a car can be recognized simply by its parts, but by the characteristic combination of the parts. In the case of the occupationally disabled, such people can be recognized by a specific behavior that all in all gives the impression of occupational disability. Such an experience, as opposed to raw, chaotic, and ambiguous experience, has a characteristic that gives it a particular name. Instead of only *having* an experience, this situation requires reflection and thought to sort out different impressions on the basis of formally organized attention.

This attention is managed through the implicit and explicit training the supervisors receive from Samhall, where different organizational routines as to how they are to behave *as* supervisors towards the occupationally disabled generate the experiences of occupational disability that they then have to interpret. The important reflection surrounding different experiences creates a difference between what the supervisors perceive and the experience itself, where the individual supervisor's previous experiences manage the experiences that are generated. Experiences by the supervisors of the occupationally disabled are not, of course, the result of pure receptivity; instead they are the result of the explicit and implicit (asymmetric) bargaining-learning between supervisors and employees, where the former are drawing on organizational codings in order to make the interaction intelligent to both parties. These codings are the necessary resources through which the supervisor becomes an authority and can thus dominate the bargaining; but it also constitutes a legitimate mechanism of making sense of the joint experiencing. Coding of various occupationally disabled behaviors are 'backed up' by a larger organizational system of experience that renders them credible as attention-cues to experience; thus the importance of authority and power in the enactment of experience. In general, the occupationally disabled are inferior to the supervisors in that they lack access to significant resources, which is proven by the fact that they have not voluntarily become members of Samhall.

Much of the daily negotiation that takes place between supervisors and occupationally disabled on the basis of the coding of the latter is further asymmetrical from the standpoint of the roles of 'leaders' and 'employees' that the different personnel groups hold. Naturally this asymmetry gives the dominant party greater opportunities than the other to influence the interpretation of the common experiences that are generated, given that the occupationally disabled regard the supervisor as a legitimate authority. There must exist a fundamental personal interest in allowing themselves to be dominated, which ultimately is based on the organizational ideas and concepts of the relationship between them and their supervisors. To the extent that the employees at Samhall feel themselves to be occupationally disabled, it is reasonable in that context to regard the supervisors at Samhall as the legitimate experts who have the resources that are needed to rehabilitate the occupationally disabled from the condition they experience. In the last resort, the domination stems from the experience that they have of themselves as handicapped, that is to say, helpless, dependent, and generally inferior to the 'occupationally fit'; that is, the supervisors. In all, this ability to dominate the day-to-day interaction is a central mechanism in Samhall's 'negotiation of the environment,' where the organization continuously imposes its worldview on its clients.

In encounters with the occupationally disabled employees at Samhall, the disability label is an important 'interpretive tool' for the supervisors in reducing the uncertainty with all the heterogeneity that meeting those around them can entail. People with different backgrounds can be experienced in a variety of ways and this can generate insecurity as to how one should act as supervisor. By understanding people as disabled on the basis of different types of disability, conflicts and confusing experiences are sorted out and many decision-making situations are substantially simplified. Rules for decision-making are generated from the specific interpretation of experiences that is made in the form of 'this is an occupationally disabled person' and more specifically, 'he is dyslexic' or 'she is mentally ill,' and so on. Hence, 'managing occupationally disabled persons' requires that supervisors act according to specific scripts as provided them by Samhall; only then can they experience that the clients are occupationally disabled according to Samhall's worldview. If not following these scripts, confusion in the individual experiencing may follow, thus threatening the overall performance of the play; namely, the effective carrying out of Samhall's mission. Supervisors must in this matter be given the tools—the disability labels—for them to sort amongst the stream of their individual experiences that they become aware of in their meetings with the employees, where each occupationally disabled employee otherwise can risk being perceived as an individual *without* an occupational disability. The organizational rules and routines that the supervisors implicitly follow permit a constant generation of certain experiences of the occupationally disabled, which are different variations on the theme of the fact that they *are* occupationally disabled. For newly appointed supervisors, it is in this context less important to integrate so to speak a *tabula rasa* with the occupationally disabled employees than to learn first the typical (theoretical) symptoms of certain disability types and thereafter to interpret their employees on the basis of the interpretive rules that are coupled with each type of handicap.

'Personnel development routines' that Samhall has built up, address the question of miscellaneous private speculations among the supervisors as to who is occupationally disabled and how the occupationally disabled are to be dealt with, in a similar way as theories on rehabilitation in general should engender credibility in 'the correct way to rehabilitate.' The integration of experiences of occupational disability in organizational frames of reference, deals in this respect with creating a comprehensive framework for observing the experiences that can be interpreted as occupational disability, implemented by a professional body, the supervisors. A supervisor's understanding of his or her daily work with the occupationally disabled can, with the help of these organizational practices use coding systems in a more understandable way in the form of disability types. To that extent, the daily flood of experiences is given form and can be dealt with more efficiently since the coding makes it easier to interpret the employees' behavior *as* occupationally disabled, which influences subsequent interactions with them. Naturally, this coding is mutual insofar as even the occupationally disabled base their interactions with the supervisors on stereotypes; but their origins do not have the same formalized character as the supervisors' experience of the employees and therefore do not have the same credibility, legitimacy, and authority, not least because they are not grounded in a medical frame of reference.

As reported, the catchwords among the occupationally disabled themselves often include 'handicap,' 'functional impairment,' 'injury,' 'problems,' 'illness' and so on. These terms become the 'socialization instruments' with which their individual experience is constituted. The language used between the occupationally disabled is not only an expression of their interlocked behaviors that is the result of a formally managed experiential learning and the collective experiences that characterize them; it also limits the generation of other experiences. Occupationally disabled employees are colleagues since they share a particular fate; they know each other's real or imagined difficulties and opinions of their situation. Employees are 'in the know' about each other's condition and on the basis of this construct collegial solidarity. To talk about one's problems is about acting correctly in organizational terms; that is, acting on the basis of Samhall's expectations that exist about each person's occupational disability, where everyone is assumed to have limitations, most of them 'hidden,' that must be ventilated if they are to be effectively dealt with and treated. Certainly the occupational disability has perhaps not always been cited as the real reason as to why an employee is working on a particular work team or with particular tasks but it can at least in such cases serve as a general explanation as to why one is employed by Samhall.

It is of lesser importance whether the medical problems that motivate a person's identity as disabled are real or imaginary; the main point is that they are experienced on the assumption that they must exist since the occupationally disabled employee *is* occupationally disabled according to

Samhall's norms and standard operating procedures. Meetings where personal problems are confronted have the important function that employees are persuaded to *sort* their experiences and to *focus* on those experiences that are consistent with the organizational role that they have been positioned to fill. Each employee lives in a stream of undifferentiated experiences that do not have any meaning in themselves when they are undergone. It is only afterwards when the employee has the opportunity to look back at them together with others in a process mediated by supervisors that he or she can focus on certain incidents and experiences and select them from the stream of ambiguous impressions that otherwise proliferate. Experiences are thereby 'frozen' in the conversation with colleagues by means of a formally managed 'spotlight' that is shone on the occupational disability that is assumed to exist. Conversations that revolve around problems and disability help the employees to create *meaningful experiences* out of what they have simply undergone, by associating these with the general types of problem that supervisors (and colleagues) talk about. Each employee's 'store of experience' must be afforded attention in a special way, namely from the standpoint of the prevailing view that he or she *has* an occupational disability. This activity, whereby experiences are thus enacted, is managed and would not have taken place if the organizational context in which the individual finds him- or herself had not existed. In their conversations, the employees take as their starting point a body of implicit rules for suitable subjects of conversation that ultimately are defined by Samhall's codified experiences of their employees as occupationally disabled. These rules stipulate, for example, that conversations are to deal with illness and other medical problems from which the employees are expected to suffer. Although experiences of self are often generated during interaction with others, it is important for the supervisor to participate in order that he or she can control the conversations so that they deal with the topics that were intended, otherwise the results can be something quite different, such as the clients not experiencing themselves as disabled.

Meaningful experience as occupationally disabled can only be generated retrospectively through selective attention. This means that a Samhall employee's behavior as occupationally disabled 'when it happens' is only a potentially meaningful experience. Only when different activities are completed and can be problematized in retrospect, can they be experienced in full as occupational disability and form the basis of behavior as occupationally disabled. To recognize occupational disability in different organizational activities receives an important confirmatory meaning for employment at Samhall. By means of the specific typing of occupational disability that is available, such as reading and writing difficulties, supervisors and other managers can guide the employee to identify and thereby concretize previously ambiguous experiences.

The supervisor, as well as older, 'disability competent' employees, act as guides, so that each person becomes aware of behavior in his or her previous life that could possibly explain the occupational disability. By and large, social interaction is necessary for employees to become aware that they are occupationally disabled—every specific experience is molded in the human interplay with other people or objects in nature; the identity is generated externally on the basis of the social interaction in which each person finds him- or herself. It is thus very plausible to assume that those who regularly mix with occupationally disabled people can more easily regard themselves as occupationally disabled than whose who does not, where the unique experience of 'occupational disability' is constructed on the basis of the interaction that takes place between these people and in so doing makes it a 'meaningful lived experience.'

The practical establishment of the experience as occupationally disabled that takes place in conversations between the occupationally disabled themselves originates partly from an association where experiences are simplified so far as possible and where all types of 'data' that can indicate a certain cluster of problems are localized together (such as defeatism, dejection, resignation; as a sign of depression and in turn of psychic occupational disability); partly through focused observation where various potentially conflicting experiences are arranged serially and are treated individually (such as fear, fatigue, pain)—for the purpose of creating clarity in the experience of the disability from which one 'suffers.' The concept 'occupational disability' results, in this respect, in an organization of the flood of experiences that arise in conversations between employees and supervisors: thus each person adapts him- or herself not to the individual members' personal experiences but to the pattern of stimuli that they generate, which involves organizing personal experiences into a common, collective experience in which all can be socialized.

In this way, the organized pattern of every person's behavior is central— the pattern confirms the occupational disability, and that also can be found described in the personal file and in the person's practical style of working. This pattern does not appear by itself but is a product of the organized interaction in which the employees are engaged—without that activity, the pattern would not emerge. The experience as occupationally disabled presupposes therefore an organizational enactment as occupationally disabled. It is always a certain type of behavior that generates certain actions that are thereafter experienced. Simply by acting as occupationally disabled, for example, by sitting in a group and talking openly about personal problems, illnesses, and the like, experiences of occupational disability can be localized for each and every one.

Focused attention plays a central role here. The employees, because of their appointment with Samhall, choose to pay attention to what they are expected to pay attention to and to ignore anything else by their experiencing being managed by supervisors enacting organizational rules and routines. Activities relating to each and every problem and the general 'disability-focused' context in which the employees live daily has in this respect an educational function. Occupational disability is thus not the result of experiences *of* occupational disability, but is instead a result of active learning from selective experience of many previous events that 'washes over the individual.' Simply living in a world of experience is not the same as being occupationally disabled; experience of the latter must be learned through conversations and activities with colleagues and supervisors, where individuals ultimately define themselves on the basis of the illness or the general problems that are assumed to lie behind the occupational disability that the individual experiences.

Supervisors do not, as a rule, discuss *their* personal problems in front of the occupationally disabled employees and this attitude is in line with the asymmetrical relationship that characterizes the interaction between supervisors and the occupationally disabled. Recounting personal matters for another person without their answering with equivalent confidences creates a situation of dependency: the information that has been imparted can always be exploited in the negotiations that characterize all social processes. It follows that the often ignominious information that the supervisor has access to regarding the occupationally disabled employees is an effective resource with which to persuade the employees to behave in the way the supervisor wants. To be open about one's private life and to talk about things that others can understand as problems is to fulfill one's duty as an occupationally disabled employee with Samhall—it is quite simply to behave according to the organizational ideas that exist about rehabilitation and personal development.

Social interaction in Samhall therefore strengthens the view, as a rule, among the occupationally disabled employees that they are occupationally disabled. Simply put, they become all the more competent in occupational disability by specializing in particular behaviors. To appreciate oneself in the group as disabled through the attitudes of supervisors is generated by a gradual learning of the established concepts as to membership in the group and in employment with Samhall as a whole, where one must assimilate a certain behavior so as to be recognized as a legitimate player. To insist on feeling well may be taken as justification both by colleagues and supervisors for believing that the employee really is disabled, where it is necessary rapidly to persuade the individual in question to absorb 'with insight' the picture of themselves that others have, namely that they *are* occupationally disabled. Much of the learning of the role as occupationally disabled in the work team comes in this case through direct teaching from colleagues who have been employed longer, and who act as proficient models (mentors) so that new employees internalize suitable attitudes about themselves and thus do not challenge the group-thinking in terms of their dominant views on illness and disability.

As is well-known, all socialization is built on a social dynamic where people observe their surroundings so as to interpret the experiences that are generated in different situations and where more experienced, and so to say, 'competent' actors function as interpreters and in that way make it easier for novices to specialize in a certain attitude about themselves and others. In a criminal gang the new recruit is socialized on the basis of certain rules as to what is suitable behavior, which helps reproduce the gang's norms and standard operating procedures as an organization. As unsuitable as it is in criminal circles to talk about how dishonest it is, for example, to steal, it is equally unsuitable in Samhall to behave as healthy and fully occupationally fit and thus not in need of the welfare services that Samhall provides. Central to the Samhall employees' experiences about themselves as occupationally disabled are thus the attitudes, experiences, and feelings that they generate about themselves, what they are capable of doing, how they ought to react to certain things, how they differ from others (such as the supervisors), how they are similar to each other (as occupationally disabled). The foundation of the organizationally enacted self-image as occupationally disabled lies in these formally managed interpretations of experiences that are a central part of Samhall's ability to reproduce itself.

As discussed above, attitudes of occupational disability are acquired to a great extent through learning processes with other occupationally disabled, where they are rewarded for behaving in a fashion that corresponds with the social identity that is reserved for the occupationally disabled. To explain a behavior as occupationally disabled on the basis of an idea that certain people have certain characteristics that predestine them to behave in this fashion, is in this context inappropriate. Behavior as occupationally disabled is generated instead with the experiences performed by the occupationally disabled; for example, performing tasks in a disabled fashion or discussing their problems and limitations in a group. It is not personal motives and attitudes towards occupational disability that lead to occupationally disabled behavior. Rather the opposite: the occupationally disabled behavior generates certain experiences that in turn enact a specific self-image and these experiences are in all relevant respects social. The work teams at Samhall create an environment for the production of certain experiences that are different variations on the theme of occupational disability, which had not been generated elsewhere, and the individual members learn that occupational disability is something qualitatively different in its respective experiences, which requires the absorption of a specific self-image.

Most new employees at Samhall do not know what it means to be occupationally disabled and must therefore be counseled by supervisors and 'older' colleagues to learn the meaning of the term. If a person is to persevere in their Samhall job, he or she must learn to appreciate that the experiences that are involved in being occupationally disabled, in the form of such things as a fixation with ill-health, dependency, stigmatization, isolation, helplessness, are, at heart, attractive and desirable. Without this experiential learning through successfully accomplished medicalization, Samhall's ability to perform its activities is at risk. During the early period in Samhall, the new employee can perhaps experience confusion and the experiences that are engendered may not always feel pleasant (in the same way that the first puff of a cigarette is seldom enjoyable). In time they must learn to appreciate their job and to reassess as positive the initial, perhaps unpleasant, experiences of acknowledging medical problems. By behaving in this fashion, the preconditions are created for the acquisition of a view of oneself as a suitable Samhall employee.

The motivation for learning this behavior comes from the attitude towards rehabilitation and personal development that is the foundation of Samhall's existence. The reason why Samhall employees have chosen to start a Samhall career is the insight that they are unable themselves to rehabilitate and normalize themselves so that they become attractive in society. It follows that to be socialized in the role of occupationally disabled, to be regarded as a 'normal' actor at Samhall and as a legitimate welfare recipient in the wider society deals to a great extent with learning the organizational rules and routines that are based on theories of occupational disability that exist at Samhall and which are reproduced in the behavior of the work teams. In this case, a significant moral and ethical component is present: to act legitimately, each individual must integrate him- or herself into the behavioral norm that distinguishes the social group of which the person has become a member. As with all organizations, there is a form of typical and standard behavior that makes the organization a recognizable whole, and specific personnel groups within it that can be identified, where specific conduct can be described as suitable or unsuitable.

A new Samhall client seldom has a personality as occupationally disabled unless he or she has previously filled this role. The new employee must therefore adopt his or her colleagues' attitudes to each other and to themselves so as to be accepted as a member of the group in general, and specifically as a legitimate Samhall employee, which in turn will influence their self-image, that is to say socialization in the work team's norms and values. By learning the dominant attitudes as to what it means to be occupationally disabled and behaving as occupationally disabled, each employee will in time be recognized as competent by those colleagues who are 'older at the game' and by the supervisors. If one looks upon oneself as occupationally disabled, it is likely that new experiences are interpreted in the light of one's disability; in the same way as other occupational groups base their perception of a problem on previous experiences and look for solutions in proximate experiences. Insofar as the 'solution' to a problem for an occupationally disabled employee is 'more' occupational disability, then this is the result of his or her specialization in the role as occupationally disabled.

DISCHARGING THE DISABLED

Samhall's transitional practices are perhaps the clearest example of Samhall's enactment of its clients as medically problematic. The 'medicalizing career' that each occupationally disabled employee at Samhall undergoes in time creates a 'competence trap' by which their individual experiences are continuously generated. 'Occupationally disabled behavior' is something that is in demand in Samhall and in the larger welfare system of which it is a part but not in most other areas in society. The more a Samhall client becomes involved with Samhall, the more she experiences herself as in need of social welfare *as occupationally disabled*. Within most occupational branches, people usually become more efficient and competent with increasing experience. This holds true generally for all specific behavior such as unemployment, the ability to make a speech, or to ride a bike, it is also the case with occupational disability. Eventually, needing social welfare becomes a vocation much in the same way as any other expert in a bureaucratic system; something one has become skilled at by reproducing certain organizational norms and routines of appropriate behavior. Competence traps and captivity in certain behavior patterns through learning is a legendary phenomenon within all organizations, and is a central factor in organizations' enactment of their environments. On the basis of positive feedback between experience and competence, people and organizations generate information and abilities that in certain contexts and during certain periods can be of great value to them, but in other circumstances can become a burden.

Previous experience always lie behind the interpretation of new experiences and can to this extent make clients 'competently myopic' and increasingly unable to generate other experiences than those that are in tune with the fundamental experience of occupational disability. Based on their learning, they tend to experience what they believe in and in so doing construct a high degree of the reality that they experience, with a self-fulfilling prophecy being the result. The process of *becoming* occupationally disabled, which starts at the National Employment Office, is in this case a process of organizational enactment where a person as a new employee is as a rule inexperienced, and then as an 'old hand' at Samhall, experienced, which is the result of the organizational learning environment that employment by Samhall involves. At the same time, as an employee is confronted with an increasing number of experiences that carry the distinguishing marks of occupational disability, his or her reality becomes progressively more that of an occupationally disabled person: the reality that is enacted with colleagues and supervisors is marked by the acquired experiences.

As a result, occupationally disabled employees at Samhall often face experiential obstacles when wanting to work outside Samhall, which is consistent with the view that the occupationally disabled need a specially adapted working environment; as a result the occupationally disabled experience illness, problems, and injuries in their interpretation of themselves. In the end occupationally disabled persons feel themselves even more occupationally disabled and in need of continued welfare support. The external stimuli that 'signal' that the labor market is really not as tough as it can appear to be, or that the person in question is less handicapped than he or she believes, is excluded as a rule or receives little attention, not least by the way such information is framed by Samhall; the occupationally disabled have quite simply learned to develop a refined opinion of themselves and the world around them from the standpoint of their employment with Samhall and therefore made themselves immune from most of the variety of experiences that could be incompatible with the role as occupationally disabled.

Typically, it is not appealing for a Samhall employee to leave Samhall after a period of employment. The person has learned the ropes within the organization and become so to speak 'street wise' there. To move to another environment where other rules and requirements prevail, can in this context become as big a come-down as an appointment with Samhall was initially. The role as occupationally disabled, where certain people are more equal than others is too valuable and has by many been internalized as a part of their personality after a long and troublesome learning process. It is a standard idea in psychology that behavior that generates success reinforces a continuation of similar behavior and behavior that results in negative sanctions tends to be weakened. For the occupationally disabled employee, a continual reinforcement takes place of their experience of themselves as occupationally disabled by selective attention to the experiences that are generated by Samhall, where earlier experiences manage future ones. A Samhall job entails an alienation from the 'occupationally fit' that can develop irrespective of the reason for the Samhall appointment and so represent a side effect of it, which, however, takes on greater significance for the person in question and his or her nearest circle than the original difficulties. The gradual resignation over their own capacity to get a job outside Samhall that several occupationally disabled express, goes hand in hand with the gradual acquisition of the role as occupationally disabled, where resistance to leaving Samhall is strengthened in tandem with the employees becoming increasingly convinced that they *are* occupationally disabled. In this way most of them also become the foremost proponents of this system.

The scenario is reminiscent of the familiar resignation that the unemployed can feel after a period of fruitless efforts to find a job. The Samhall employees only need to look around them through their learned organizational lenses. Their own experience tells them something other than what was put forward at the introductory meeting and in Samhall's publications; the accepted behavior seems to be to stay in the system rather than to leave it, and that in itself contributes to its further institutionalization. This behavior has nothing to do with lack of intelligence or laziness on the part of the occupationally disabled employees, but with medicalizing management, where a gradual construction of experiences *as* occupationally disabled makes it increasingly difficult to leave their present role for a radically different one; namely that of an 'occupationally fit' person in society. This process is at the core of Samhall's institutionalization by enacting demands and requirements among prospective and existing clients that can be fulfilled by the organization. In this way, its services become something that takes on a life of its own.

11 Enacting the Welfare Disabled Client

Overall, my study suggests how the Swedish social welfare organization Samhall, which is devoted to assisting 'occupationally disabled individuals' essentially enacts the 'occupationally disabled' person; and how this construction respects the organization's aim to 'develop people with occupational disabilities.' Unemployed individuals that apply for welfare support eventually become instruments in the fulfillment of Samhall's activities by learning the organized role of occupational disability that makes them competent players in the overall societal activity of assisting and rehabilitating 'people with occupational disabilities.'

This familiar observation of formally organized management activity can fruitfully be extended through the concept of medicalization in order to explain the institutionalization of this kind of social welfare. By enacting its prospective and existing clients' behavior through a number of concrete 'medicalizing management' activities of diagnosis and treatment, Samhall effectively creates its most important environment to which it subsequently adapts. Unemployed individuals in Sweden who are assigned organized social welfare by Samhall are not 'disabled,' but may become disabled by adopting the organizational norms, rules, and routines that specify what is expected of them as disabled; what is morally and ethically acceptable and unacceptable, suitable and unsuitable behavior, and good and bad ways of thinking. Disability in this welfare context is an experientially learned role that has been created for the rational pursuit of welfare management. An 'occupationally disabled' person's behavior is not a bio-medical problem, simply waiting to be discovered, but is a result of formal organization.

Samhall illustrates how a social welfare organization manages by medicalizing its environment, at the same time becoming all the more medicalized by continuously adapting its management practices of recruitment, development, and transition to its environment's increasingly medicalized behavior. As with most other programs of social welfare (e.g. Butcher, 2002; Considine, 2001), the ultimate idea with Samhall is that the occupationally disabled should leave the welfare program on which he or she has become dependent. This is what is meant by the internationally popular notions of 'empowerment' and 'inclusion' in social welfare policy. Most transitions from Samhall fail as a result of its medicalizing management that enacts clients' behavior as disabled concurrently with the medicalization of Samhall that makes the organization all the less able to experience any other solutions for its clients than the organization can provide. In enacting clients as disabled, Samhall's medicalizing management practices of selection, classification, confirmation, training, counseling, and discharging are fundamental. The success of Samhall's enactment of its environment is evidenced by the fact that the vast majority of Samhall's clients remain occupationally disabled once they have been diagnosed and treated as such.

Effectively identifying and placing the 'right' and 'correct' welfare clients according to some dominant organizational norms and codes is an activity that is central to any social welfare organization (e.g., Patti, 2000; Slavin, 1985; Stone, 1985). The process of enacting individuals as 'disabled' is part of their program of offering disadvantaged individuals help and assistance adapted to their individual requirements and demands *as disabled*. A central prerequisite for the rational management of this activity is the segregation of them into a distinct social category, that of 'disabled.' By segregating them from the rest of the population it is believed that the social welfare organization can more effectively operate upon them in order to accomplish a successful rehabilitation and restoration to a 'normal life' (Albrecht, 2002; Thomas, 2002). These 'sheltering activities' are commonly appreciated as to how they contribute to manage welfare clients as disabled; that is, as deviant on medical grounds. A less common analysis revolves, however, around how they act to reinforce and institutionalize the practice of social welfare in society.

The segregation of the disabled in social welfare programs has promoted the development of standardized principles for the identification, analysis, and development of the disabled (Abberley, 2002). The fact that there exist organizations exclusively dedicated to organizing people who are experienced as 'needy' has also favored the growth of a distinct competence in the organization of the disableds' development in society. A social welfare organization's experiential focus, its 'organizational gaze' (Foucault, 1977), is *the disabled* and without a social welfare organization it is quite unlikely that the internationally popular term 'disability' would have the institutionalized status that is currently attached to it. In other words, without social welfare organizations, there would be no disabled in society; without disabled there would be no social welfare organizations. The term 'organization' refers to those human relations that must be present in order for something to exist. It is by means of social welfare organizations' medicalizing management that disabled people are enacted in society; hence they are 'formed in correlation with a set of institutions of control' (Foucault, 2003: 323). An isolated and solitary individual lacks identity. They can only attain a personality by acquiring the goals and meaning that organizations have which at the same time becomes a fundamental mechanism of the organization's reproduction. The individual experience of disability arises solely in certain specific circumstances that can be found, amongst other places, within a social welfare organization: by organizing behavior certain experiences are established as meaningful, in this case disability. The individual's behavior can therefore only be understood through an analysis of the behavior of the organization.

Learning disabled behavior based on experience must not be simply left to the clients' own uncertain trial and error. This could produce many different experiences for them and not necessarily those that are suitable for the organizations that aim to develop them personally *as* disabled. Instead, it is important to implement, as is the case of social welfare organization, a standardized and organized manner of behaving for the purpose of organizing the perceptions of activity that the clients produce in their experiences. Through the organizational activities that social welfare clients participate in, which are 'disability adapted' (Albrecht, 1992; Lane, 1997; Scott, 1980), each client's view of him- or herself as disabled is enacted and the client becomes a suitable 'object' for a disability-focused personal development. Segregation of the disabled in social welfare programs also affects the attitude of those surrounding the disabled, and this is significant for the disableds' view of themselves. Theories on the 'nature of the disabled' rationalize not only formal programs for personal development and create a subtle mechanism for maintaining a social distance from the disabled, with the accompanying stereotypical views on their behavior and how they are to be treated. They also create an important basis for the maintenance of the opinion that there exists a qualitative and fundamental difference between 'able' and 'disabled.' The management practices of social welfare organizations, where theories on disability and rehabilitation are applied, do not therefore deal so much with reducing the gap between the 'disabled' and 'able' citizens. Instead, it maintains and reinforces the distinction by systematically contrasting a disabled behavior by a group of people with the 'non-disabled' behavior in another group of individuals. Assistance by a social welfare organization means to this extent to institutionalize the constructed categorization between someone who is 'disabled' and someone who is 'fit,' 'non-disabled'—which is a difference with significant moral and social qualities with regard to people's self-image.

In all, it is reasonable to conclude that much disability in contemporary welfare society originates initially from within the formally organized social welfare system. This is not because this system is the place where disabilities invent themselves, but because of the fact that the system is the organized environment that makes possible the assimilation of certain experiences of needy individuals into an experience *of* disability. Medicalizing management routines of analysis have been developed over the years in social welfare programs that seek to effectively identify the disabled by organizing them in specially adapted activities, where the activities result in the client ceasing to behave as individuals and behaving instead in an organized fashion on the basis of certain assumptions as to how the disabled typically behave. Organizational practices of medical classification of disability are less concerned with identifying a medical problem than with constructing it.

Social welfare can be seen as a centralized, public enterprise to interpret disadvantaged persons' complex of individual needs as signs of the single problem *disability*. By managing the transformation of able people into disabled people, social welfare organizations medicalize such social states as unemployment and poverty as part of an agenda of organizational and societal normalization. The way in which this enterprise is successfully accomplished is ultimately based on a medical model's standard ideas of diagnosis and treatment. By medicalizing people's behavior, a social welfare organization enacts its environment by implying that some people are 'in need on medical grounds' that are justified through medical examinations. The fact that it is, for instance, the possibility of getting a job that ultimately defines a disability, and not a personal medical condition, is necessarily ignored by the organized welfare system by the fact that it adapts its behavior to an organizationally enacted idea of disability and to nothing else. This is the crux of social welfare organizations' enactment of their environments that is concretely realized through medicalizing management.

The construction of the role as disabled is not a private matter but in essence an organizational experience through the individual's participation in the formally organized relations, discussions, and practices for the disabled. Most of the disabled at a social welfare organization can be expected to behave as disabled since they understand the behavior to be legitimate and socially acceptable. This acceptance is the basis on which the authority of any social welfare organization must rest and with it the fundamental precondition for the development of individuals as disabled. Significantly, the welfare disabled are part of the social arrangement whose purpose it is to develop them as disabled; to rehabilitate them by respecting their individual requirements and needs. Their behavior is therefore organizationally rational. The rationality of the disabled in behaving in a way the organization is able to understand given its experiences, is a social welfare organization's most important instrument for the development of the disabled.

If people are to recognize themselves as being in need of social welfare, they must learn to focus on their experiences in a certain fashion—in a disabled fashion. The logic behind this behavior lies in the view that experiences are instilled in people's consciousness through their five senses deriving from the external objects with which they interact throughout their lives. To focus on earlier acts in retrospect is the way in which distinct experiences can be generated from the memory of lived experiences. As noted previously, to this extent, all experience is retrospective—it is when one first remembers something that previously lived experiences take on a distinct form and are connected with a comprehensible objectification; for example, in the form of disability categories at a social welfare organization. As Kierkegaard said: 'Life must be lived facing forward, but can only be understood looking backwards.' Thus only lived experiences can become meaningful experiences.

To this extent, social welfare organizations deal with teaching disadvantaged individuals to regard themselves and their backgrounds differently from the way they have done previously, so as to be able to function in an effective and technically rational fashion in an organized welfare system. It is not a question of falsifying one's past so that it fits in with a particular social role, but of interpreting it differently, by focusing on certain experiences that have previously been ignored and by ignoring certain experiences that have previously received attention. The role as disabled makes it possible to aggregate personal experiences of disability to a common 'savings bank' of experiences, that in the future can be used to help others to realize that they also are disabled and that can be presented in the annual official statistics of welfare clients. If future generations of welfare disabled are to learn from earlier generations it naturally presupposes that even they will experience themselves as disabled on the basis of the equivalent organized experiences that are deposited in the role as disabled. By enacting each individual experience by means of this formally organized role, meaning is constructed in the collective experience. To be confronted with one's own failure in society can be confusing. It becomes meaningful if people can say to themselves: 'I am dyslectic like many others and also need welfare support and assistance' and thus experience their actions as different expressions of a common experience of disability that requires help as offered by a particular social welfare system.

There is no doubt that a person who is partially sighted, has cancer, or has lost an arm has greater difficulty than others in functioning 'normally' in society and that social welfare services can be of much importance to him or her. However, it is not necessarily the case that the person regards him- or herself as disabled in the way the organized system of social welfare does. According to this analysis disability can have two meanings: it is in part an abnormal biological and personal situation the existence of which can be confirmed on real or false grounds by the individual, doctors, or other medical experts; in part it is the social role as disabled, which can be self-experienced or assigned. This latter does not always imply the former but the former often implies the latter. It may be the case that there is a 'biomedical abnormality' on which the experience as disabled is based, but that abnormality is still not the 'objective' disability. A visually-impaired person is not necessarily blind; that is, he or she has adopted the social role as blind with all the behavioral expectations that accompany this. Similarly, epileptics can have physiological problems, without experiencing themselves as epileptics in their interactions with themselves and others. The central difference between a bio-medical divergence and a social divergence with respect to welfare services, lies in the person's experiences of their behavior; experiences that are the result of an organized system's activities.

A person who is biologically 'incomplete,' but does not have problems with doing or keeping a job is generally not regarded as disabled. A person who, on the other hand, is 'bio-medically perfect' (do they exist?) but still has problems in getting or keeping a job, can easily be regarded as disabled in modern welfare society. In the same way as most mental illnesses are defined from the standpoint of a person's behavior and not from physiologically-based diagnoses, disability is defined from the standpoint of a person's behavior in a certain social environment. From this perspective, the definition of disability becomes closely connected with the question of what the organizations for the disabled in society actually *do*, which in turn emphasizes that disability is not something that people have; rather it is something they enact. All 'illnesses' are not deviations in a biological sense; they are more a question of ethical and moral problems than physiological disorders that consequently can be construed as an explanation for some 'divergent behavior.'

It is not the case that an 'abnormal behavior' in the form of disability comes first: it is the organizational practices carried out at a social welfare organization that precede the experience of disability and underlie a person's knowledge of him- or herself as 'abnormal.' These practices enable a person in need to understand herself, interpret herself, and acknowledge herself as disabled. In the whole process from an initially non-disabled to a disabled behavior which distinguishes not only the sorting, segregating, and socializing practices by a social welfare organization; but also establishes a welfare disabled person's career, it is a matter of making oneself known as disabled on the basis of an interpretation of one's personal experiences as indications of disability. This 'admission' is a personal responsibility but takes place with the help of the organizational practices in which the individual participates and which encourage the people to appreciate themselves as disabled. In substance, help by a social welfare organization creates the pre-conditions for self-examination and self-deliberation that make it clear that the problem is the individual's own and only he or she can solve it, through participation in the social rehabilitation that is available.

By means of the medicalizing management practices, which lead to the generation of an experience of self as disabled so that the person eventually performs the organizational assignment for which they were identified, recruited, and trained, the final result may become a confirmatory insight into the personal responsibility for the extensive and complex system of rehabilitation for the disabled that society has organized. This individual insight is the foremost means by which social welfare is institutionalized through humans' interlocked behaviors. By medicalizing prospective and existing welfare clients, social welfare management is eventually medicalized by it increasingly adapting to medicalized behavior in its environment. The organizationally constructed personal responsibility does not imply an exhortation to independent activity, but to submit to the organizational system of social welfare that adapts to its own experience of people's disabilities and to nothing else. Therefore, before one can become 'non-needy,' the disabled must learn the role disabled. To be able to be rehabilitated and developed, a person must first become disabled: to be able to be helped in modern welfare society, a person must first be helpless. The person's problems, born in the form of a feeling of being sick, handicapped, and the like by so many disabled people in society, depends to this extent not on possible personal short-comings, but on the learning of these as disabled for which they receive the appreciation and praise of society's main instrument of normalization: social welfare. Essentially, becoming disabled does not constrain; it empowers.

Paradoxically, the further one penetrates into this system, the more difficult it becomes to answer the question why a person is there; that is to say, what the basis is for the person's problems in the form of bio-medical disorders; and the longer the period of involvement, the more difficult it becomes to leave the system. This institutionalization as a result of experience-based learning is legendary. The answer a person could perhaps give when newly assigned to social welfare seems after a while naïve and simple, since all the extensive assessments the newly recruited client typically undergoes and the activities he or she carries out as disabled makes it clear for the client that their complex of problems is more multifaceted and complicated than they initially believed. Consequently it also becomes increasingly difficult for them to answer the question as to what they want to do with the rest of their lives. To leave a social welfare system would be to leave themselves and the identity as disabled that through learning has become their own, as well as to 'run away' from the responsibility for their rehabilitation that is still regarded as necessary, and thereby 'shirk their responsibility.' The mental integration that has taken place with the system that numerous welfare clients have belonged to for many years, means that they become their own watchmen, which effectively hinders attempts to 'flee' from the responsibility they are assumed to have for their personal problems.

To leave the system would not only involve running away from one's responsibility, it would also involve running away from the responsibility one has for one's fellows. Culpability for the disability is, in substance, shared and therefore the responsibility of others who are in the same category, for it is similarly shared. The mutual dependency between human behaviors that all organizations rest on becomes more obvious when members are bound together not only by common interests, but also by means of a common, learned guilt. The gradually accumulated experience by means of a number of imperceptible and, looked at individually, fairly harmless steps (for example from unemployment to coding as disabled), lures the individual into a trap, where he or she becomes a victim of their own previous actions. The solidarity that can be generated between the disabled in society is a result of the paradox of the trap: people cannot become free without involving themselves further.

The contempt for social welfare that some may feel as new clients is no longer so apparent after a period of support and assistance. Unlike a broken leg or an injured eye, from which a person can get better, it is very difficult to get 'cured' from a 'welfare disability,' for both psychological and sociological reasons. Certainly disability is defined as a medical condition; but not in the 'regular' medical sense; instead it is a result of medicalization. Hence, once having been caught in a social welfare organization's cone of light, discharging from social welfare becomes very hard. Basically, this common 'lock-in' effect of social welfare is the result of medicalizing management that makes clients helpless and dependent 'for medical reasons,' thus at the same time reinforcing the organization's enactment of its environment in terms of disabled clients.

It may naturally be very easy to reach the conclusion that if a 'disability' does not exist in an objective, medical sense among welfare clients, then why should government policies for the disabled, organizations for the disabled, work for the disabled exist? The existence and growth of formal organizations and systems of welfare is sometimes taken as evidence for the existence and growth of disability among individuals, which implies that the system's task is to seek out these people and offer them appropriate support. Disability coding, the formal process of defining personal limitations in one's social ability is, in this connection, a central mechanism in a larger social undertaking, by highlighting a social problem that needs to be attended to, establishing a number of needs, stimulating demand for support, and describing who has the right to certain services. In this respect, classifying someone as disabled is not a mechanism for social exclusion but rather for social integration, since it offers a form of sanctioned social deviation in the Parsonian sense of a 'sick role': Once a person has been coded as disabled the individual is divested of personal responsibility for his or her deviation from social norms, as well as the duty to 'do what they have to do' (Parsons, 1951: 285). This opportunity is, however, not without obligations versus the formal organization that makes this possible: the individual is expected to cooperate fully with those who have made it possible. If this does not happen, the legitimate deviation is transformed into something illegitimate with diverse social and economic sanctions as a result. Medicalization acts in this way to transform deviant behavior into socially normal behavior. Since it is generally assumed that disability is a personal characteristic, this means that the individual can implicitly be saddled with responsibility for the medical problems that social welfare organizations experience: it is the individual's 'fault,' thus making the person responsible for the organizationally designated role he or she is assigned (Ryan, 1971).

Ultimately, it is not a technical/administrative definition that determines who will or will not be classified as disabled in any welfare system and thus enjoy its privileges: the final decision, and with it the practical sorting of disabled in society, rests with the disabled themselves who accept the formal labeling on the basis of their personal behavior that is experienced as problematic. As a result of social welfare organizations' activities, some people start acting disabled by fulfilling roles and organizational identities, which in essence become their 'self-management' and 'technology of self' (Foucault, 2003). The imaginary or real existence of health and illness are used as templates for managing the potentially infinite range of human behaviors that constitute a source of uncertainty to any organization or society. By objectifying people as medical cases they become subject to a medical organization's systematic control. To a very large extent, this is a learning process, where the person acquires norms, codes, standard operating procedures, and other expressions of society's dominance and control. In this learning activity the individual enacts a role, such as the social role of blind person, thus making him or her likely to behave 'normally' in a specific social environment. From this perspective medicalization is a central mechanism in society for influence (Simon, 1997), inculcation (Barnard, 1968), and indoctrination (Selznick, 1984); hence management.

When turning increasing aspects of individuals' behaviors into medical issues, individuals are then expected to more intensely cooperate in their medical and social rehabilitation, or to more intensely participate in programs for 'staying healthy' and promoting an overall well-being (Conrad, 1987). These management practices, which are common in discourses on public health and welfare constitute situated learning activities by which individuals' behavior becomes medicalized based on their individual experience of their selves, hence legitimate and normal given certain social norms. Regarded in this way medicalization risks becoming a kind of 'totalitarianism'; it is a way by which more and more of people's behaviors and attitudes become the subject of extensive social control (e.g., Rose, 1999; Sennett, 2003). Of course, in contemporary society there is no point in asking whether over the span of an individual's life she should or should not be enacted as a medical case: the significant question becomes instead how often and severe a case. In any modern welfare society the question of *who is* healthy or ill, disabled or non-disabled must necessarily be *who becomes* healthy or ill, disabled, or non-disabled as a result of medicine's management of social welfare? Given this observation, few if any persons in contemporary society are likely to escape the institutionalizing forces of organized social welfare.

As already said, medicalization is not just negative and repressive, as is sometimes implied in the literature; it is also productive, formative, and positive (Lupton, 1997). Organizations are encoded experiences (Levitt and March, 1988) and corpuses of knowledge (Weber, 1978), which are necessary to generate certain medical experiences among people in order to enact them as 'medical subjects.' To become 'sociologically sick or healthy' is to learn something, to take part in an educative experience. The learning of the role of blind person, the role of impotent person, the role of mental patient, and so on, operates according to the same mechanisms as any learning activity does. A person who learns a social role and internalizes it as part of her identity is transformed and changed. Medicalization is not only a means by which individuals gain 'technical' knowledge about themselves and the world around them; it is also a mechanism for transferring morals and ethics that are necessary for them to successfully contribute to the activities of particular social institutions (e.g., social welfare organizations). Human development, whatever its result, thrives on conscious organization that operates through conceptual models. Without organization a sense of self can hardly be created; a person becomes a subject only in relation to certain organizational practices in which she is an active agent. A medical model's authority is in this regard something exercised rather than held; something that people do voluntarily based on their individual experiential learning. It is not something that is repressive, operating on something or someone; instead people become medical objects by taking part in certain organizational activities and procedures through which their self and identity are enacted. Learning the role of blindness, for example, not only totalizes, it also individualizes; that is, it makes the person more identifiable vis-à-vis others and his or her previous conception of self.

Once again this social and organizational approach stresses the idea that 'the disabled' is not a self-evident phenomenon, an observable reality that is to be appraised, observed, and documented. The disabled person, as a subject, is necessarily the organizationally enacted person, a person whose attitudes and behaviors are managed in relation to particular organizational norms that the person helps to maintain; he or she is continuously constituted and constructed through organized relationships and practices. To understand medicalization one cannot only focus on people's individual behavior that generates certain individual experiences. Any complete analysis of medicalization must include the organized and consciously coordinated aspect of this enterprise; that is, management. Thus, a crucial concept is management in analyzing medicalization; that is, the transformation of previously non-medical behavior into medical behavior. More than anything else, formal organizations are *effective* mechanisms to breed medicalization. They guide people's individual learning by providing them with medically-based behavioral plans, routines, and standard operating procedures. Certainly, such properties do not guarantee progress toward betterment; but they guarantee progress toward behavioral change; in this case from non-medical behavior to medical behavior. According to this analysis, medicalization is the managed learning from medical experience, resulting in organizational enactment of human behavior. As such it constitutes a powerful mechanism of organized institutionalization.

12 Conclusions

Despite their familiarity, the empirical observations that have been reported in this book are theoretically intriguing. They seem to be partly inconsistent with some standard and valuable treatments of institutionalization. While institutional research has illuminated institutionalization to a large extent, the observations proposed in my study capture essential aspects of institutionalization that have received inadequate attention. Therefore I believe this book can contribute to a revised understanding of the general process of organized institutionalization, and of the institutionalization of social welfare in particular.

A standard analysis of the institutionalization of organized social welfare would have focused on a social welfare organization as a more or less perfect or more or less genuine product of its external environment. This environment would be seen to consist of the objective and genuine existence of 'disabled individuals'—a social status conceived as a highly institutionalized rule—that a social welfare organization adapts to, albeit sometimes in a ceremonial sense only. An essential idea in much current institutional theory is that environments exist in a real and objective manner that determines organizational behavior including its discourses. That some people are seen to objectively suffer from various disabilities that make them needy of social welfare organizations' services is a central assumption according to this framework. However, such an analysis largely ignores the crucial idea that organizations essentially do not 'react' or 'respond' to their 'objective' environments; they enact them. A social welfare organization's environment does not consist of the objective existence of disability among prospective and existing clients; but of its experience of disability. This experience is the result of social welfare organizations' enactment of individuals' behavior through various 'medicalizing management' activities that stress the importance of organizations' internal operations for understanding their institutionalization.

Certainly, students of institutionalization have emphasized the need to focus on organizations' own activities such as sense-making and interpretation in explaining how organizations' adaptation to the environment comes about. This important development of institutional theory needs to be continued by exploring the full implications of such an approach. To this end, taking into account how organized practices of social welfare *create* the environments to which they adapt (whether ceremonially or not) based on their own experience seems to be a particularly relevant route. The concept of enactment embodies a strong recognition of how agency and constructive cognitive processes are critical elements in institutionalization.

According to an 'enactment view of institutionalization,' a social welfare organization responds to external pressures to conform; but these external pressures are the result of its own experiential learning. Organizations are agents of experiences rather than entities that simply undergo experiences. The enactment concept does not suggest a representation of the world 'out there' through interpretation and sense-making; but an ongoing bringing forth of a world through the process of individuals' experiencing. This world is no imaginary phenomenon; it is made up of concrete human behaviors acting in a way that the organization is competent to understand and that become critical components in the organization's self-maintenance and reproduction. Simply put, this view of institutionalization focuses attention on how organizations experientially produce the environments to which they subsequently adapt. They become institutions through their own dynamics; the changes that result from the interplay between the organizations and their environments may be brought about by the environment but are always determined by the organization. In this way the organization, whether it is concerned with managing social welfare or not, creates the institutionalized environment that permits it to continue operating, otherwise it disintegrates.

Most students of institutionalization have so far behaved with a certain reserve toward the concept of enactment as offered by organization theory. However, it has an undeniable prominence since it suggests a potentially more complete analysis of institutionalization than the dominating one. It is an important concept in order to better explain how formal organizations tend to perpetuate themselves beyond their original intentions by enacting increasing aspects of their environments based on their own experiential activities. This observation is a particularly important one to explain social welfare organizations' common propensity to eventually ignore disadvantaged persons' individual requirements and instead become concerned with the organizations' own needs. By generating positive feedback between experience and competence social welfare organizations (like all organizations) become increasingly 'myopic' (Levinthal and March, 1993); that is, unresponsive to the clients' experiences. This has nothing to do with brute exploitation of clients or unintelligence and stupidity in the overall management of social welfare; it is the result of standard processes of institutionalization. Indeed, this behavior is unavoidable when formally managing social welfare; eventually *any* formal organization becomes primarily concerned with its own activities as a result of it adapting to an enacted environment; not to an objective one. Enacting prospective and existing welfare clients according to a social welfare organization's own experiences is the foremost means by which the organization secures its institutionalization.

Overall, by framing institutionalization as enactment, this study challenges the still dominating idea in institutional theory that environments, at least partially, exist independently of organizational activity. Whether or not adaptation is complete or partial through discriminative attention and interpretation, the full or partly objective existence of the environment remains a central component in most institutional analyses. Most critics of a traditional framing of institutionalization that is said to have resulted in an 'over-socialized' view of organizations, still share the idea of the existence of an objective environment that acts as a source of legitimacy for organizations. Essentially, recent critics' social-constructivist approach is framed around how organizations adapt to their environments in a discriminative way, but not around how organizations create and produce their environments on experiential grounds. For instance, in their critique of institutional theory's weak conceptualization of how institutions are created, altered, and reproduced, Barley and Tolbert (1997: 99) argued that '[u]nless an institution exists prior to action, it is difficult to understand how it can affect behavior and how one can examine its implications for action or speak of action's subsequent affects on the institutionor An analysis of institutionalization based on the enactment concept, however, necessarily challenges this view by emphasizing that organization action is prior to institutions, not the other way around; hence an analysis of institutionalization that assumes that organizations' environments are *fully* of their own making.

As observed by Weick et al. (2005: 417), discussions of enactment and similar notions often include such words as 'construct,' 'product,' 'generate,' and 'create'; less often 'react,' 'discover,' and 'adaptor This asymmetry indicates that my approach may exaggerate agency and that '[i]nstitutionalists might well argue that the causal arrow in this assertion points in the wrong direction. The causal arrow in this neglects evidence showing that organizational members are socialized (indoctrinated) into expected sense-making activities and that firm behavior is shaped by broad cognitive, normative, and regulatory forces that derive from and are enforced by powerful actorsor I have already answered this potential criticism above by outlining a framework for the enactment of institutions that is based on the idea that when *experiencing*, individuals act upon experience and *do* something with it, and then they *suffer* the consequences of their experience. Actors do something to experience, and experience does something to them because experience has both an *active* and a *passive* element. This framing is not fully consistent with Weick et al.'s 'solution' to this critique, namely that 'macro states at one point in time influence the behavior of individual actors, and how these actions generate new macro states at a later time'

(Hedström and Swedberg, in Weick et al., 2005: 417). 'Macro states' are not prior to the behavior of individual organizations that the above-mentioned quote indicates. Environments may trigger organizational activity, but they are always determined by organizations as they have previously enacted certain experiences: hence the fundamental idea that organizations generate their environments, not the other way around.

According to my observations 'medicalization' is a particularly potent mechanism of enactment that can explain why social welfare seems to be the subject of an extraordinary successful institutionalization. Today the phenomenon of organized social welfare is largely taken for granted. Given its comprehensiveness from both a social and economic point-of-view (Considine, 2002; Butcher, 2002; Lewis, 2004; Lindert, 2004), in contemporary society most people constitute organized social welfare's environment, and to a smaller or greater degree participate in its institutionalization by enjoying its services. In the course of their lives few if any people are exempt from social welfare organizations' enactment that is concretely realized through various programs of help and assistance; most of 'modern' society's citizens are prospective or current 'welfare disabled clientsor Indeed, the more 'civilized' a society, the more likely that organized social welfare has an important role to play in enacting some central behavioral characteristics of that society. The reason why the official number of 'disabled people' is the largest in countries with a comprehensive welfare system, whether public or private (Fujiura and Rutkowski-Kmitta, 2001: 78–79) does not have anything to do with there being relatively more people suffering from various bio-medical disorders. Instead it has to do with there being a relatively large formal organization of social welfare that continuously institutionalizes itself by enacting all the more people as disabled.

Throughout this book I have suggested that the institutionalization of social welfare is the result of rational and effective 'medicalizing management' practices undertaken by formal organizations. Their medicalization is realized through a number of management practices devoted to organizing welfare clients that draw on both standard medical ideas and standard management ideas. In this enterprise the management of medicalization generates medicalization of management that illustrates how medicine is a management relevant phenomenon and how management is a medically conditioned phenomenon. This activity has implications both for the management of prospective and existing welfare clients, and the overall organization of social welfare. As a result of medicalizing management, social welfare clients' behavior becomes all the more medicalized, concurrently with the medicalization of social welfare. These twin forces are instrumental to the institutionalization of social welfare.

In each step of identification, classification, codification, and so on of welfare clients by social welfare organizations, medicalization is reinforced so that eventually the individuals start behaving according to the organizations' experience. The efficiency, speed, and rationality of this process indicate its reliance on a bureaucratic model in the standard Weberian sense (Weber, 1978: 987ff). It is revealed through the fact that the many people who are not needy begin, after a period, to behave as if they were so, and from a very heterogeneous population of prospective welfare clients a considerable degree of homogeneity is created in the form of 'the disabledor A person that becomes identified by others as disabled may eventually experience herself as disabled and accept a formal classification of disability. This in its turn may induce her to accept being organized as disabled. These institutionalizing processes are significant where the individual is medicalized through individual experiential learning, *and* where the organization behind this is medicalized through its unique learning from experience. As Hedberg (1981: 6) said: 'Organizations influence their members' learning, and they retain the sediments of past learning after the original learners have leftor This activity is not about adapting to external demands; it is about enacting behavior according to organizational experience as retrieved in ordinary management routines and practices.

Medicalization is not only a source of organization regarded as a technical mechanism for interlocking human behaviors based on individual experience; it is also a source of institutionalization regarded as the taking on of values beyond the technical requirement at hand. A 'medicalized individual' is necessarily an 'institutionalized individual' by her particular view of herself as dependent and helpless; hence in need of assistance and help. The medicalized individual, in this study the welfare client, is someone that has been transformed from a 'neutral' technician to someone that is committed and loyal to her organizationally enacted role that she eventually requires to be maintained. Hence, this is not about fulfilling the role of 'the disabled' in a 'neutral' and 'technical' sense; it is about becoming disabled as part of one's fundamental identity that constitutes a fundamental prerequisite of its institutionalization. Certainly as suggested in my study, there are those that try to resist the institutionalizing forces of medicalization as exercised by social welfare organizations by insisting on not behaving as disabled. As a rule, resistance is not easy for moral, social, and economic reasons. Medicalizing management is a particularly effective mechanism of experiential learning through its reliance on both medical and management ideas for regulating human activity; by it being linked to the activities of social welfare organizations—that aim to help and assist people in need—it further gains an aura of benignity. Enacting oneself as disabled becomes the foremost means by which one helps oneself in contemporary welfare society to develop and act 'normallyor Essentially the concept 'disabled' in a welfare context is not a constraining stigma, but an enabling mechanism for human development.

By managing social welfare on medical grounds, both institutional legitimacy and administrative rationality can effectively be accomplished. The medicalization of individuals in a particular social welfare organization extends to a 'medicalization of welfare'; hence to a 'medicalization of societyor This means that a social problem is 'managed' by viewing and treating it as a personal, bio-medical problem, thus transforming it from a source of societal uncertainty and threat to a source of individual dependency and need. When someone becomes labeled as 'disabled' on medical grounds, his or her condition becomes an issue of social welfare management (i.e., society's foremost instrument of normalization). By medicalizing more aspects of individuals' behavior, eventually most people will start behaving in a medically problematic way as they learn this behavior is appropriate and legitimate in the relevant social context, thus demanding further medically-oriented practices by society. Any organized system that manages its environment by medicalizing it, is destined to become all the more medicalized itself by increasingly responding to its enacted environment in a 'medically-oriented' way through all the more normalizing activities of 'rehabilitation,' 'reformation,' and 'curingor

As suggested by my study, medicalizing management may be a particularly relevant concept for explaining the successful institutionalization of social welfare in society. However, medical ideas and medical models play a more or less prominent role for the institutionalization of *all* organizations. By managing humans in corporations, public organizations, religious organizations, and military organizations based on medical models and ideas, their behavior is likely to eventually reflect these models and ideas, thus contributing to the medicalization of the management activities themselves. All management is concerned with the ordering of human behavior as grounded in their individual experience, which is accomplished by organizations enacting their environments much in the same way as a doctor enacts a patient through examinations, investigations, tests, diagnoses, prognoses, and therapies. Medical models and ideas are therefore not only important as metaphors for our understanding of the general process of organizing (cf. Simon's [1997] ideas on the 'anatomy of organizations' or Beer's [1981] the 'anatomy of management'). As each individual is an immensely complex, variable, and uncertain being from both a bodily and mental point of view, much organizing in society is about managing people's 'medical conditionor

Indeed, the vast sociological literature on health and illness, impairment and disability, the human relations literature on occupational health, discourses on 'public health' and 'health promotion,' the history of medicine, and so on illustrate the fact that throughout history, people's health and illness conceived as their individual and social ability or disability, has been a central source of uncertainty for the stability and even growth of organizations and societies (Canguilhem, 1991: 76–79; Durkheim, 1982: 86–93; Parsons, 1951: 429–433); hence a central source for organized intervention and control, both in a preventive and in a restorative sense. Medical classification is a particularly important mechanism for reducing behavioral variety since this practice targets the very foundation of a human beings' 'personal condition'—sickness or health; disability or fitness. A medical model provides a powerful and influential method of managing the most basic components of human behavior; it therefore provides a powerful method of control: No human being is exempt from health or non-health. Without medicalization, classification and organization of the most basic human behaviors into medical concepts and labels, much human variability would remain, to the detriment of the activities of organized society.

In all, a key idea in my analysis of the institutionalization of social welfare is that social welfare organizations manage by medicalizing, thus at the same time becoming all the more medicalized themselves. The organization becomes medicalized when managing medicalization by experientially adapting to its clients' behavior. This is the result of the organization learning how to adapt to its own medicalized experiences that are continuously enacted through individual experiencing. Management will increasingly be drawing on a medical model to accomplish its purpose, namely to effectively manage its environment. In this way a 'medicalizing organization' becomes all the more medicalized itself. When medicalizing, management turns all the more technical, rational, scientific, programmatic, and rule-bound—hence *clinical*. It eventually becomes efficient and coldly detached, drawing on the same fundamental methods as in any medico-clinical analysis, which are different variations of activities oriented to 'objective rules,' that is, to calculable routines and 'without regard for persons.'

Since medicalization is an extraordinary management mechanism potentially it is also an extraordinary mechanism of institutionalization. This suggestion can potentially explain the observation that social welfare is one of contemporary society's most enduring institutions. Since social welfare is concerned with normalizing human activity, medicalization is a very plausible means. As such, effectively managing social welfare becomes a mechanism that is central to the effective maintenance of societies. A society that allows for much organized social welfare generates conditions of social stability and 'securityor By medicalizing, social welfare becomes a keystone of modern society's institutionalization. Consequently, if there is a desire on the part of a particular society to continue exercising its unique norms and morals, formally organized social welfare seems to be a particularly attractive instrument. By targeting the foundation of human behavior, medicalizing management is potentially not limited to certain organizational contexts such as social welfare; rather it pervades social life and is a crucial mechanism for better understanding the institutionalization of all social *organon*.

ENDNOTE

A possible reaction on my study may be surprise at the way disadvantaged individuals in Sweden, a model country in much international conversation on social welfare, are organized as 'disabled' and are taught that they can only get the various privileges that come with being helped by society if they accept a view of themselves as disabled, something that appears not only to medicalize them, but also to degrade them. However, as one of the anonymous reviewers of a draft version of this book stressed: One should remember that Sweden has a long history of being very highhanded when it comes to certain segments of the population, especially those who Karl Marx (in his own highhanded way) called the *Lumpenproletariat*. The key ideologists of Swedish social welfare, Alva and Gunnar Myrdal, suggested, for instance, in the 1930s that individuals of 'low quality' did not belong in the welfare state; it was only for people of 'good qualityor Sweden also allowed sterilization of young working class women until the 1970s. From this perspective, the story of what happens to people in Samhall is perhaps not so surprising.

But even for the reader who is not familiar with the practice of social welfare in Sweden, the Samhall story should not be so surprising. A number of famous American sociological studies have reported on the propensity of organizations that are designed 'to do good' in many cases ending up doing the reverse (e.g., Goffman, 1961; Resnick and Patti, 1980; Scott, 1969; Rosenhan, 1975). One may not even have to relate to scholarly work to acknowledge the validity of this observation, but instead turn to such classic fiction as, for instance, *One Flew Over the Cuckoo's Nest*. Hence, to the extent that my study has an empirical contribution it is hardly in my report of a hitherto unknown phenomenon.

Nevertheless, what may be surprising about organized social welfare that has been reported here and elsewhere, is its ability to continue its activities despite the sometimes morally disturbing results. I believe that this issue can be fruitfully explained by the framework that I have suggested in this book. Enacting people as 'disabled' and treating them as such is not an expression of some dysfunction or pathology in the formal organization of contemporary social welfare. By making clients experience themselves as the organized system does, namely as disabled and more specifically as helpless, dependent, and incapacitated, a crucial prerequisite of organized social welfare's institutionalization is attained. The success of this enterprise is complete if people eventually start behaving as disabled.

Appendix
Notes on Methodology

By conceptualizing the enactment concept for institutional analysis this book aims to contribute to the advancement of organizational research on institutions and institutionalization from an interpretive perspective (Burrell and Morgan, 2000: 114–117). Following Smircich and Stubbart (1985: 733–734), this interpretive research of institutionalization can avoid a detached Olympian perspective on an industry or firm, by exploring what organization members are experiencing in their learning of specific behavior. Interpretive studies of institutionalization aim to understand organization members' institutionalized thoughts and actions at an experiential level, not at the far removed level of abstract, aggregate statistics. Necessarily, such an approach requires analyses of individuals' experiencing, such as in detailed case studies of how particular human behavior unfolds. In their analysis of enactment and strategic management, Smircich and Stubbart (Ibid: 734) asked what prevents scholars from doing interpretive analyses more frequently and gave the following answer that is highly relevant for institutional analysis as well: '[A] general acceptance of a deceptively persuasive "organization-environment" metaphor blinds one to the largely symbolic, social nature of organized life. That metaphor leads theorists to adopt the frame or reference of a focal organization or industry, rather than the perspective of an undisciplined environment enacted by multiple interest groups.'

In standard organizational analyses of institutionalization, individuals' experience-as-lived receives little systematic analysis despite its fundamental importance to the institutionalization of organization. One must be careful about reifying the organization and understanding it as 'institutionalizing.' All institutionalization is grounded in individual human heads; an organization is institutionalized only by the experiential learning of its members. An enactment approach to institutionalization seeks to advance an analysis of institutionalization that brings into focus how organization members experientially construe the situations in which they eventually learn to adapt in a taken-for-granted and organized way. As Durkheim (2001: 310–322) manifested in his seminal study of religious beliefs, institutions can exist only in individual minds and through them. Hence, any interpretive approach to institutionalization is done from the point of view of the participants' individual, social, and organized experience and how they contribute to generating the world in which their behavior becomes manifested (Berger and Luckmann, 1966; Schutz, 1967).

The present approach to the analysis of institutionalization should be most relevant for detailed case studies where humans' experiential learning processes can be closely examined. This 'micro-sociological' approach to institutionalization is, of course, not new (Clark, 1956; Selznick, 1949; Scott, 1969), nor unique in today's conversation on institutionalization (Czarniawska and Sévon, 1996; Greenwood et al., 2002). The concept of enactment can be an important trigger to further methodological explorations into the micro-sociology of institutions. Institutionalization in an enacted world necessarily alters the way research on institutions is done by emphasizing the obvious idea that institutions exist only in people's minds and through them; hence the need for in-depth case studies of how humans experientially generate the institutions to which they subsequently respond.

There is a large literature that gives helpful advice on doing 'qualitative case study research,' for instance on how to design archival studies, how to do interviews, how to set up and analyze questionnaires, and how to pursue various types of observations (e.g., Barley, 1990; Eisenhardt, 1989; Miles and Huberman, 1994; Yin, 1994). When completing my study I benefited from this literature in a casual sense. As my research design very much evolved as the study progressed, I did not strictly adhere to any *a priori* rules of how to complete my data collection and analysis. However, I have tried to be faithful to the following idea:

> Careful observation of ordinary organizational life is critical. If there are insights to be found in modern perspectives on organizational choice, they are borrowed from the fine detail of good field observations (March, 1981: 207).

Overall, I would say that my study is 'based on the view that one can only understand the social world by obtaining first-hand knowledge of the subject under investigation...by "getting inside" situations and involving oneself in the everyday flow of life' (Burrell and Morgan, 1979: 6). Other qualitative studies have been very helpful in informing me on how to concretely exercise various methods. In Scandinavia there is a long tradition of doing field studies among students of organization; thus I have been lucky to work in an environment where much valuable experience is at hand. Likewise, I have found much guidance and inspiration in classic American case studies of institutionalization (e.g., Hammond, 1964; Scott, 1969; Selznick, 1949), as well as in a host of reputable field studies on various topics (e.g., Kunda, 1992; Latour and Wolgar, 1986; Orr, 1996).

If I should try to label my research process by using the terminology that is popular in the literature on qualitative methods, perhaps I have followed what Strauss and Corbin (1990) and Miles and Huberman (1994) have respectively termed 'an iterative process,' that is, a journey back and forth between the data and an emerging structure of theoretical arguments and ideas. As I have pursued my research, I have concurrently worked with 'empirical data' and 'theory.' I started off with some conceptual ideas that made Samhall a potentially interesting case; these ideas proved to some extent useful when trying to make sense of this organization. But I also continuously experienced surprise and puzzlement when pursuing my study, thus stressing a need for further conceptual analysis by reading relevant literature, and so on. Since this 'iterative strategy' seems to be very popular among students of organizations (perhaps because it is necessary), there is, of course, nothing original or unique about my approach.

As is customary in many field studies, I have relied on the following sources:

- **Documents,** such as government reports, internal Samhall documents, books written by former Samhall managers or by clients: I have benefited very much from the trust shown to me by Samhall regarding access to internal documents. I have also benefited very much from the famous Swedish 'transparency' regarding official reports and inquiries; thus enabling me to use a host of government reports on Samhall;
- **Interviews and socializing** with managers and clients of Samhall and administrative officials of the National Employment Office: Throughout my study, no restrictions were obvious to me regarding whom to see and talk to. Supervisors at Samhall and administrative officials at the National Employment Office, as well as Samhall clients have in general answered my questions or agreed to discuss various issues that I have deemed important;
- **Participant observation** was the most important source of data for this study. The opportunity for me to participate in Samhall's activities as a 'regular' client has, of course, been indispensable to my understanding of this organization. Samhall has been very accommodating and helpful in arranging periods of observation and in supporting these activities. I have also experienced much interest and support by the clients with whom I worked; they too have very much contributed to my data collection through observing regular work situations in Samhall.

I will now give a chronological account of the research process.

In December 2002 I contacted Samhall's CEO, and suggested that I would undertake a study of how Samhall's occupationally disabled employees were recruited and put to work. As a student of organization with a particular interesting in change and learning, I was intrigued by Samhall's mission to 'rehabilitate individuals with occupational disability.' Thus, I explained to him that I was an Associate Professor with a particular interest in learning more about how 'people with occupational disabilities develop in Samhall.' He agreed to the project and assigned a group consisting of four of his deputies to act as my contact group. The research was carried out during 2003 through 2005, and complemented with updated information in 2006 for the completion of this book. Throughout the project I acted as an independent researcher, and at no time did Samhall interfered in my activities, at least as I experienced it. The contact group initiated some contacts in the organization to help me get started. Soon, however, I could freely make any contacts that I found important without having to check with anyone. My informants often enabled me to contact other important informants, both within and outside Samhall (e.g., at the National Employment Office). The study was funded by a research grant from two national research foundations in Sweden without any obligations versus Samhall. Overall, Samhall had no influence on the design of my study or on the evolving text.

On two occasions I made presentations of my findings to members of Samhall's top management team. As it seemed to me, their reaction was neither enthusiastic nor critical. Largely, they remained supportive of the project and allowed me to continue my studies. When my Swedish report was finished and the same day it was published (see Holmqvist, 2005), I presented my findings to Samhall's leading officers. Several of those present disputed my findings. When the report was published, it was given much publicity in Sweden in leading newspapers, radio, and TV. Samhall officially chose to dispel my findings by stating 'we do not recognize what Holmqvist describes.' Why did Samhall accept my presence during these years, allowing me to move freely in the organization, even gaining access to their internal network of documents and reports? Of course, I cannot answer this question. A number of economic, social, and political expectations and desires were probably behind the decision to allow me to do my study, and to the continuously support it. Suffice it to say that Samhall's leading officials had probably expected me to come up with a radically different result that, perhaps, would have been useful for the organization's further institutionalization in Swedish society.

I started the study by visiting around 10 Samhall sites as part of a pilot study. I presented myself as a researcher doing field studies regarding 'work for the disabled.' The purpose was to gain some first impressions. The sites were suggested to me by my contacts at Samhall. They respected my request that the sites would reflect both operations in cities and on the countryside; as well as the production of both goods and services. I did not experience that the sites were chosen to represent any particular aspect of Samhall's activities; overall I found that they gave me a general picture of the organization. To gain some preliminary verification regarding this, I consulted a number of Samhall magazines that were distributed to employees, and that gave various reports on the situation in Samhall, at least as it was suggested by Samhall itself. I also studied five government reports on Samhall that had been published between 1980 and 2005, which provided additional information on the company and its clients.

During the pilot study I conducted both 'formal' and 'informal' interviews and participant observation. The formal interviews took place with managers and supervisors, enabling me to rely on a recorder as a complement to my notes. Each interview lasted around one hour. My questions were broad but, by and large, centered on these issues: How did the managers look upon themselves in relation to managers in other organizations? How did they look upon themselves in relation to the occupationally disabled? How did they perceive the occupationally disabled? How did they socialize with them? In most cases I did only informal or 'conversational' interviewing with the clients, typically during lunch breaks or during work, asking them about their work, their background, and their view of themselves as occupationally disabled. Few of them wanted to be interviewed formally, perhaps from fear of what I would do with tape-recorded materials; in most cases it would moreover interfere in their work. During the informal interviewing I continuously took notes, often experiencing a high degree of openness after promising the respondent that I would not disclose his or her identity.

Further, I participated in various work activities to gain a preliminary impression of the organization. Through this technique, I could systematically observe the design of the workplaces and the conduct of the employees (e.g., by paying attention to social interactions between supervisors and clients, between clients themselves, between clients and machines, and so on). By working at Samhall myself I also gained a sense of what 'work for the occupationally disabled' was all about. For instance, at one site I was given the opportunity to work as a cleaner during some hours that allowed me to get some first-hand impressions of the work as an occupationally disabled cleaner. The work was not different from regular cleaning work at Samhall's competitors with whom I sometimes interacted making comparisons regarding such elements as work content and speed of operation, with the exception of some important differences (e.g., regarding speed of activity). Intermittently I stopped my observational activities and wrote down my impressions in my notebook that were later transcribed together with the interviews. During my pilot study some preliminary themes and ideas 'emerged' (not least after having reflected upon some of the relevant literature that I was reading at the moment) that were grouped into 'logical' categories in a Word document. These were complemented with information from Samhall documents and secondary sources such as government reports. In all, the pilot study not only helped me to gain some first impressions of Samhall; it also helped me to understand the importance and problems of various research methods. Formal interviewing did not turn out to be a very fruitful strategy in terms of collecting information from clients; on the other hand, participant observation seemed to be a highly fruitful avenue.

After a three-month break, I started working at around 10 sites for one week or more. In some cases these sites were the same as those I had studied during the pilot study. Upon entrance at a site I was introduced by the plant manager as a researcher from a university who would stay there for about a week. Some plant managers stressed that I had 'understood' what Samhall was all about, and that the clients should feel relaxed in their interaction with me. During my study of Samhall there was information on Samhall's internal website about my research project, thus manifesting that it was undertaken 'with the blessing of top management.' This piece of information seemed to be more necessary in relation to supervisors and plant managers than to the clients. Some clients initially looked upon me with suspicion because some of them, as it appeared to me, remained hostile to Samhall as an organization. Overall, however, I experienced that I was well accommodated by the clients in the different work groups, particularly after having described my project in less formal terms and on a more personal basis.

I worked in the following Samhall premises with the following tasks that were either located at a contractor's premises or at Samhall's own workplaces:

Härnösand (Northern Sweden). *Distribution of food.* Together with eight of Samhall's clients that were employed by Samhall in Härnösand I stowed ready-cooked food and beverages in plastic bags that were then distributed by us by car to private persons (mostly elderly) that were living in Härnösand. We distributed the packages according to a set distribution route each morning. *Eldercare.* I visited three houses for the elderly run by the City of Härnösand where 10 Samhall clients were working on a contract basis with feeding, clothing, and washing elderly persons. I did not actively participate myself in the work activities as they were regulated by certain rules. Instead I closely observed how the Samhall clients interacted together and with the individuals that they were assisting. *Cleaning* of private houses commissioned by the City of Härnösand. This work involved ordinary cleaning of private persons' homes. I worked in a team of three Samhall clients, both in apartments and in homes.

Stockholm (Southern Sweden). *Book conversion.* This work entailed the 'conversion' of paperbacks into hardcover for distribution to libraries. The activity was contracted by an organization that sells books from all publishers to libraries in Sweden. The work consisted in ripping off the front and back cover of the paperback, and then sorting the converted books into various sizes that were later sent off for binding in hard cover. I worked on a team consisting of around eight Samhall clients. *Working in two warehouses* receiving goods, distributing the items on shelves, sorting them for external distribution, etc. This work was contracted by two corporations that used the units as their central warehouses in Scandinavia. I worked with around 15 Samhall clients with different tasks in the two locations. *Cleaning.* I did cleaning with one or two other clients at companies' premises or in the lobby of apartment buildings. Sometimes I cleaned the stairs of tall buildings several days in a row. *Packaging* various items at one of Samhall's packaging units. Together with eight other clients and sitting around a table, I packaged bulbs, condoms, lipstick, pencils, etc., that were to be distributed to various customers that had commissioned the packaging work.

Sundsvall (Mid-Sweden). *Manufacturing ladders* at one of Samhall's factories. I was given the opportunity to work with the different steps of producing ladders to be sold by Samhall. Each step consisted of various activities that were carried out by several teams. *Visiting a riding-school* that employed five Samhall clients on a contract basis. Here I did not participate in the work activities as I only visited the site for a couple of hours. The clients were working with ordinary tasks related to the maintenance of the horses and the buildings, as well as teaching horsemanship. *Visiting a site where Samhall clients were sorting clothes* on commission by a relief organization. The clothes had been donated by private individuals and were now sorted into bags according to color, size, type (winter, summer, etc), and so on. I observed the work that was carried out in different stations by around 40 Samhall clients.

Lund and Malmö (Southern Sweden). *Production and distribution of food* for private persons. The work was carried out in one of Samhall's large-scale kitchens where I participated in preparing the food (e.g., by washing and peeling large amounts of vegetables) and in the cooking itself (e.g., broiling meatballs). I worked together with Samhall clients in teams of around three persons. After having produced the food, it was frozen in parcels according to a specific procedure in which a number of clients were engaged. The parcels were then distributed to clients by car. *Shopping for everyday commodities* in a food store. Working in a team of eight persons I shopped for such commodities as milk, marmalade, butter, yoghurt, and so on according to a list set up by each client (mostly staple foods). After having shopped at the food store, we distributed the commodities by car to the clients. *Working in a cleaning unit.* Samhall is under contract to provide clients with laundry service, delivering the clean laundry to clients. I participated in activities that focused on cleaning and ironing, working in a facility with around 40 Samhall clients.

Uppsala (Southern Sweden). In Uppsala I participated in the work activities at two Samhall workplaces. In one of them work revolved around sorting and cataloguing hospital documents. The workplace was located at a major hospital. The Samhall team consisted of around 10 persons. At the other site I worked together with other clients sorting large amount of documents from various customers that were to be archived either on CD or by microfilming. I participated in various activities on different teams that specialized in the relevant activities.

Gävle (Mid-Sweden). In Gävle Samhall has a large factory that produces metal cabinets and safes. I worked together with Samhall clients carrying out various operations relevant to the production of these goods, such as working with a milling-machine or with a turning lathe, painting, and so on.

Fagersta (Mid-Sweden). Here I worked at Samhall's factory for producing bathroom cupboards, one of Samhall's best-selling products. The work was similar to the one that I carried out in Gävle, that is, a typical industrial labor activity.

Ludvika (Mid-Sweden). In Ludvika Samhall produces advanced electrical fittings under contract from a leading Swedish design firm. As in Gävle and Fagersta, the factory consisted of around 90 employees and the work was organized according to a traditional division of labor. I worked in various teams with various assignments, such as assembling, installation, and testing.

When staying at a Samhall workplace I wore the same clothes as the clients wore, ate lunch with them, took coffee breaks with them, and so on, thus trying to share their everyday routines. As reported above, depending on the particular work at a site, I participated in a host of activities, such as cleaning, maintenance, archival work, production of food, manufacture of furniture, that gave me a good chance to get to know the organization and how it operated. During work I chatted with the employees, and wrote down their statements about Samhall, about their careers, and about their jobs in particular. My approach was necessarily tentative, even though I tried to ask people some particular questions as my conceptual focus became all the more distinct. Further, I observed how people worked—if they worked with highly repetitive tasks or not, how often they were allowed to take breaks, how they confronted new and unexpected situations, such as when a machine broke down, and so on. These 'ethnographic' activities were important to gain some deeper understanding of what was going on in Samhall; how people looked upon themselves, how their careers progressed, how the supervisors organized the work. I continuously wrote down statements by employees and supervisors and my own impressions in a notebook that I transcribed at the weekend after the session was concluded.

Throughout my continued study I made around 50 interviews with Samhall managers and supervisors as well as around 20 interviews with administrative officials at the National Employment Office. Most of them were tape-recorded. The interviews were focused on understanding how the organization, through its officers' statements, operated upon the clients; how they expected clients to behave and develop; how they concretely organized their time, how they tried to shape the clients' view of themselves; how they looked upon themselves as managers and supervisors; how they regarded the phenomenon of Samhall and social welfare in general, and so on. Much time was also spent going through relevant documents pertinent to the activities of Samhall and the National Employment Office.

In ending this Appendix, I wish to stress the merits of my methodological approach that has centered on a longitudinal field study. This type of research, as I see it, has both contributed to testing the validity of the conceptual mechanisms as found in the standard literature, as well as calling for revisions of established ideas of institutionalization. An approach by which the student of organization participates in the organized activities that are being studied is, of course, not unique, but, unfortunately, still relatively uncommon in organization studies. Still, students of organizations generally agree upon the need for 'field studies' in order to explain organizational behavior.

Given the need for such undertakings, what may be the reason why such projects are relatively rare? A first potential explanation may be lack of time. 'Nevertheless, such obstacles can be overcome by juggling one's schedule creatively to allow solid blocks of time for research,' as Barley chose to put it (1990: 244). Naturally we are all struggling with having too much to do and too little time at our disposal. But, it would indeed be a bad sign for any research program if lack of time militated against important research methods, so that scholars resort to potentially less favorable methods, given their theoretical interest. In that regard, time would ultimately characterize what is organization science, which surely some of us would feel uncomfortable with.

A second reason may be the problem of obtaining access to relevant data, which, of course, is a crucial requirement for conducting field studies. This, however, should not discourage any scholar from doing such research: in most cases, this is more of an imagined than a real problem even though there clearly may be empirical issues that are more difficult to study than others.

A third explanation for the relative lack of field studies may be skepticism regarding the efficiency of the method in itself, particularly regarding the ability to generalize the findings. A simple answer to that issue, given that students of organizations may wish to overcome the lack of processual and contextual depth in quantitative studies is, however, that a sample of one in-depth case study is better than a sample of none. By conducting longitudinal field studies, the student gradually gains knowledge about differences and similarities in organizations' behavior; about what needs to be studied in order to draw valid generalizations; and what precautions must be taken in order to avoid biases in their samples and analyses.

Finally, a fourth reason for the general lack of ethnographic field studies may be a belief among scholars that there is a trade-off between producing good conceptual ideas, and conducting good empirical research. As Stern and Barley put it:

The reputations of the most renowned organizational theorists rest less on the rigor of their research than on the importance of the ideas they have contributed.... To be sure, methods matter. Without them we would not be able to judge the quality of a researcher's claims or put theories to the test. But measured in terms of contributions to the field, methods are always, and will undoubtedly remain, secondary to ideas, theories, and perspectives (Stern and Barley, 1996: 158).

For sure, the organization studies literature, including the institutional literature, has created an impressive conceptual framework that relies on insightful and powerful ideas. But for the literature as a whole, there should not be a trade-off between producing concepts and producing empirical data. If the institutional literature is to advance any further, it must certainly produce convincing and relevant ideas, theories, and perspectives; but it must also continuously examine if those ideas, theories, and perspectives are valid descriptors of the empirical reality that they ultimately seek to explain.

Notes

CHAPTER 1

1. Such an interpretation of the enactment concept was suggested by Hannan and Freeman (1989: 31–32) who, like most students of organizational institutionalization assume the environment to be an objective and external entity. They criticized the concept of enactment by arguing that 'the imagery of enactment suggests that the environment is in the eye of the beholder, an organizational dream. If organizations are understood to relate to social, economic, and political changes in such a surreal way, they can hardly shape the broader processes.'
2. Internal Revenue Services of the United States. IRC section 501 (c) (4) on "social welfare organizations." Downloaded from http://www.irs.gov on October 10, 2006.

CHAPTER 5

1. For the sake of simplicity and since all written sources (government reports on Samhall, internal Samhall documents, etc.) are only available in their original Swedish, in the following I only refer to them by stating what type of source is being used in the particular case. Example: 'According to a government report, Samhall...'; 'One Samhall document emphasized the following....' For the reader who is conversant with Swedish, a complete specification of written sources is available in Holmqvist (2005: 403–434).
2. In Swedish, the word 'arbetshandikappad' is the product of two words, 'arbete' (work) and 'handikapp' (disability).

CHAPTER 7

1. According to the yearly polls by Samhall regarding employees' satisfaction at work, most of the occupationally disabled employees are pleased with their employment with Samhall.

Bibliography

Abberley, P. (2002), 'Work, Disability, Disabled People and European Social Theory.' In C. Barnes, M. Oliver, and L. Barton (Eds.), *Disability Studies Today*. Cambridge: Polity, pp. 120–138.

Albrecht, G. (1992), *The Disability Business: Rehabilitation in America*. Newbury Park, CA: Sage.

Albrecht, G. L. (2002), 'American Pragmatism, Sociology and the Development of Disability Studies.' In C. Barnes, M. Oliver, and L. Barton (Ed.), *Disability Studies Today*. Cambridge: Polity, pp. 18–37.

Albrecht, G., K. Seelman, and M. Bury (2001) (Eds.), *Handbook of Disability Studies*. New York: Paul Chapman.

Arendt, H. (1968), *The Origins of Totalitarianism*. New York: HBJ/Harvest.

Ballard, K. and M. A. Elston (2005), 'Medicalization: A Multi-Dimensional Concept.' *Social Theory and Health*, 3, pp. 228–241.

Bandura, A. (1986), *Social Foundations of Thought and Action: A Social Cognitive Theory*. Englewood Cliffs, NJ: Prentice-Hall.

Bandura, A. (2001), 'Social Cognitive Theory: An Agentic Perspective,' *Annual Review of Psychology*, 52, pp. 1–16.

Barley, S. and P. Tolbert (1997), 'Institutionalization and Structuration: Studying the Links between Action and Institution,' *Organization Studies*, 18, pp. 93–117.

Barley, S. R. (1990), 'Images of Imaging: Notes on Doing Longitudinal Field Work,' *Organization Science*, 3, pp. 220–247.

Barnard, C. I. (1968), *The Functions of the Executive*. Cambridge, MA: HBR Press.

Beer, S. (1981), *Brain of the Firm*. 2nd ed. Chichester: John Wiley.

Bengtsson, T. (1994) (Ed.), *Population, Economy, and Welfare in Sweden*. New York: Springer.

Berger, P. and T. Luckmann (1966), *The Social Construction of Reality*. London: Penguin Books.

Blackler, F. and S. Regan (2006), 'Institutional Reform and the Reorganization of Family Support Services,' *Organization Studies*, 27, pp. 1843–1861.

Blau, P. and W. R. Scott (1967), 'The Concept of Formal Organization.' In G. D. Bell (Ed.), *Organizations and Human Behavior*. Englewood Cliffs, NJ: Prentice-Hall, pp. 77–81.

Blumer, H. (1969), *Symbolic Interactionism:Perspective and Method*. Berkeley: University of California Press.

Branson, J. and D. Miller (2002), *Damned for Their Difference: The Cultural Construction of Deaf People as Disabled. A Sociological History*. Washington, D.C.: Gallaudet.

British Medical Journal (2002), Special Issue on Medicalization ('Too Much Medicine'), 324, No. 7342.

Brown, J. S. and P. Duguid (1991), 'Organizational Learning and Communities of Practice: Toward a Unified View of Working, Learning, and Innovation,' *Organization Science*, 2, pp. 40–57.

Brunsson, N. and J. P. Olsen (1997), *The Reforming Organization*. Bergen: Fagboksforlaget.

Bull, M. (1990), 'Secularization and Medicalization,' *British Journal of Sociology*, 41, pp. 245–261.

Burrell, G. and G. Morgan (1979), *Sociological Paradigms and Organisational Analysis*. Aldershot: Arena.

Burrell, G. and G. Morgan (2000), 'Two Dimensions: Four Paradigms.' In P. Frost, A. Y. Lewin, R. L. Daft (Eds.), *Talking About Organization Science*. London: Sage, pp. 107–122.

Butcher, T. (2002), *Delivering Welfare*. 2nd ed. Buckingham: Open University Press.

Canguilhem, G. (1991), *The Normal and the Pathological*. New York: Zone Books.

Christensen, T. and P. Laegrid (2001), *New Public Management: The Transformation of Ideas and Practices*. Ashgate: Aldershot.

Clark, B. (1956), *Adult Education in Transition*. Berkeley: University of California Press.

Clark, J. and J. Newman (1997), *The Managerial State*. London: Sage.

Conrad, P. (1987), 'Wellness in the Work Place: Potentials and Pitfalls of Work-site Health Promotion,' *The Millbank Quarterly*, 65, pp. 255–275.

Conrad, P. (2005), 'The Shifting Engines of Medicalization,' *Journal of Health and Social Behavior*, 46, pp. 3–14.

Conrad, P. (2007), *The Medicalization of Society: On the Transformation of Human Conditions into Treatable Disorders*. Baltimore: Johns Hopkins University Press.

Considine, M. (2001), *Enterprising States. The Public Management of Welfare-to-Work*. Cambridge: Cambridge University Press.

Corker M. and Shakespeare, T. (2002), *Disability/Postmodernity: Embodying Disability Theory*. London: Continuum.

Cyert, R. M. and J. G. March (1992), *A Behavioral Theory of the Firm*. Cambridge, MA: Blackwell.

Czarniawska, B. and B. Joerges (1996), 'Travels of Ideas.' In B. Czarniawska and G. Sévon (Eds.), *Translating Organizational Change*. Berlin: Walter de Gruyter, pp. 13–48.

Czarniawska B. and G. Sévon (1996) (Eds.), *Translating Organizational Change*. Berlin: Walter de Gruyter.

Davis, L. J. (1997), 'Constructing Normalcy.' In L. J. Davis (Ed.), *The Disability Studies Reader*. London: Routledge, pp. 9–28.

Dewey, J. (1916), *Democracy and Education*. New York: The Free Press.

Dewey, J. (1934), *Art as Experience*. New York: Perigee Books.

Dewey, J. (1938), *Experience and Education*. New York: Touchstone.

DiMaggio, P. J. and W. W. Powell (1991a), 'Introduction.' In W. W. Powell and P. J. DiMaggio (Eds.), *The New Institutionalism in Organizational Analysis*. Chicago: University of Chicago Press, pp. 1–38.

DiMaggio, P. J. and W. W. Powell (1991b), 'The Iron Cage Revisited: Institutional Isomorphism and Collective Rationality in Organization Fields. In W. W. Powell and P. J. DiMaggio (Eds.), *The New Institutionalism in Organizational Analysis*. Chicago: University of Chicago Press, pp. 63–82.

Drake, R. F. (1999), *Understanding Disability Policies*. London: MacMillan.

Durkheim, E. (1982), *The Rules of Sociological Method*. New York: The Free Press.

Eisenhardt, K. M. (1989), 'Building Theories from Case Study Research,' *Academy of Management Review*, 14, pp. 532–550.

Emerson, R. M. (1962), 'Power-Dependence Relations,' *American Sociological Review*, 27, pp. 31–41.

Fitzpatrick, M. (2001), *The Tyranny of Health: Doctors and the Regulation of Lifestyle*. London: Routledge.

Flood, B. A. and W. R. Scott (1987), *Hospital Structure and Performance*. Baltimore: Johns Hopkins University Press.

Foucault, M. (1977), *Discipline and Punish: The Birth of Prison*. London: Penguin Books.

Foucault, M. (1989), *The Birth of the Clinic*. London: Routledge.

Foucault, M. (2003), *Abnormal*. New York: Picador.

Freidson, E. (1970), *Profession of Medicine*. New York: Dodd, Mead.

Freud, S. (2001), *On Dreams*. New York: Dover.

Fujiura, G. T. and V. Rutkowski-Kmitta (2001), 'Counting Disability,' In Albrecht, G., K. Seelman, M. Bury (2001) (Eds.), *Handbook of Disability Studies*. New York: Paul Chapman, pp. 69–96.

Giddens, A. (1984), *The Constitution of Society: Outline of the Theory of Structuration*. Cambridge: Polity Press.

Goffman, E. (1961), *Asylums. Essays on the Social Situation of Mental Patients and Other Inmates*. Garden City, NY: Anchor.

Greenwood, R. and C. R. Hinings (1996), 'Understanding Radical Organizational Change: Bringing Together the Old and the New Institutionalism.' *Academy of Management Review*, 21, pp. 1022–1054.

Greenwood, R., R. Suddaby, and C. Hinings (2002), 'Theorizing Change: The Role of Professional Associations in the Transformation of Institutional Fields,' *Academy of Management Journal*, 45, pp. 58–80.

Gummer, B. (1990), *The Politics of Social Administration: Managing Organizational Politics in Social Agencies*. Englewood Cliffs, NJ: Prentice-Hall.

Hammond, P. E. (1964) (Ed.), *Sociologists at Work: Essays on the Craft of Social Research*. New York: Basic Books.

Hannan, M. T. and J. Freeman (1989), *Organizational Ecology*. Cambridge, MA: Harvard University Press.

Hasenfeld, Y. (2000), 'Social Welfare Administration and Organizational Theory.' In R. J. Patti (Ed.), *The Handbook of Social Welfare Management*. London: Sage, pp. 89–112.

Hasselbladh, H. and J. Kallinikos (2000), 'The Project Rationalization: A Critique and Reappraisal of Neo-institutionalism in Organization Studies,' *Organization Studies*, 21, pp. 697–720.

Hedberg, B. (1981), 'How Organizations Learn and Unlearn.' In P. C. Nystrom and W. H. Starbuck (Eds.), *Handbook of Organizational Design*. Oxford: Oxford University Press, pp. 3–27.

Hedberg, B., P. C. Nystrom, and W. H. Starbuck (1976), 'Camping on Seesaws: Prescriptions for a Self-Designing Organization,' *Administrative Science Quarterly*, 21, pp. 41–65.

Holmqvist, M. (2004), 'Experiential Learning Processes of Exploitation and Exploration Within and Between Organizations: An Empirical Study of Product Development,' *Organization Science*, 15, pp. 70–81.

Holmqvist, M. (2005), *Samhall. Att bli normal i en onormal organization.* (In English: Samhall—To Become Normal in an Abnormal Organization). Stockholm: SNS Förlag.

Illich, I. (1975), *Medical Nemesis:The Expropriation of Health.* London: Ideas in Progress.

Jahoda, M., P. F. Lazarsfeld, and H. Zeisel (2002), *Marienthal: The Sociography of an Unemployed Community.* New York: Transaction.

James, W. (1981), *The Principles of Psychology.* Cambridge, MA: Harvard University Press.

Janis, I. J. and L. Mann (1977), *Decision Making.* New York: The Free Press.

Jennings P. D. and R. Greenwood (2003), 'Constructing the Iron Cage: Institutional Theory and Enactment.' In R. Westwood and S. Clegg (Eds.), *Debating Organization.* Cambridge: Blackwell.

Jepperson, R. L. and J. W. Meyer (1991), 'The Public Order and the Construction of Formal Organizations.' In W. W. Powell and P. J. DiMaggio (Eds.), *The New Institutionalism in Organizational Analysis.* Chicago: University of Chicago Press, pp. 204–231.

Kahneman, D., P. Slovic, A. Tversky (1982), *Judgment under Uncertainty: Heuristics and Biases.* Cambridge: Cambridge University Press.

Köhler, W. (1970), *Gestalt Psychology.* New York: Liveright.

Kunda, G. (1992), *Engineering Culture: Control and Commitment in a High-Tech Corporation.* Philadelphia: Temple University Press.

Lane, H. (1997), 'Construction of Deafness.' In L. J. Davis (Ed.), *The Disability Studies Reader.* London: Routledge, pp. 153–171.

Lave, J. and E. Wenger (1991), *Situated Learning: Legitimate Peripheral Participation.* Cambridge: Cambridge University Press.

Le Fanu, J. (2000), *The Rise and Fall of Modern Medicine.* London: Abacus.

Levinthal, D. A. and J. G. March (1993), 'The Myopia of Learning,' *Strategic Management Journal,* 14, pp. 95–112.

Levitt, B. and J. G. March (1988), 'Organizational Learning,' *Annual Review of Sociology,* 14, pp. 319–340.

Lewis, J. (2004), *Welfare State Change: Towards a Third Way?* Oxford: Oxford University Press.

Lindert, P. H. (2004), *Growing Public.* Cambridge: Cambridge University Press.

Loe, M. (2004), *The Rise of Viagra.* New York: New York University Press.

Lupton, D. (1995), *The Imperative of Health:Public Health and the Regulated Body.* London: Sage.

Lupton, D. (1997), 'Foucault and the Medicalisation Critique.' In A. Petersen and R. Bunton (Eds.), *Foucault. Health and Medicine.* London: Routledge, pp. 94–110.

March, J. G. (1981), 'Decision Making Perspective.' In A. H. Van de Ven and W. F. Joyce (Eds.), *Perspectives on Organization Design and Behavior.* New York: John Wiley, pp. 205–248.

March, J. G. (1994), *A Primer on Decision Making.* New York: The Free Press.

March, J. G. and J. P. Olsen (1979) (Eds.), *Ambiguity and Choice in Organizations,* 2nd ed. Bergen: Universitetsforlaget.

March, J. G. and H. A. Simon (1993), *Organizations.* Cambridge: Blackwell.

March, J. G. and J. P. Olsen (1989), *Rediscovering Institutions: The Organizational Basis of Politics.* New York: The Free Press.

McLaughlin, K., S. P. Osborne, and E. Ferlie (2002) (Eds.), *New Public Management: Current Trends and Future Prospects.* London: Routledge.

Mead, G. H. (1967), *Mind, Self, and Society:From the Standpoint of a Social Behaviorist.* Chicago: University of Chicago Press.

Meyer, J. W. and B. Rowan (1991), 'Institutionalized Organizations: Formal Structure as Myth and Ceremony.' In W. W. Powell and P. J. DiMaggio (Eds.), *The New Institutionalism in Organizational Analysis*. Chicago: University of Chicago Press, pp. 41–62.

Miles, M. B. and A. M. Huberman (1994), *Qualitative Data Analysis*. 2nd ed., London: Sage.

Mills, C. W. (2000), *The Sociological Imagination*. Oxford: Oxford University Press.

Myrdal, G. (1962), *An American Dilemma: The Negro Problem and Modern Democracy*. New York: Harper & Row.

Nee, V. (2005), 'The New Institutionalisms in Economics and Sociology.' In N. J. Smelser and R. Swedberg (Eds.), *The Handbook of Economic Sociology*. 2nd ed. Princeton, NJ: Princeton University Press, pp. 49–74.

Nelson, R. R. and S. G. Winter (1982), *An Evolutionary Theory of Economic Change*. Cambridge, MA: Belknap.

Oliver, C. (1991), 'Strategic Responses to Institutional Processes,' *Academy of Management Review*, 16, pp. 145–179.

Orr, J. (1996), *Talking About Machines: An Ethnography of a Modern Job*. Ithaca, NY: Cornell University Press.

Parsons, T. (1951), *The Social System*. New York: The Free Press.

Patti R. J. (2000) (Ed.), *The Handbook of Social Welfare Management*. London: Sage.

Perrow, C. (1979), *Complex Organizations:A Critical Essay*. Glenview, IL: Scott, Foresman.

Pfeffer, J. and G. R. Salancik (2003), *The External Control of Organizations: A Resource Dependence Perspective*. Stanford, CA: Stanford University Press.

Phillips, N., T. Lawrence, and C. Hardy (2004), 'Discourse and Institutions.' *Academy of Management Review*, 29, pp. 635–652.

Piaget, J. (1952), *The Principles of Genetic Epistemology*. New York: Basic Books.

Pitts, J. (1968), 'Social Control: The Concept.' In D. Sills (Ed.), *International Encyclopedia of Social Sciences*, Vol. 14. New York: MacMillan.

Polsky, A. J. (1991), *The Rise of the Therapeutic State*. Princeton, NJ: Princeton University Press.

Powell W. W. and P. J. DiMaggio (1991) (Eds.), *The New Institutionalism in Organizational Analysis*. Chicago: University of Chicago Press.

Praddock, D. L. and S. L. Parish (2001), 'An Institutional History of Disability.' In G. Albrecht, K. D. Seelman, and M. Bury (2001) (Eds.), *Handbook of Disability Studies*. London: Sage, pp. 11–68.

Resnick, H. and R. J. Patti (1980) (Eds.), *Change from Within: Humanizing Social Welfare Organizations*. Philadelphia: Temple University Press.

Rose, N. (1999), *Powers of Freedom: Re-framing Political Thought*. Cambridge: Cambridge University Press.

Rosenhan, D. L. (1975), 'On Being Sane in Insane Places.' In T. J. Scheff (Ed.), *Labeling Madness*. Englewood Cliffs: Prentice-Hall, pp. 54–74.

Ryan, W. (1971), *Blaming the Victim*. New York: Vintage Books.

Sahlin-Andersson, K. (1996), 'Imitating by Editing Success: The Construction of Organizational Fields.' In B. Czarniawska and G. Sévon (Eds.), *Translating Organizational Change*. Berlin: Walter de Gruyter, pp. 69–92.

Schmid, H. (2000), 'Agency-Environment Relations: Understanding Task Environments.' In R. J. Patti (Ed.), *The Handbook of Social Welfare Management*. London: Sage, pp. 133–154.

Schram, S. F. (2000), 'In the Clinic: The Medicalization of Welfare,' *Social Text,* 18, pp. 81–107.

Schumpeter, J. H. (1955), *Imperialism and Social Classes.* Cleveland: Meridian Books.

Schutz, A. (1967), *The Phenomenology of the Social World.* Evanston, IL: Northwestern University Press.

Schutz, A. and T. Luckmann (1973), *The Structures of the Life-World.* Evanston, IL: Northwestern University Press.

Scott, R. A. (1969), *The Making of Blind Men: A Study of Adult Socialization.* New York: Transaction.

Scott, R. A. (1980), 'The Selection of Clients by Social Welfare Agencies: The Case of the Blind.' In H. Resnick and R. J. Patti (Ed.), *Change from Within: Humanizing Social Welfare Organizations.* Philadelphia: Temple University Press, pp. 96–109.

Scott, W. R. (1995), *Institutions and Organizations.* London: Sage.

Scott, W. R. and J. W. Meyer (1991), 'The Organization of Societal Sectors: Propositions and Early Evidence.' In W. W. Powell and P. J. DiMaggio (Eds.), *The New Institutionalism in Organizational Analysis.* Chicago: University of Chicago Press, pp. 108–140.

Selznick, P. (1949), *TVA and the Grass Roots: A Study in the Sociology of Formal Organization.* Berkeley: University of California Press.

Selznick, P. (1984), *Leadership in Administration: A Sociological Interpretation.* Berkeley: University of California Press.

Sennet, R. (2003), *Respect: The Formation of Character in a World of Inequality.* London: Allen Lane.

Sévon, G. (1996), 'Organizational Imitation in Identity Transformation.' In B. Czarniawska and G. Sévon (Eds.), *Translating Organizational Change.* Berlin: Walter de Gruyter, pp. 49–68.

Shionoya, Y. (2005), *Economy and Morality: The Philosophy of the Welfare State.* Cheltenham: Edward Elgar.

Simmel, G. (1971), *On Individuality and Social Forms.* Chicago: University of Chicago Press.

Simon, H. A. (1996), *The Sciences of the Artificial.* 3rd ed. Cambridge, MA: MIT Press.

Simon, H. A. (1997), *Administrative Behavior.* New York: The Free Press.

Skinner, B. F. (1953), *Science and Human Behavior.* New York: The Free Press.

Slavin, S. (1985) (Ed.), *Social Administration: The Management of Social Services.* New York: Haworth Press.

Smircich, L. and C. Stubbart (1985), 'Strategic Management in an Enacted World,' *Academy of Management Review,* 10, pp. 724–736.

Starbuck, W. H. (1976), 'Organizations and Their Environments.' In Dunette, M. D. (Ed.), *Handbook of Industrial and Organizational Psychology.* Chicago: Rand McNally, pp. 1069–1123.

Stern, R. N. and S. R. Barley (1996), 'Organizations and Social Systems: Organization Theory's Neglected Mandate,' *Administrative Science Quarterly,* 41, pp. 146–162.

Stinchcombe, A. L. (1968), *Constructing Social Theories.* Chicago: University of Chicago Press.

Stone, D. A. (1985), *The Disabled State.* Basingstoke: Macmillan.

Swedberg, R. (2005), *The Max Weber Dictionary.* Stanford: Stanford University Press.

Szasz, T. S. (2003), *The Myth of Mental Illness.* 2nd ed. New York: Perennial.

Taylor, F. W. (1998), *The Principles of Scientific Management.* New York: Dover.

The Concise Oxford Dictionary (1999), Edited by Judy Pearsall. 10th ed. Oxford: Oxford University Press.

Thomas, C. (2002), 'Disability Theory: Key Ideas, Issues and Thinkers.' In C. Barnes, M. Oliver, and L. Barton (Ed.). *Disability Studies Today*. Cambridge: Polity, pp. 38–57.

Thompson, J. D. (2003), *Organizations in Action: Social Science Bases of Administrative Theory*. New Brunswick, NJ: Transaction.

Tolbert, P. S. and L. G. Zucker (1996), 'The Institutionalization of Institutional Theory.' In S. R. Clegg, C. Hardy, W. R. Nord, *The Handbook of Organization Studies*. London: Sage, pp. 175–187.

Tsoukas, H. (1996), 'The Firm as a Distributed Knowledge System: A Constructionist Approach.' *Strategic Management Journal*, Winter Special Issue, pp. 11–25.

Walsh, J. P. and G. R. Ungson (1991), 'Organizational Memory.' *Academy of Management Review*, 16, pp. 57–91.

Watzlawick, P., J. H. Weakland, R. Fisch (1974), *Change. Principles of Problem Formulation and Problem Resolution*. New York: W. W. Norton.

Weber, M. (1946), 'Politics as a Vocation.' In H. H. Gerth and C. W. Mills (Eds.), *From Max Weber: Essays in Sociology*. Oxford: Oxford University Press, pp. 77–128.

Weber, M. (1949), *Methodology of the Social Sciences*. New York: Free Press.

Weber, M. (1978), *Economy and Society*. Vols. 1 and 2. Berkeley: University of California Press.

Weick, K. E. (1969), *The Social Psychology of Organizing*. Reading, MA: Addison-Wesley.

Weick, K. E. (1976), 'Educational Organizations as Loosely Coupled Systems,' *Administrative Science Quarterly*, 21, pp. 1–19.

Weick, K. E. (1979a), *The Social Psychology of Organizing*. 2nd ed., New York: McGraw-Hill.

Weick, K. E. (1979b), 'Cognitive Processes in Organizations,' *Research in Organizational Behavior*, 1, pp. 41–74.

Weick, K. E. (1995), *Sensemaking in Organizations*, London: Sage.

Weick, K. E., K. M. Sutcliffe, and D. Obstfeld (2005), 'Organizing and the Process of Sensemaking.' *Organization Science*, 16, pp. 409–421.

Wertz, R. and D. Wertz (1989), *Lying in: A History of Childbirth*. New Haven, CT: Yale University Press.

Yin, R. K. (1994), *Case Study Research*, 2nd ed. London: Sage.

Zilber, T. (2002), 'Institutionalization as an Interplay between Actions, Meanings, and Actors: The Case of a Rape Center in Israel.' *Academy of Management Journal*, 45, pp. 234–254.

Zola, I. K. (1972), 'Medicine as an Institution of Social Control.' *Sociological Review*, 20, pp. 487–504.

Index